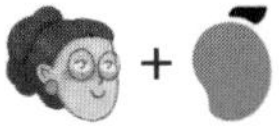

Bad at Adulting, Good at Feminism

Comics on Relationships, Life & Food

Planet Prudence
Prudence Geerts

Published by Mango Publishing Group, a division of Mango Media Inc.
Cover + Interior Illustrations: Prudence Geerts
Cover and Layout Design: Elina Diaz

For permission requests, please contact the publisher at:

Mango Publishing Group
2850 Douglas Road, 3rd Floor
Coral Gables, FL 33134 USA
info@mango.bz

For special orders, quantity sales, course adoptions and corporate sales, please email the publisher at sales@mango.bz. For trade and wholesale sales, please contact Ingram Publisher Services at customer.service@ingramcontent.com or +1.800.509.4887.

Bad at Adulting, Good at Feminism: Comics on Relationships, Life and Food

Library of Congress Cataloging

ISBN: (print) 978-1-63353-758-3, (ebook) 978-1-63353-759-0
Library of Congress Control Number: 2018933361
BISAC category code: CGN008000 COMICS & GRAPHIC NOVELS / Contemporary Women
HUM001000 HUMOR / Form / Comic Strips & Cartoons

Printed in the United States of America

This book is dedicated to you, because without you,
I wouldn't be where I am today!

"Life from Prudence's point of view is fun, colorful and shameless. Something to make fun at because life is too short!"

—@sweetcornandlettuce

"Struggling with the whole "mature adult" thing? Illustrator Prudence Geerts feels your pain."

—Brittany Wong, *Huffington Post*

"Perfect read for when the struggle is too real."
—@elina_designs

"Prudence's comics are highly relatable and a large portion of them highlight the issues of the modern woman (or man). A truly wonderful comic artist!"

—@relatabledoodles

"Prudence is an inspiring person and illustrator in the comic community. Her work portrays her honest vulnerability with all its raw authenticity and a big chunk of creativity-something many of us could relate to. She is an absolute talented darling."

—@vicscribs

"Planet Prudence proves that the struggle is real for millennials."

—@PopSugar.

"Prudence is an amazing artist who knows just how to capture the daily struggles of life as a female. Her work is entertaining, relatable and makes you want to be her best friend."

—@goodbadcomics

Table of Contents

Introduction

My name is Prudence. I'm twenty-five years old at the time of writing and I'm loving it, even though I'll admit that it's very challenging and awkward to be in your mid-twenties. To this day, I don't even feel like a proper adult yet. Taxes still scare the crap out of me, I don't own a house yet, and I laugh at dirty jokes—heck, I still *make* dirty jokes. I feel as if I'm still sixteen years old on the inside while, in reality, that was a decade ago. Sometimes I feel as though I should stop acting this way. Like if I acted more in the style of what society would expect from an "adult," then people would probably feel a lot more comfortable around me.

Honestly, I'm really socially awkward and that has put me in situations that

are worth exploring and sharing with you. Because aren't we all a bit like this—like everything my blog Planet Prudence embodies? Apparently we are, because I've seen it firsthand. Young and old can relate to my comics. How awesome is that?

I grew up and lived my entire life in Belgium. Rainy, cloudy, tiny but beautiful Belgium. Currently I live in an even smaller town, where all the kids knew each other growing up and, today, they still know each other or they've grown up to be colleagues or sisters-in-law. Everyone probably knows *everyone* around here.

I didn't go to high school here, though. I wanted to study art, so I went to Bruges. It is a big city, full of potential, and I had endless fun. If I could go back anywhere, even for just one day, I most definitely would return there. I'd probably hug everyone in the classroom and thank them for the amazing experience, the great friendships, and the laughter.

Despite the great experience, however, many teachers didn't like my work. I faced huge academic obstacles and could not find a way to overcome them. After trying to be the best student possible for many years, I was faced with a situation that forced me to drop out. A teacher, who was my mentor for my final piece, threatened me. He looked seventeen-year-old me in the eyes and crushed my dreams with the words "You won't get your degree if you don't have sex with me." This was the cherry on top of an already hard enough youth.

At that point, my life changed forever. I entered a terrible depression, which was only the start of other mental issues I still battle with today.

Years later, when I returned for a reunion, my mentor didn't recognize me at all. Disturbingly enough, he tried to flirt with me. I looked him in the eyes—being the badass that I was—and told him, "I'm Prudence, I think you know pretty damn well who I am."

He turned pale and ran from the café. I felt like a boss. And I knew at that point that, even though I dropped out, he'd never be the one who would make the decision for me to stop drawing. If I *ever* stopped drawing, it certainly wouldn't be because I wasn't passed by a teacher because I didn't have sex with him. It would be because I just didn't want to draw.

That moment has never come, though. I love drawing, always have.

The reason that I wanted to go to art school was because I was always drawing no matter where I was. Ever since I can remember, I've walked around with a pencil and sketchbook. I've also always been living in my own world—in the imaginary world that books provide and in the world that I've created through my drawings. Some of my favorite books were (and still are) *Eat Pray Love* and *#Girlboss.*

This need for connection to a world more like myself is kind of like what I'm doing now with Planet Prudence. If I feel lonely in real life or awkward or hurt—or I feel like I need to talk about something—then I write about it. Suddenly, I find there's an entire group that agrees or feels the same way. This connects us and makes us all feel less alone.

I'm glad I never stopped doing what I was born to do. And I love that I never gave up on the person that I was meant to be when I entered the world. Because, through my art and the capability of reaching a large crowd of amazing people, my perspective on life has changed. I love life a little more and appreciate every little flaw I own. I've learned to embrace myself as I am—with every freckle or inch of cellulite on my body.

As a three-year-old, I wanted to make a change in the world. As a twenty-five year old, I'm glad that I can. I've received so many messages from people who love the way I portray myself, how I portray the most awkward of situations, and how I demonstrate how *human* we are all allowed to be. It makes people fight and beat eating disorders, depression, and low self-esteem. These people may not really realize it, but they make me happier and healthier as well. They make me see myself as worthy—that I'm good enough—and they make me feel less lonely.

I want to thank my three-year-old self for being strong enough to have dreams and for believing that they could come true. And I want to thank all the people who are following me—you are the reason why I'm writing this book and why I'm drawing on a daily basis.

Art means more to me than anyone could ever imagine. Without art, I don't think I would even be here.

Someone already tried to take my passion away from me and make me feel as if everything was lost. But by losing myself entirely afterwards, and being at the lowest I could ever be, I was able to start over, pick myself up again, and keep going. Moving forward, and going uphill again, was only because of art. Art is the blood in my veins, the oxygen in my lungs, the life I was given at birth.

I hope you'll hold on to this book and that it provides comfort in the tough and awkward times of your life. If you ever look in the mirror and feel less than yourself, or have days when you feel you aren't good enough, or days when *everything* that could possibly go wrong has gone wrong, I hope—when you open this book—that you suddenly feel good again. That you are able to smile, love life, and feel happiness and acceptance once more. With this book comes laughter, joy, and a bundle of love from me to you!

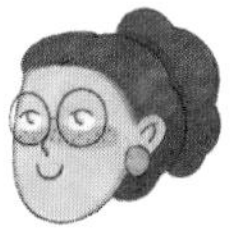

I Love Me

Just like she has for you, Mother Nature has given me a beautiful body, which I love very much. I get to feed myself, take care of myself, see myself grow, and love myself everyday. I get to touch every bit of my body and spend my whole life in it—taking care and appreciating it. We all have flaws that we can't really control, such as cellulite, or acne, or things we'd rather not have. But we *can* all decide whether we love it or not. And I'd rather spend my wonderful and short life loving my body than hating it. Appreciation takes less energy <3.

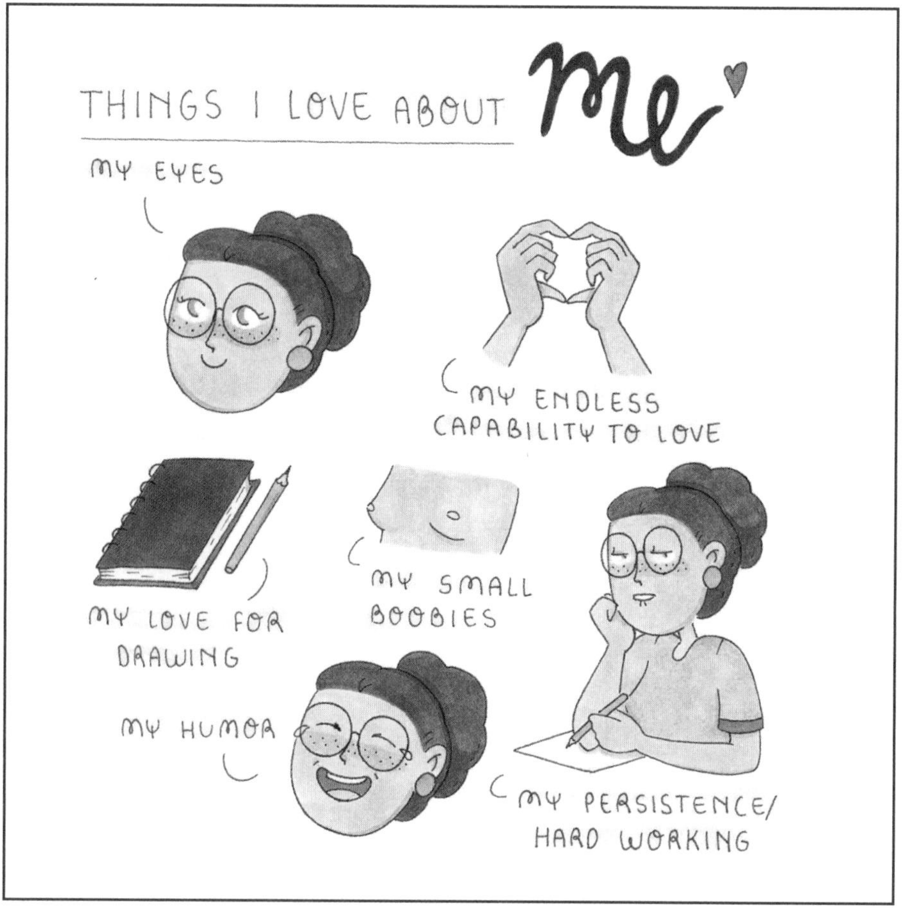
THINGS I LOVE ABOUT me
MY EYES
MY ENDLESS CAPABILITY TO LOVE
MY LOVE FOR DRAWING
MY SMALL BOOBIES
MY HUMOR
MY PERSISTENCE/ HARD WORKING

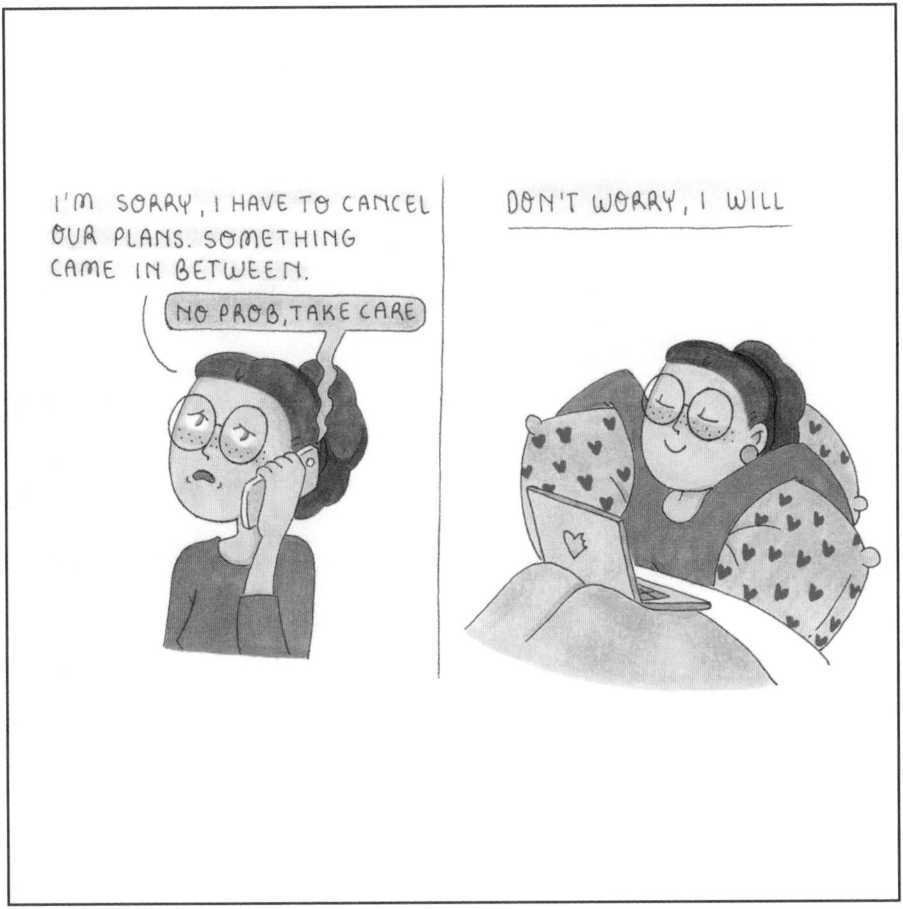
I'M SORRY, I HAVE TO CANCEL OUR PLANS. SOMETHING CAME IN BETWEEN.
NO PROB, TAKE CARE
DON'T WORRY, I WILL

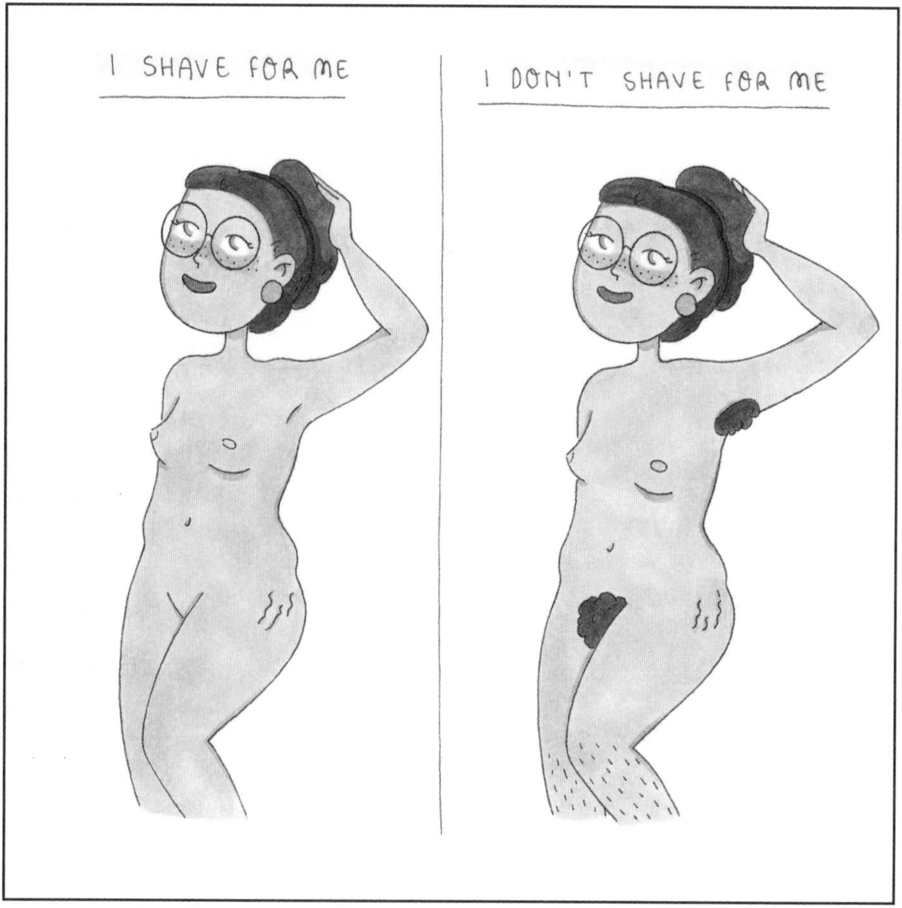
I SHAVE FOR ME
I DON'T SHAVE FOR ME

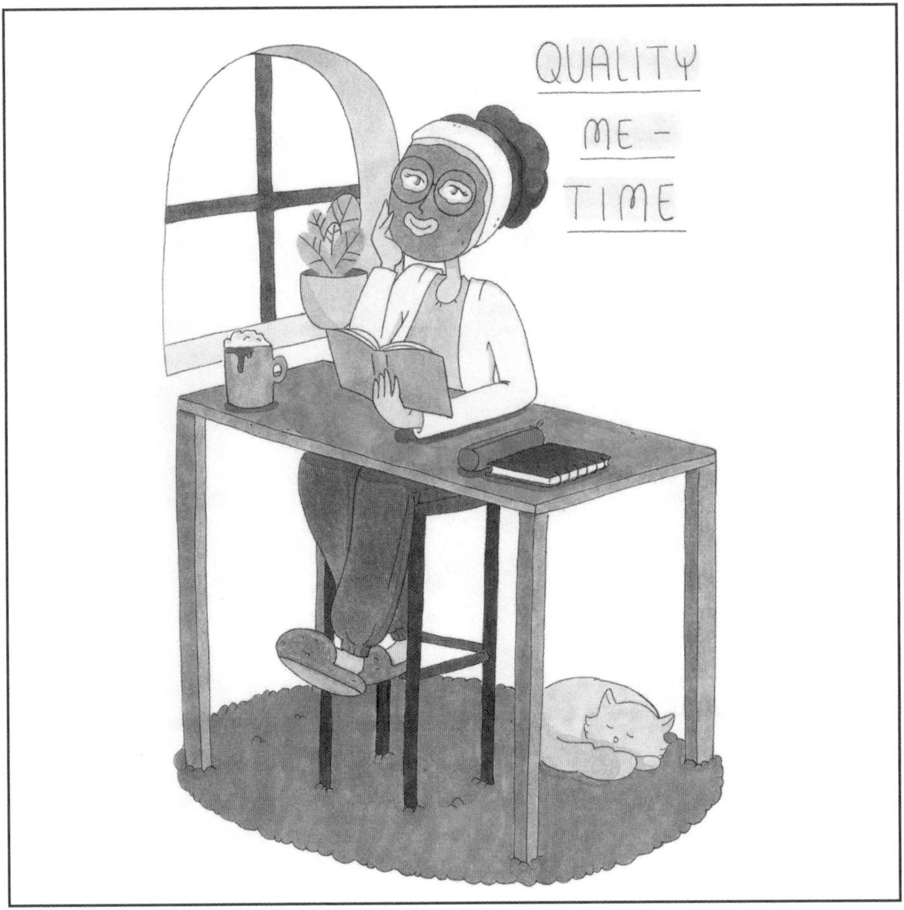
QUALITY
ME -
TIME

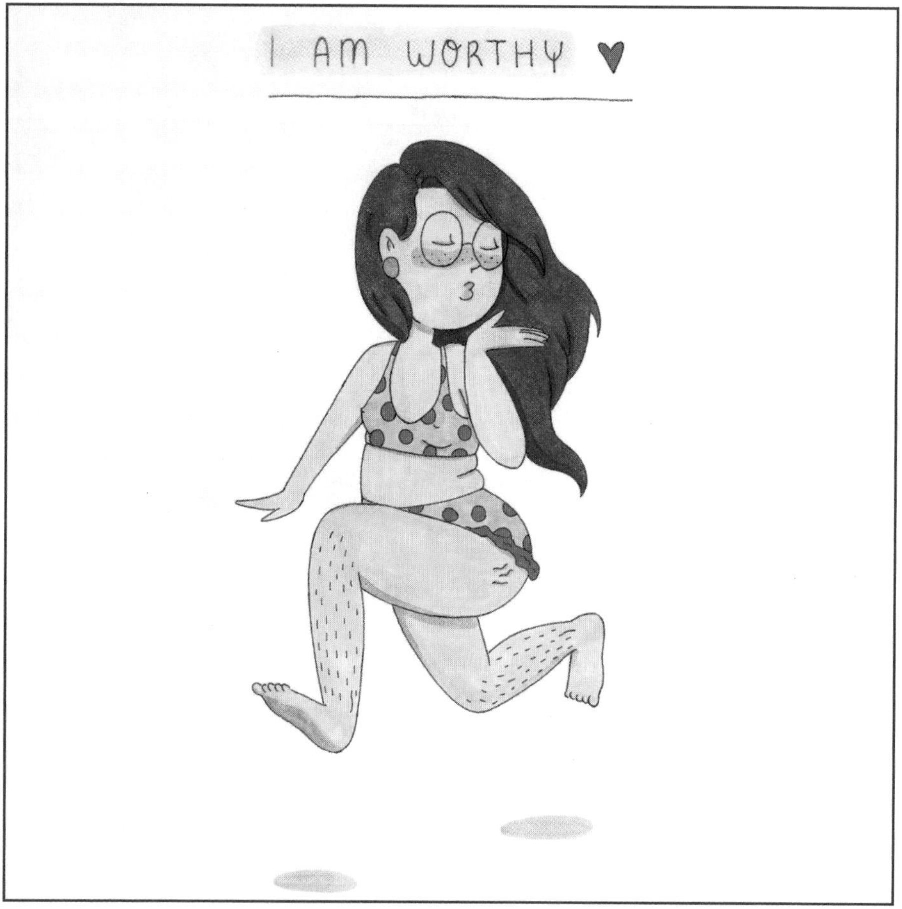
I AM WORTHY ♥

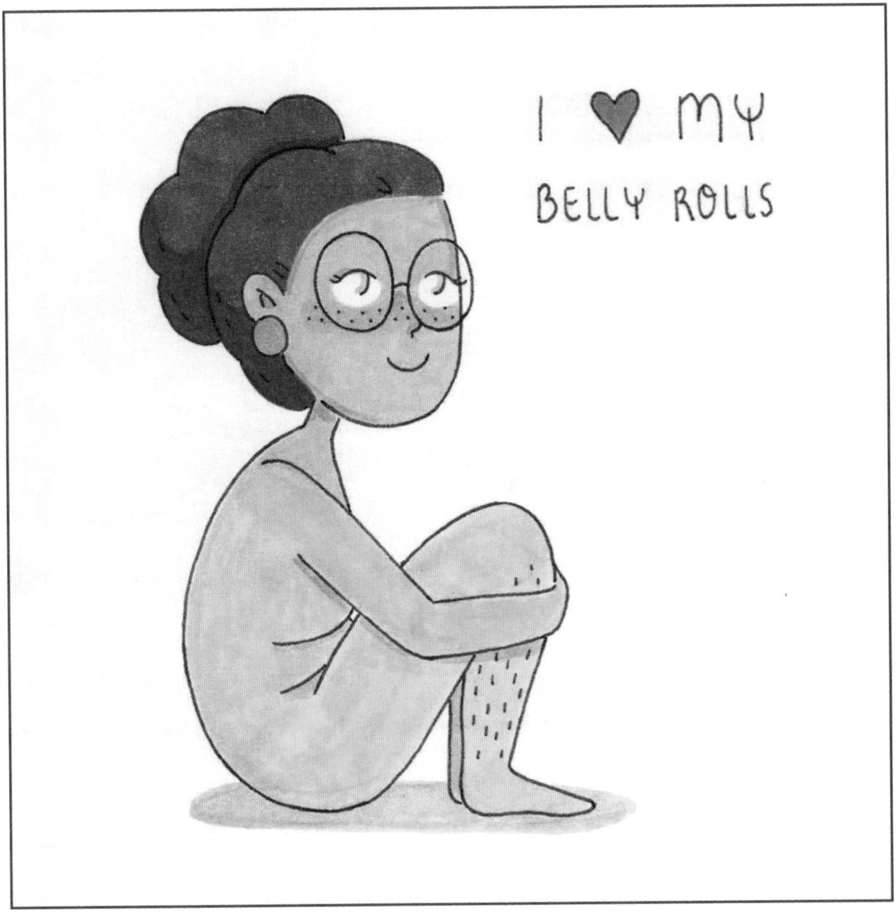
I ♥ MY
BELLY ROLLS

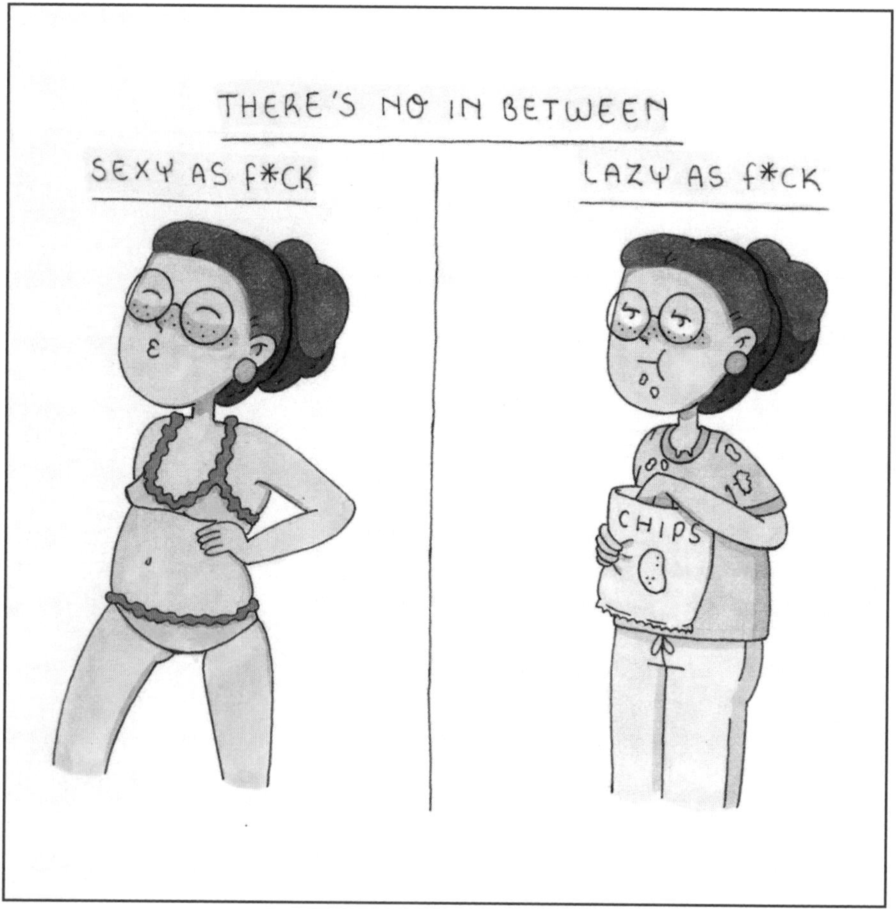
THERE'S NO IN BETWEEN
SEXY AS F*CK
LAZY AS F*CK
CHIPS

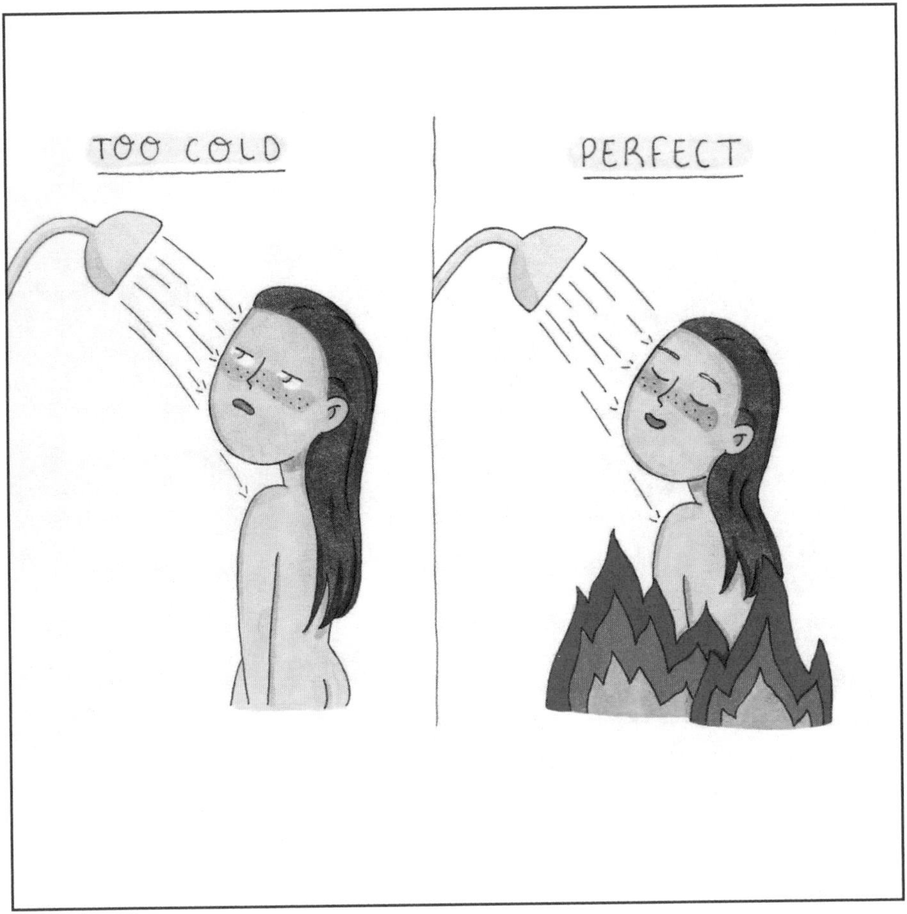
TOO COLD
PERFECT

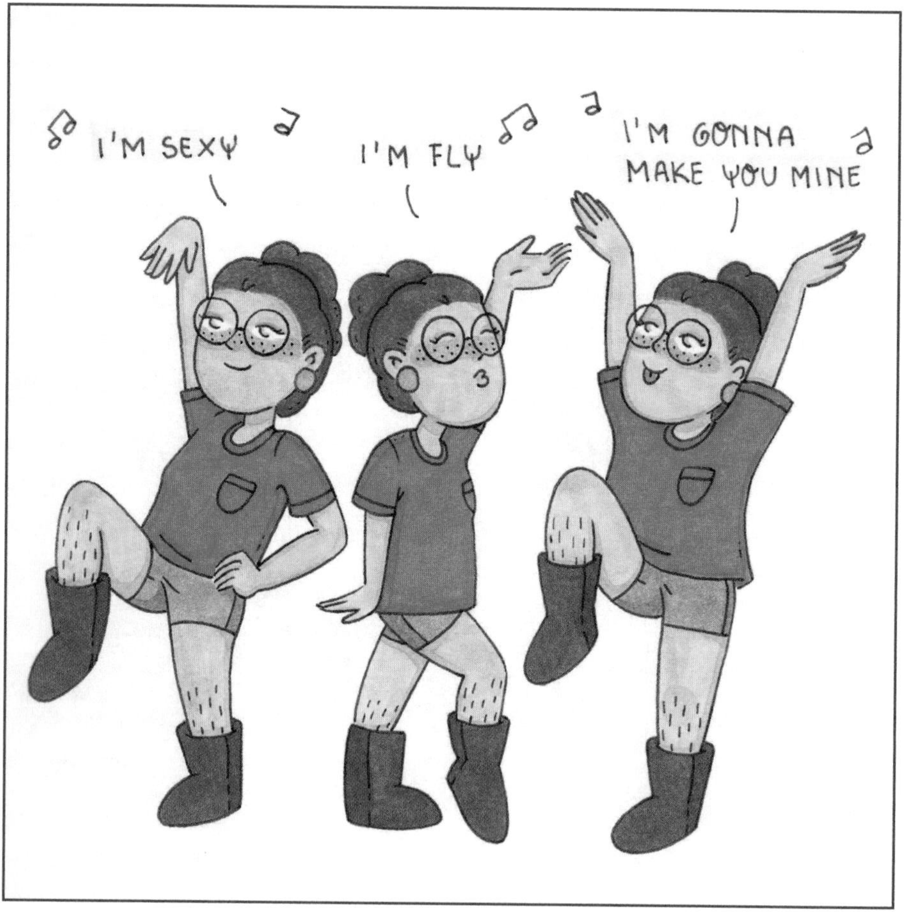
I'M SEXY
I'M FLY
I'M GONNA MAKE YOU MINE

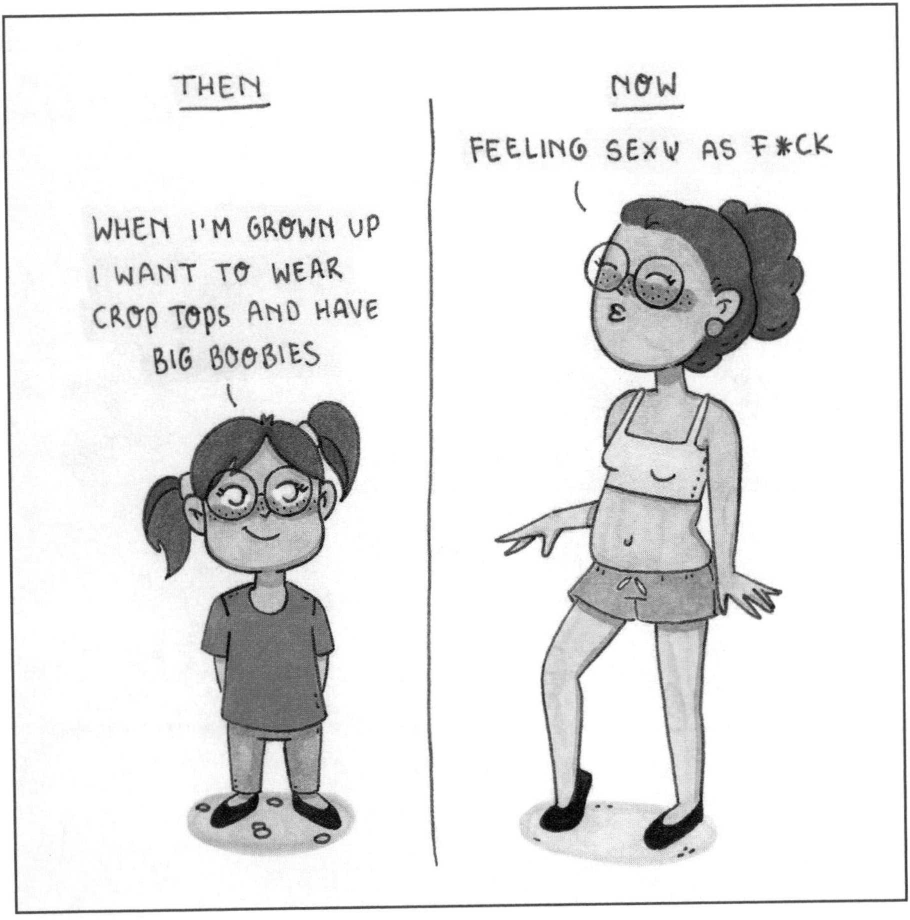
THEN
NOW
WHEN I'M GROWN UP I WANT TO WEAR CROP TOPS AND HAVE BIG BOOBIES
FEELING SEXY AS F*CK

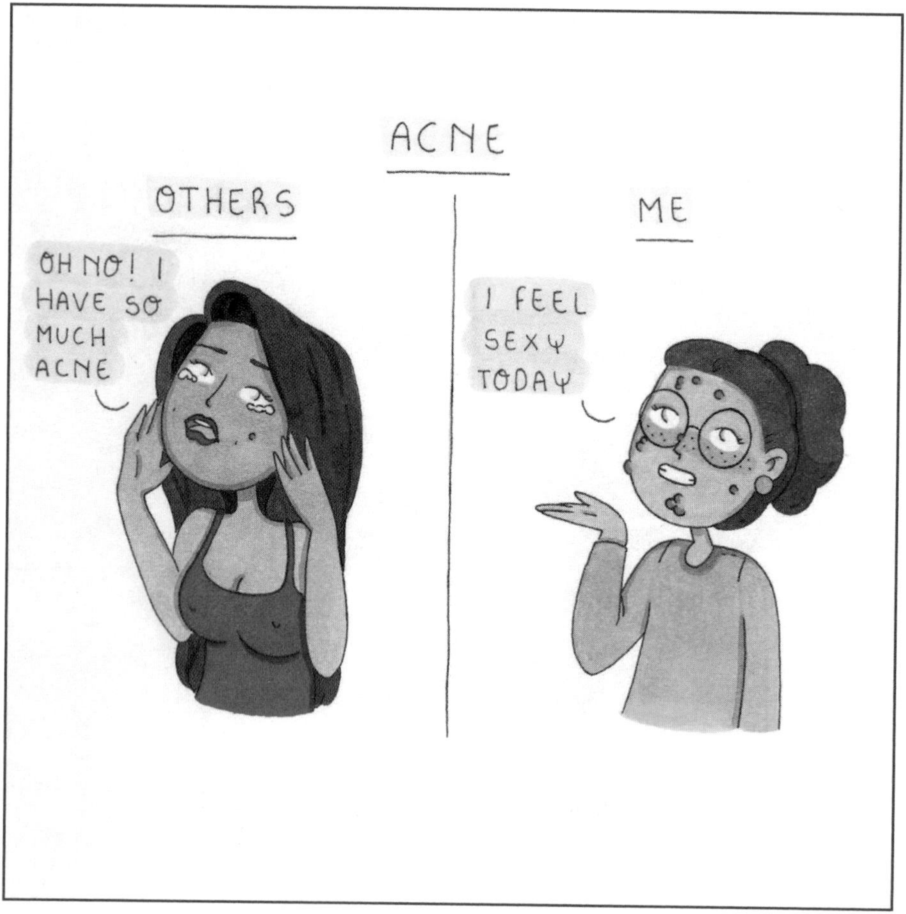
ACNE
OTHERS
OH NO! I HAVE SO MUCH ACNE
ME
I FEEL SEXY TODAY

Om Nom Nom

Food is life and life is food. There's no other way to put it.
We can accept the fact that cabbage is healthy, yet mostly
tastes like water, and that kale is meant to taste funny (and I
often nourish my body by eating my veggies) but—let's face it—
chocolate, chips, and cookies are also part of a balanced diet...
right? I hope! And on top of this we are lucky enough to live in a
world where some genius invented fast-food and there's just no
way to escape it. It's everywhere—even on my plate! So embrace
the good with the bad and try to make more good decisions than
not-so-great ones and you'll be OK.

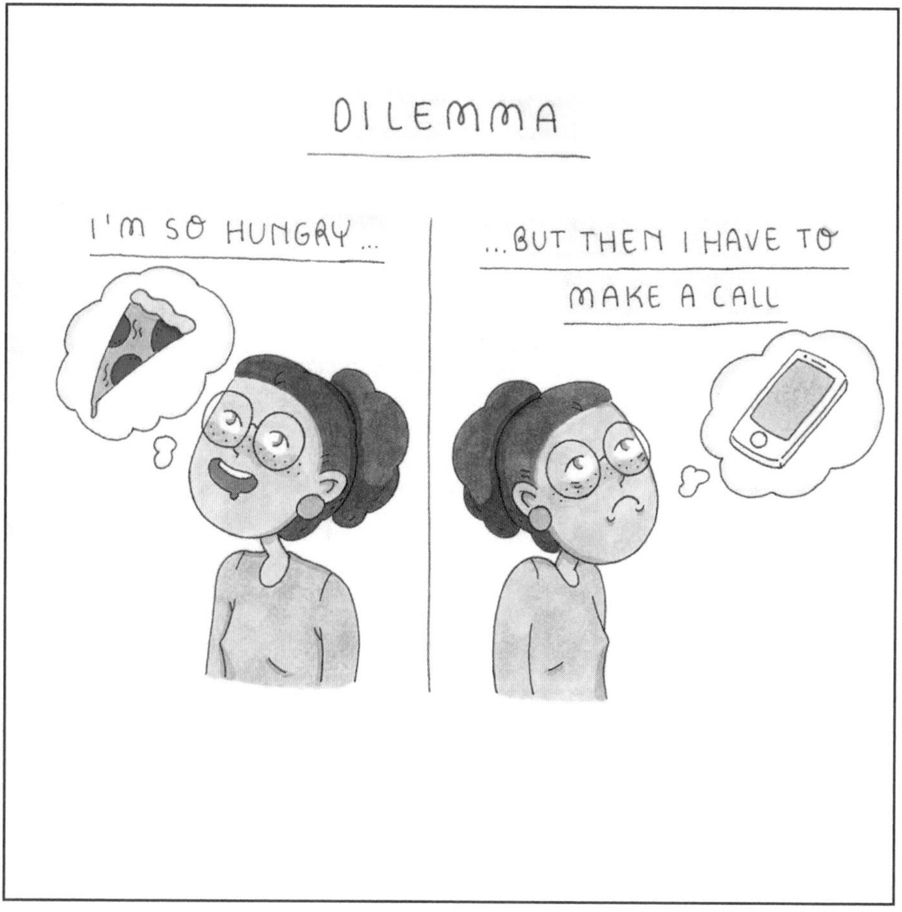
DILEMMA
I'M SO HUNGRY...
...BUT THEN I HAVE TO MAKE A CALL

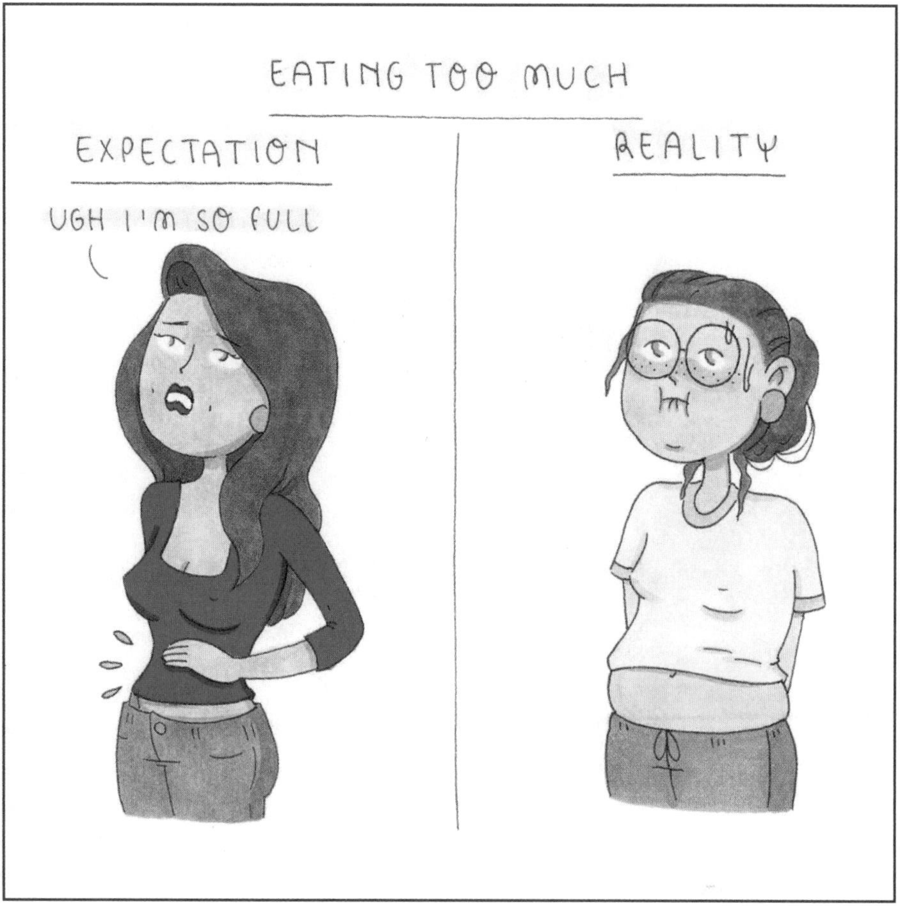
EATING TOO MUCH
EXPECTATION
REALITY
UGH I'M SO FULL

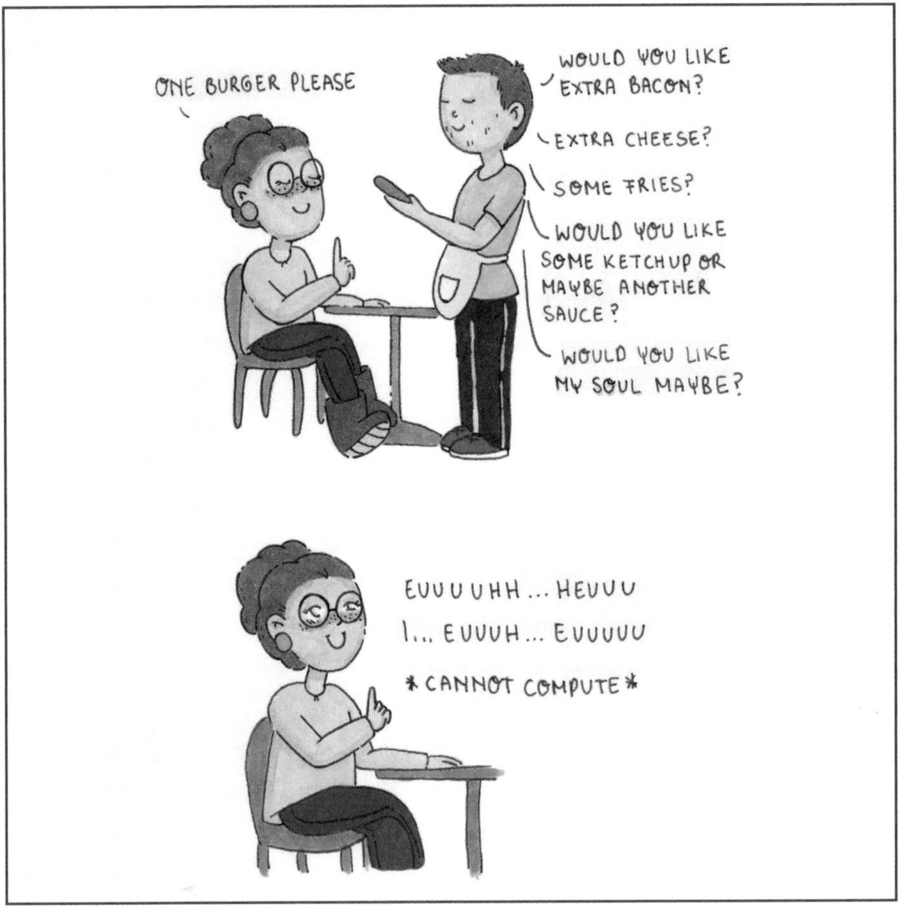
ONE BURGER PLEASE
WOULD YOU LIKE EXTRA BACON?
EXTRA CHEESE?
SOME FRIES?
WOULD YOU LIKE SOME KETCHUP OR MAYBE ANOTHER SAUCE?
WOULD YOU LIKE MY SOUL MAYBE?
EUUUUHH... HEUUU
I... EUUUH... EUUUUU
CANNOT COMPUTE

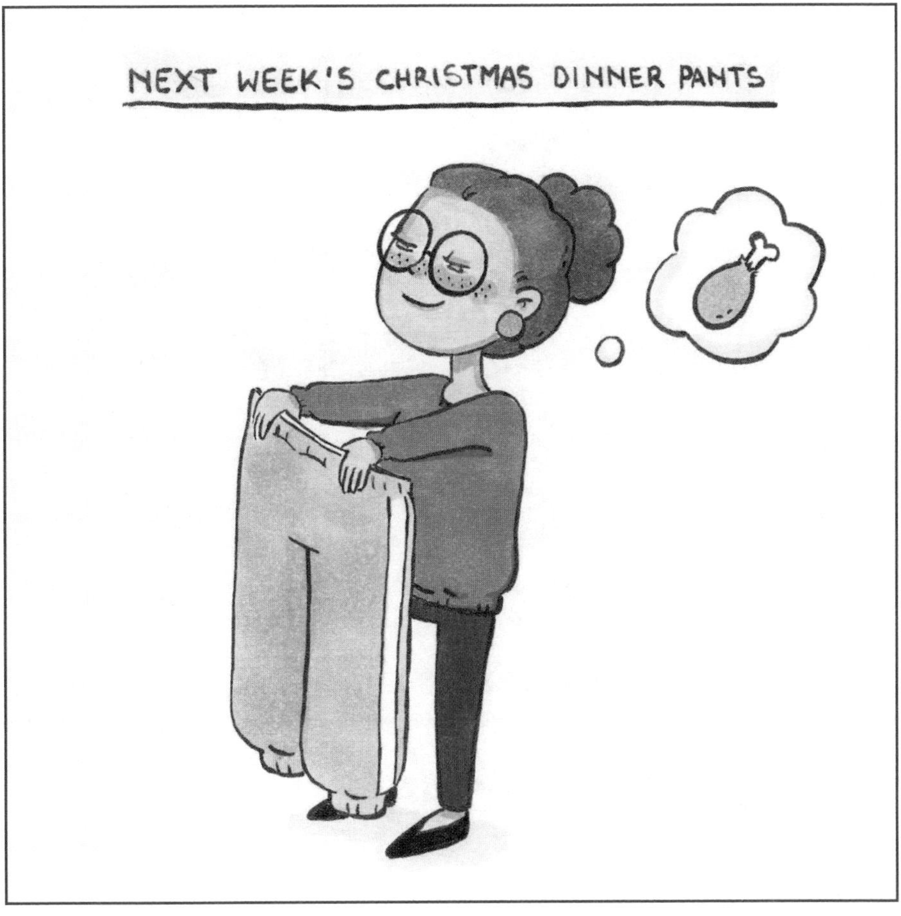
NEXT WEEK'S CHRISTMAS DINNER PANTS

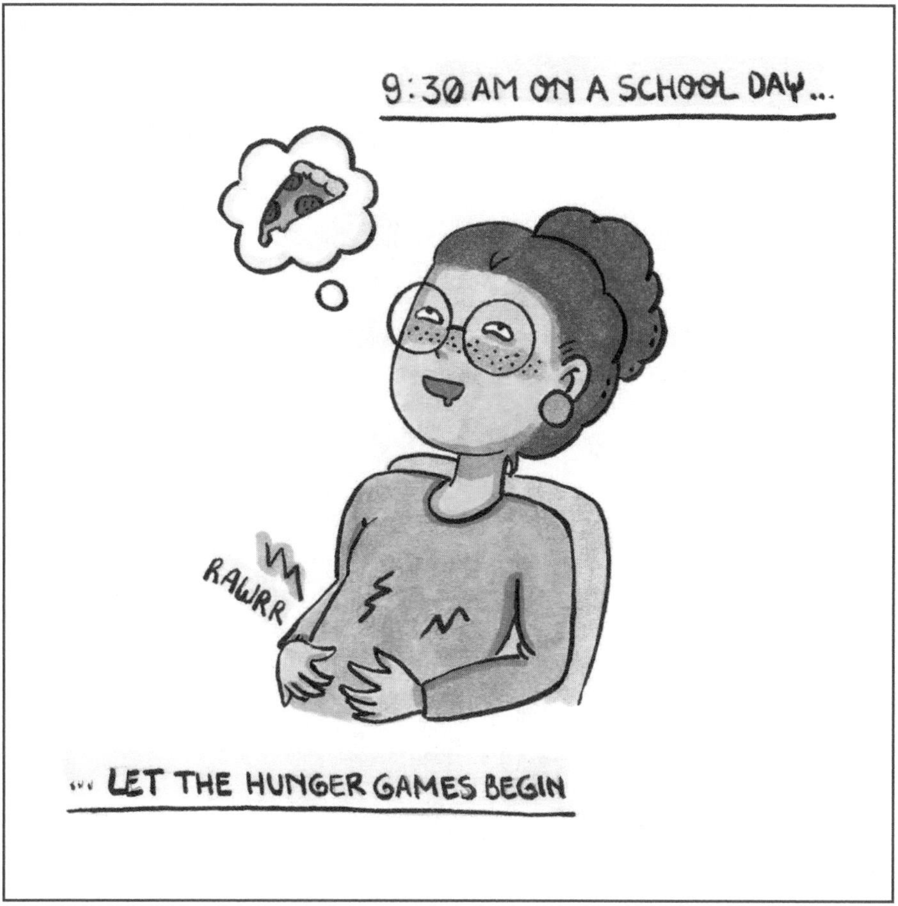
9:30 AM ON A SCHOOL DAY...
RAWRR
... LET THE HUNGER GAMES BEGIN

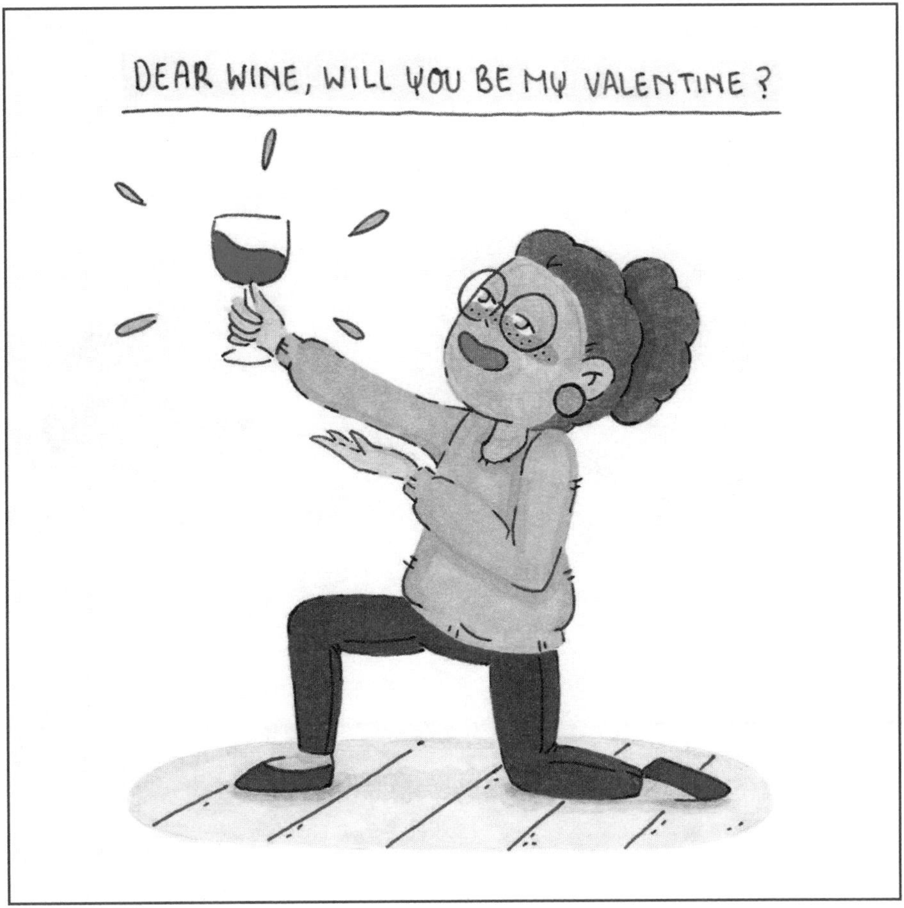
DEAR WINE, WILL YOU BE MY VALENTINE ?

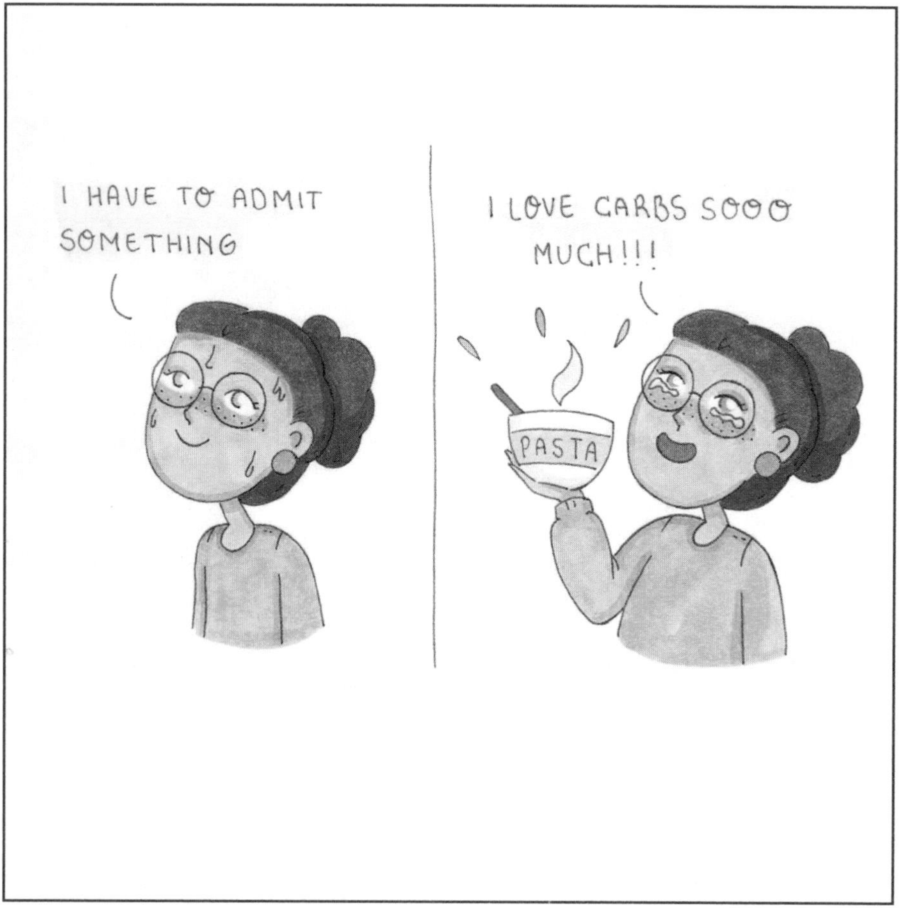
I HAVE TO ADMIT SOMETHING
I LOVE CARBS SOOO MUCH!!!
PASTA

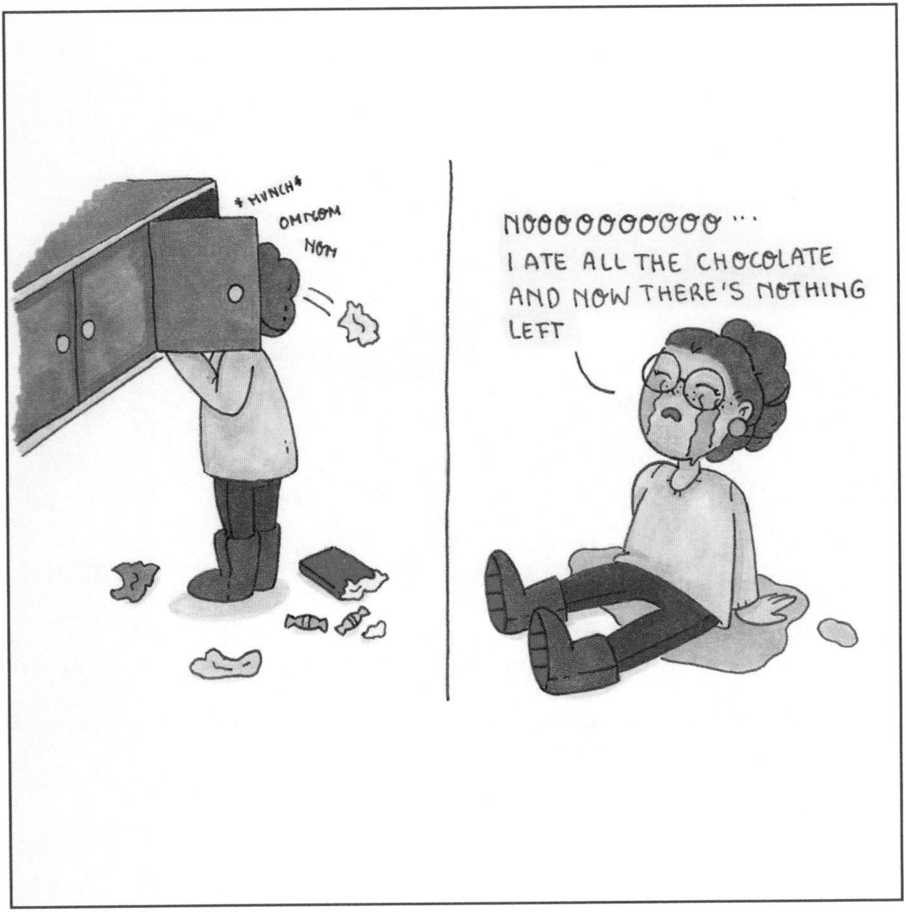
MUNCH
OMNOM
NOM
NOOOOOOOOOO...
I ATE ALL THE CHOCOLATE AND NOW THERE'S NOTHING LEFT

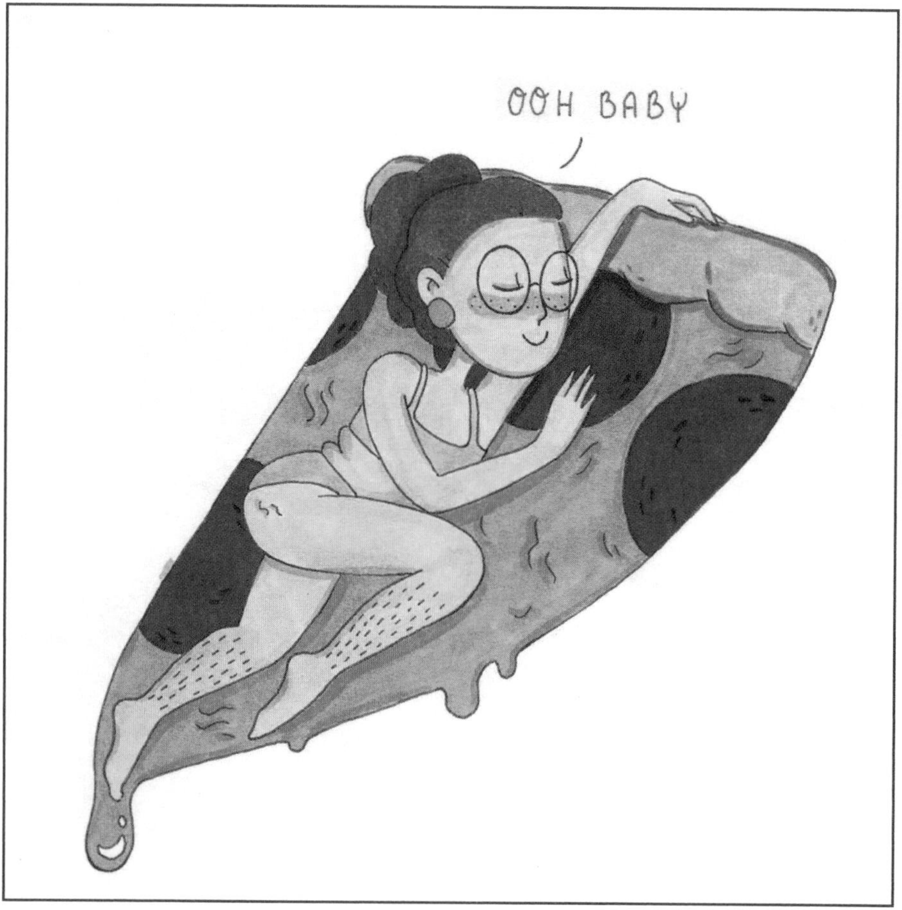
OOH BABY

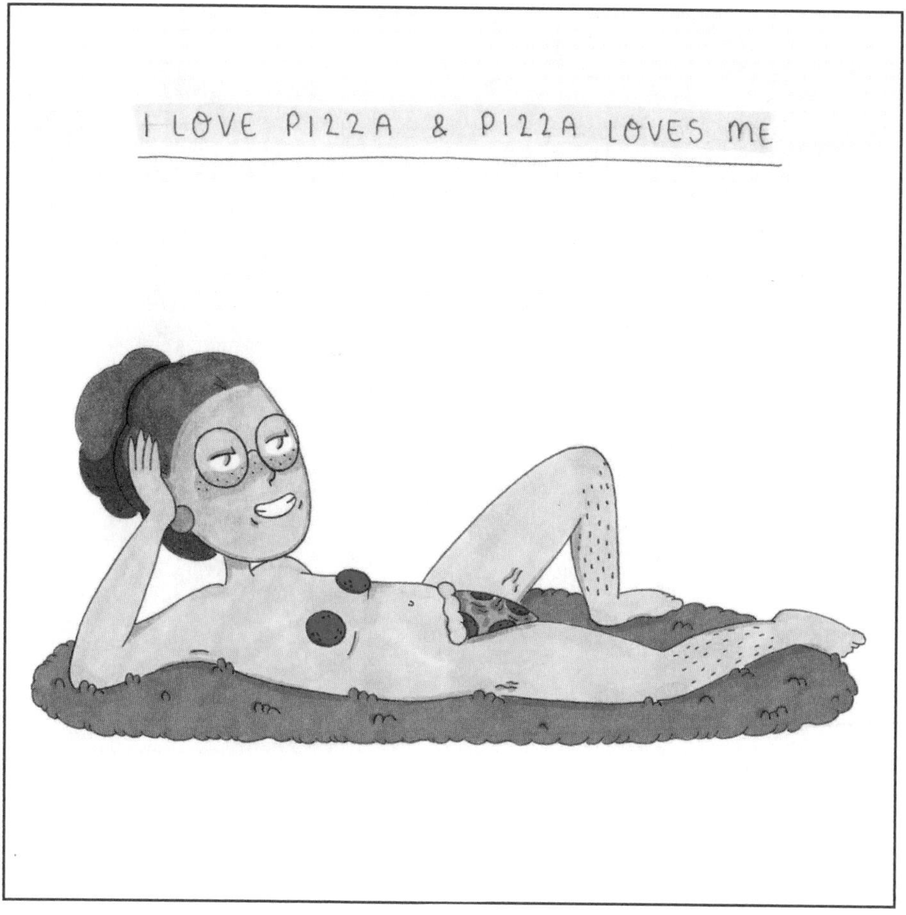
I LOVE PIZZA & PIZZA LOVES ME

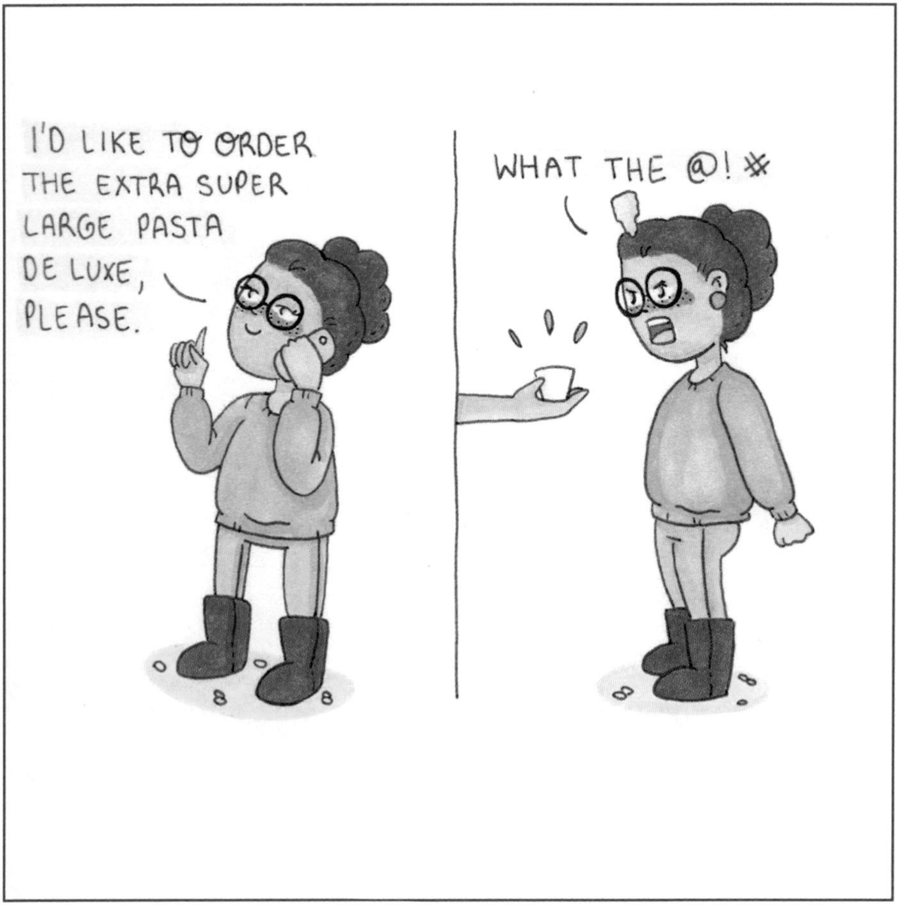
I'D LIKE TO ORDER THE EXTRA SUPER LARGE PASTA DE LUXE, PLEASE.
WHAT THE @!#

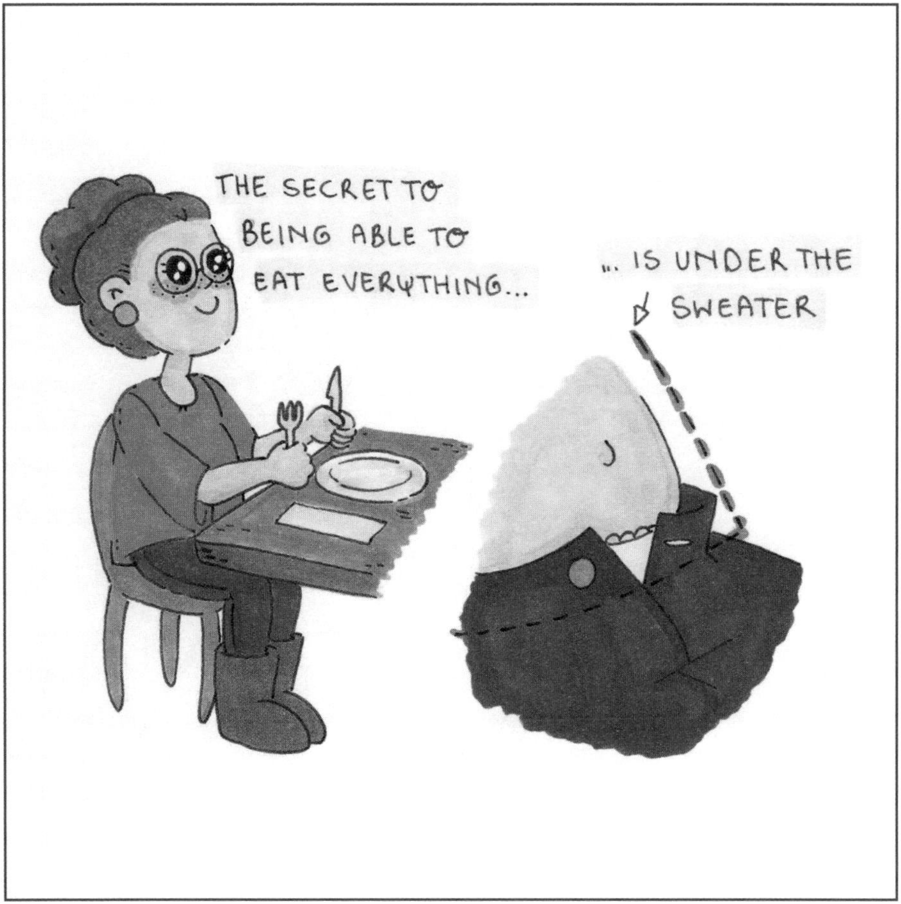
THE SECRET TO BEING ABLE TO EAT EVERYTHING...
... IS UNDER THE SWEATER

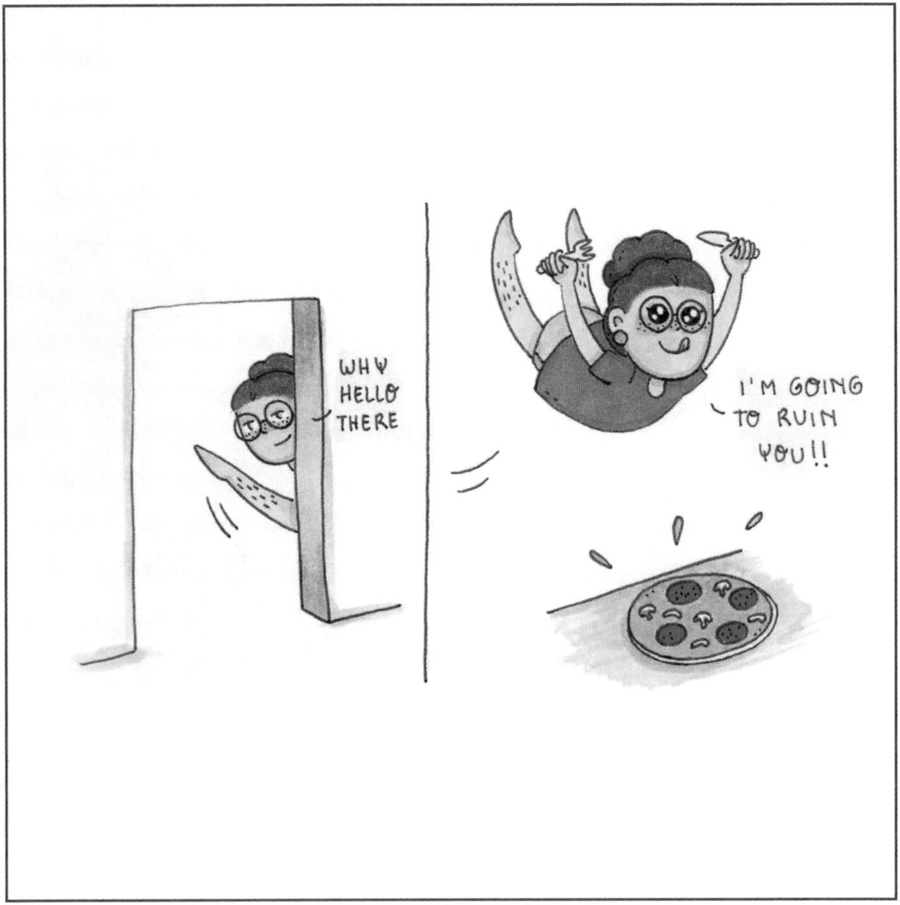
WHY HELLO THERE
I'M GOING TO RUIN YOU!!

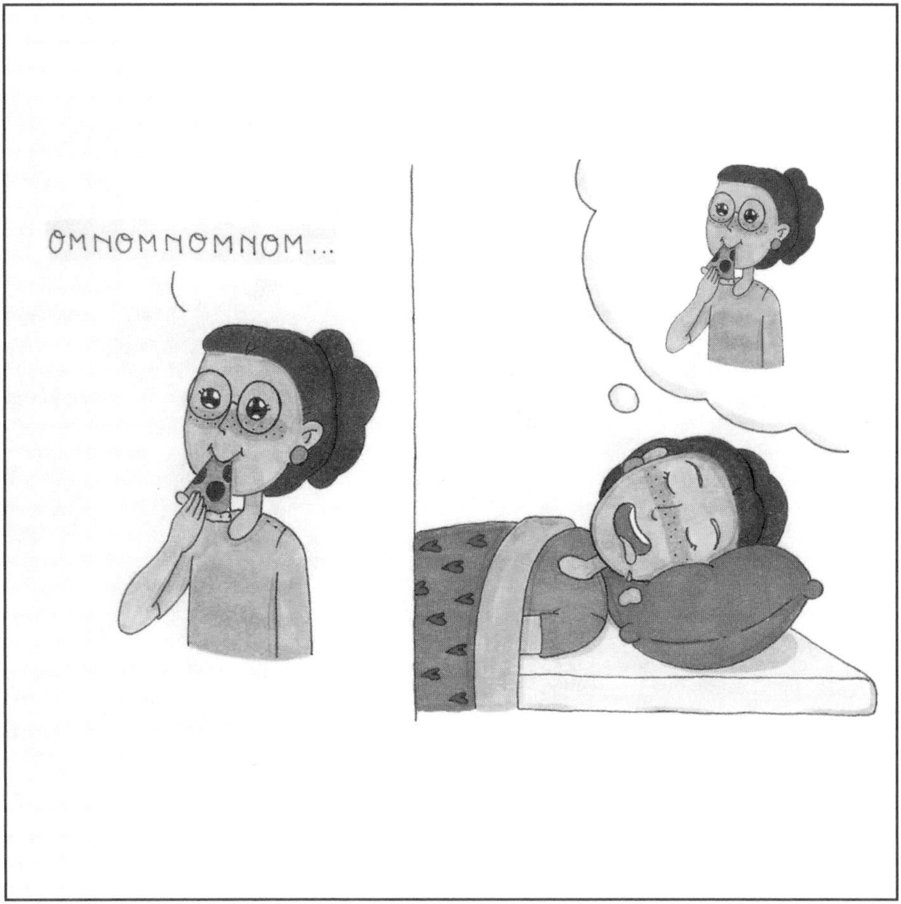
OMNOMNOMNOM...

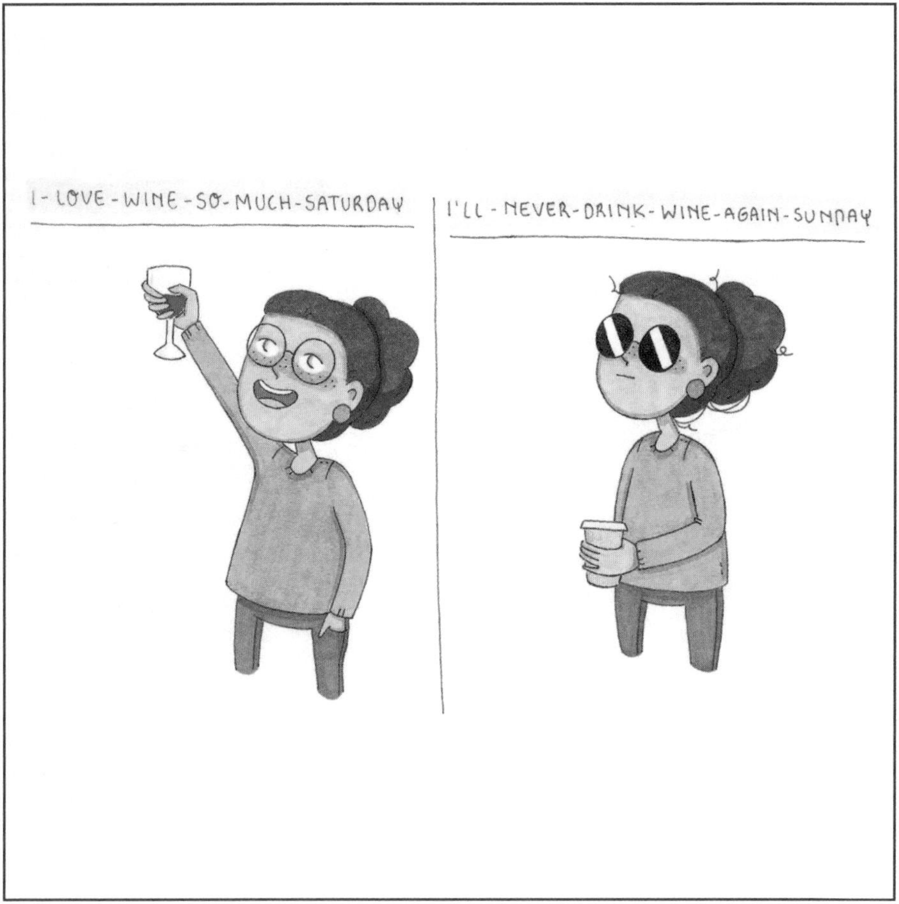
I-LOVE-WINE-SO-MUCH-SATURDAY
I'LL-NEVER-DRINK-WINE-AGAIN-SUNDAY

Social Butterfly–
Anti-Social Butterfly

I often find myself drowning in a bath of sadness and despair. It won't kill me and it'll probably make me a lot stronger in the end, but it happens. Also, there's sunshine and rainbows after the rain. However, we do not remember this when we're in the moment of sadness. In the moment, the world will end, demons will haunt us at night, and things will never be good again.

But I want you to know that things *do* get better and these moments will pass. Let's just embrace our weaknesses and look forward to brighter days.

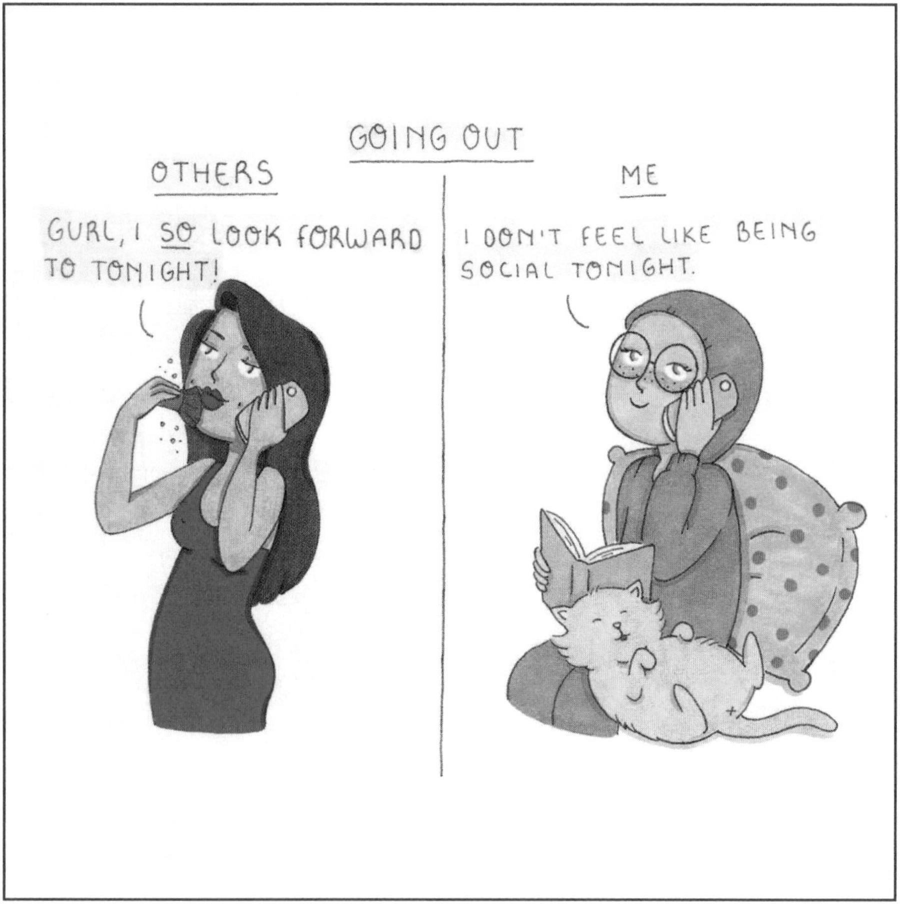
GOING OUT
OTHERS
ME
GURL, I SO LOOK FORWARD TO TONIGHT!
I DON'T FEEL LIKE BEING SOCIAL TONIGHT.

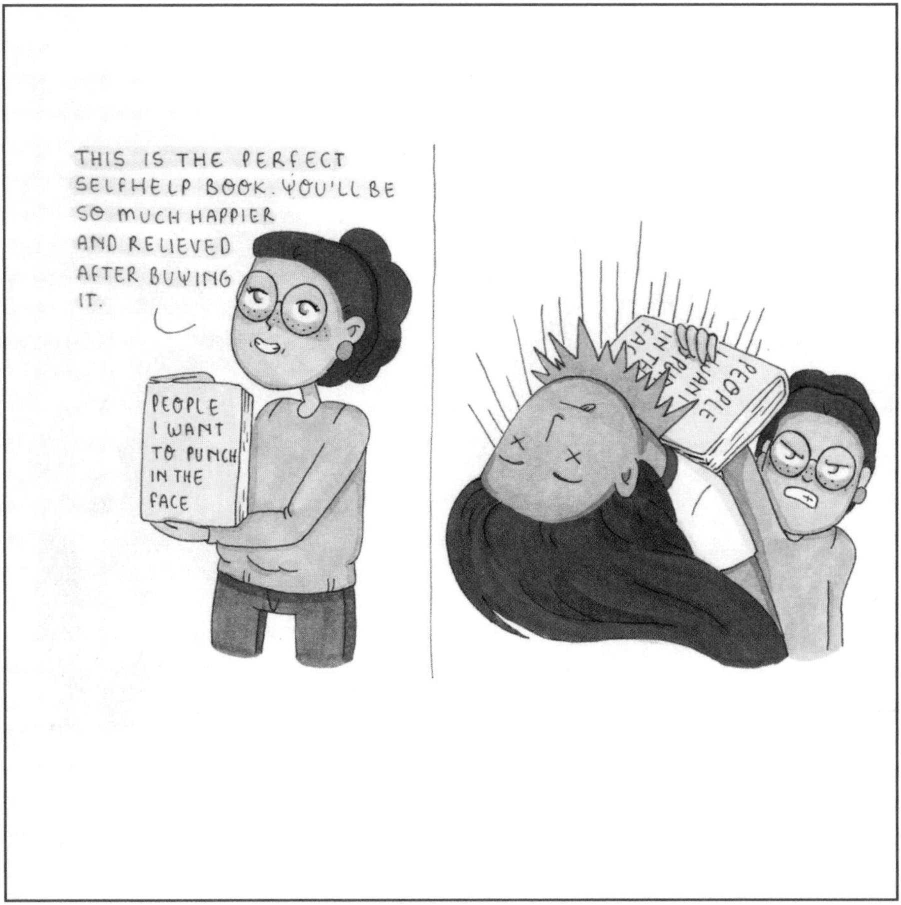
THIS IS THE PERFECT SELFHELP BOOK. YOU'LL BE SO MUCH HAPPIER AND RELIEVED AFTER BUYING IT.
PEOPLE I WANT TO PUNCH IN THE FACE

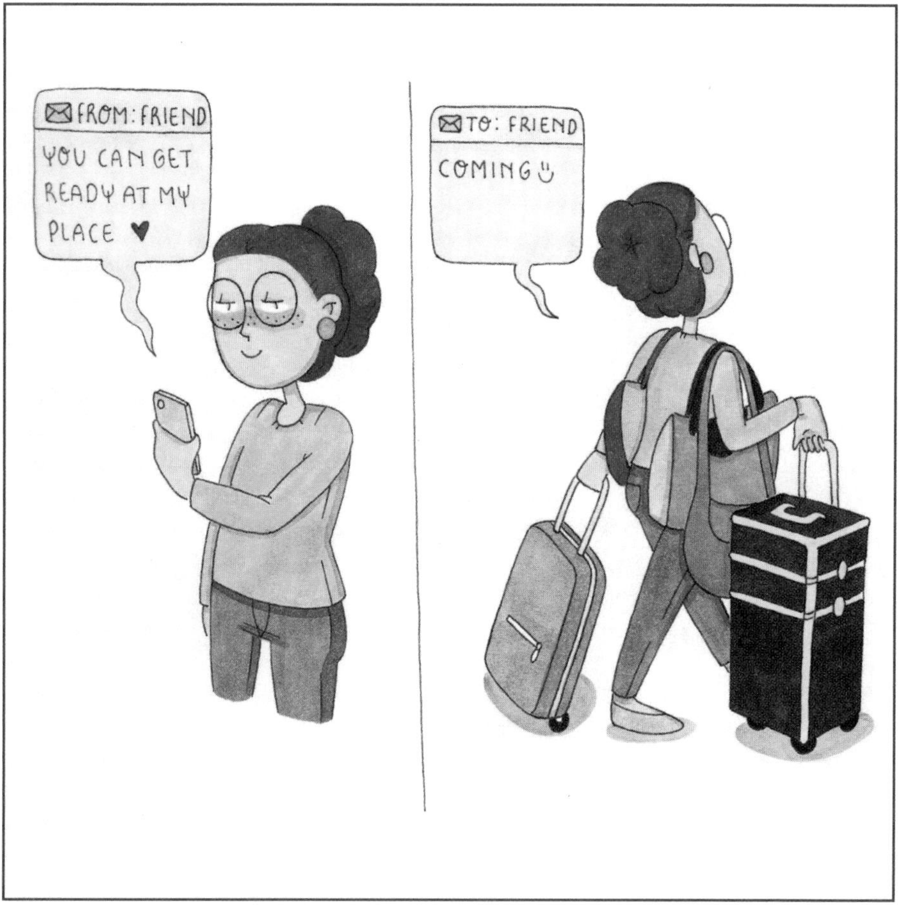
FROM: FRIEND
YOU CAN GET READY AT MY PLACE ♥
TO: FRIEND
COMING

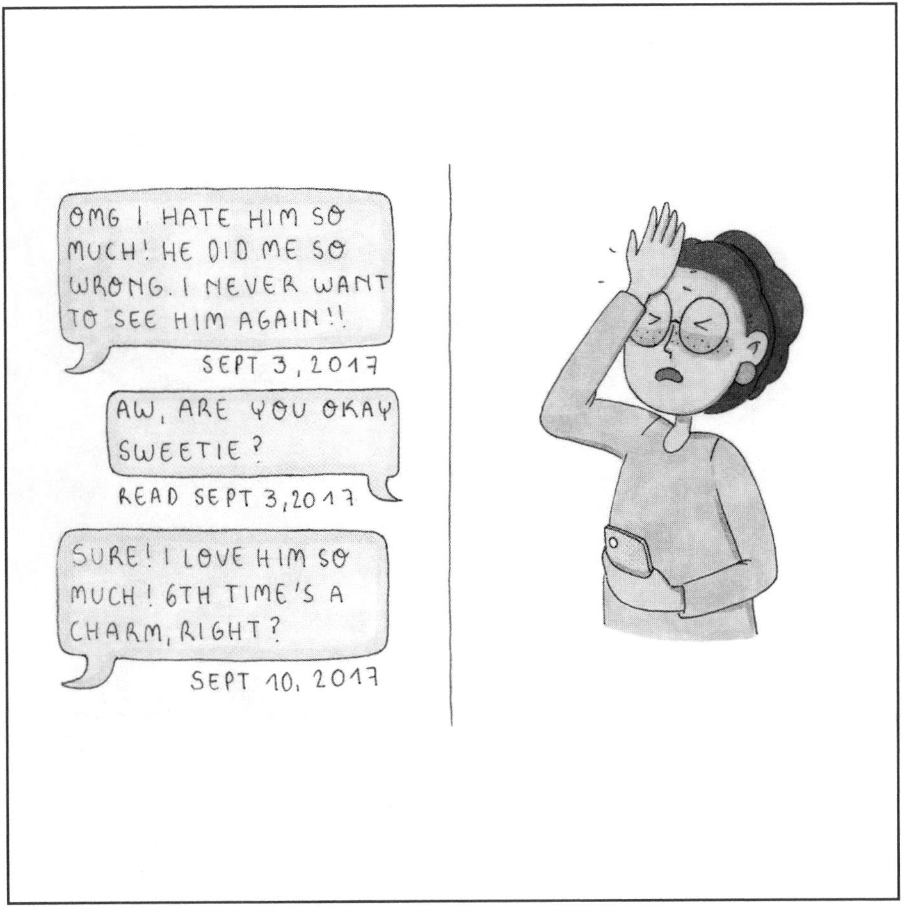
OMG I HATE HIM SO MUCH! HE DID ME SO WRONG. I NEVER WANT TO SEE HIM AGAIN!!
SEPT 3, 2017
AW, ARE YOU OKAY SWEETIE?
READ SEPT 3, 2017
SURE! I LOVE HIM SO MUCH! 6TH TIME'S A CHARM, RIGHT?
SEPT 10, 2017

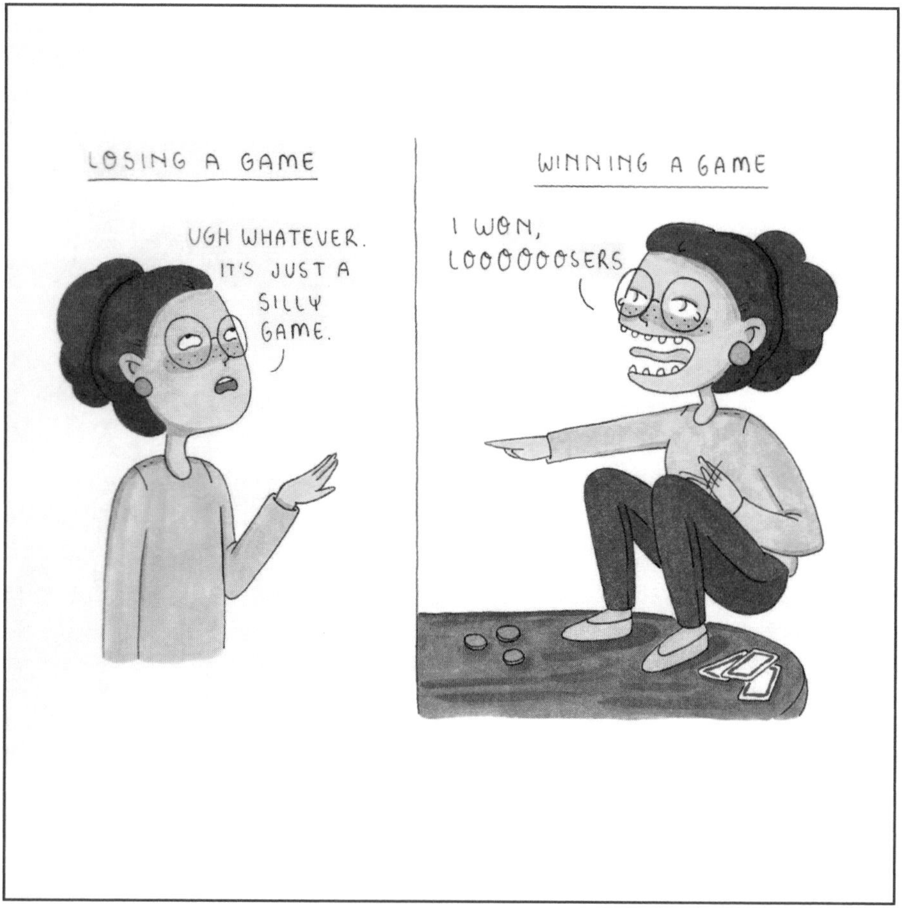
LOSING A GAME
UGH WHATEVER. IT'S JUST A SILLY GAME.
WINNING A GAME
I WON, LOOOOOOOSERS

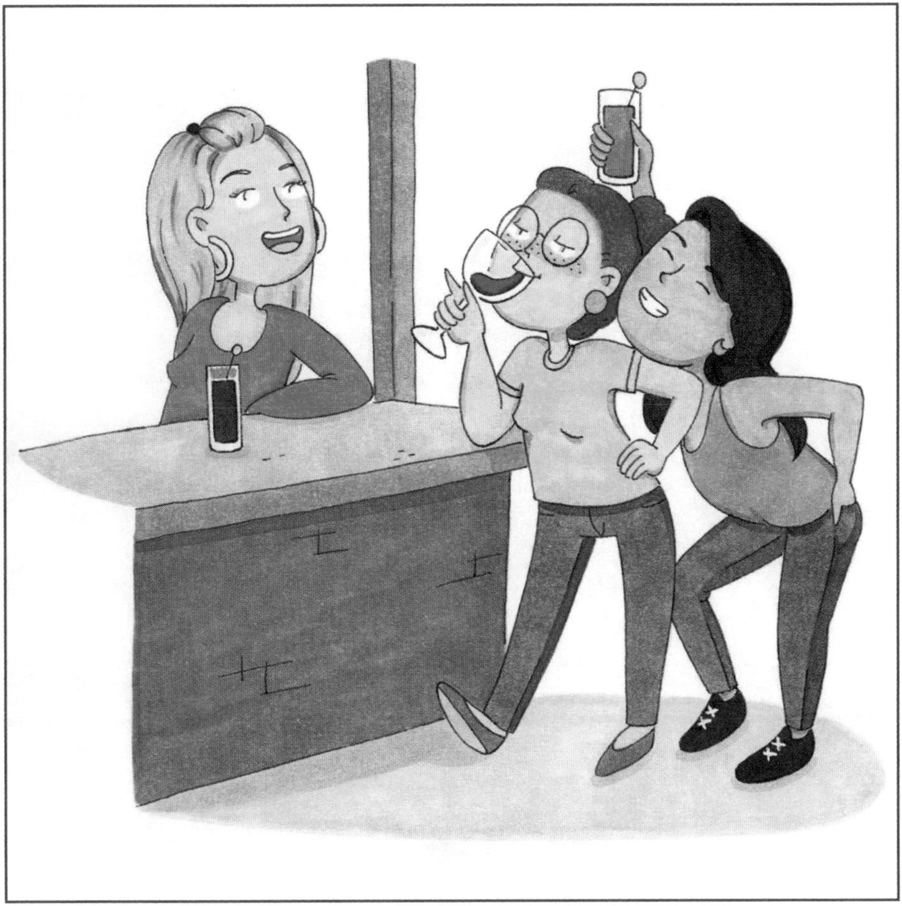

Inside and Out

Well...the truth is that life is a struggle for everyone. From the very rich to the very poor, we all have our own set of unique problems that might not seem so bad to someone else—but that doesn't mean they aren't real. Being a woman is challenging from time to time. For example, I love to decorate my face with makeup. I don't always do so, though, but I am lucky enough to feel confident with or without it. Some aren't so lucky. Let's face it—pun intended—many people watch makeup tutorials for a reason. And those of us who do wonder how some are able to apply makeup and end up looking like flawless dolls. If you are like me, you end up frustrated and just go for the Panda look...which looks great!

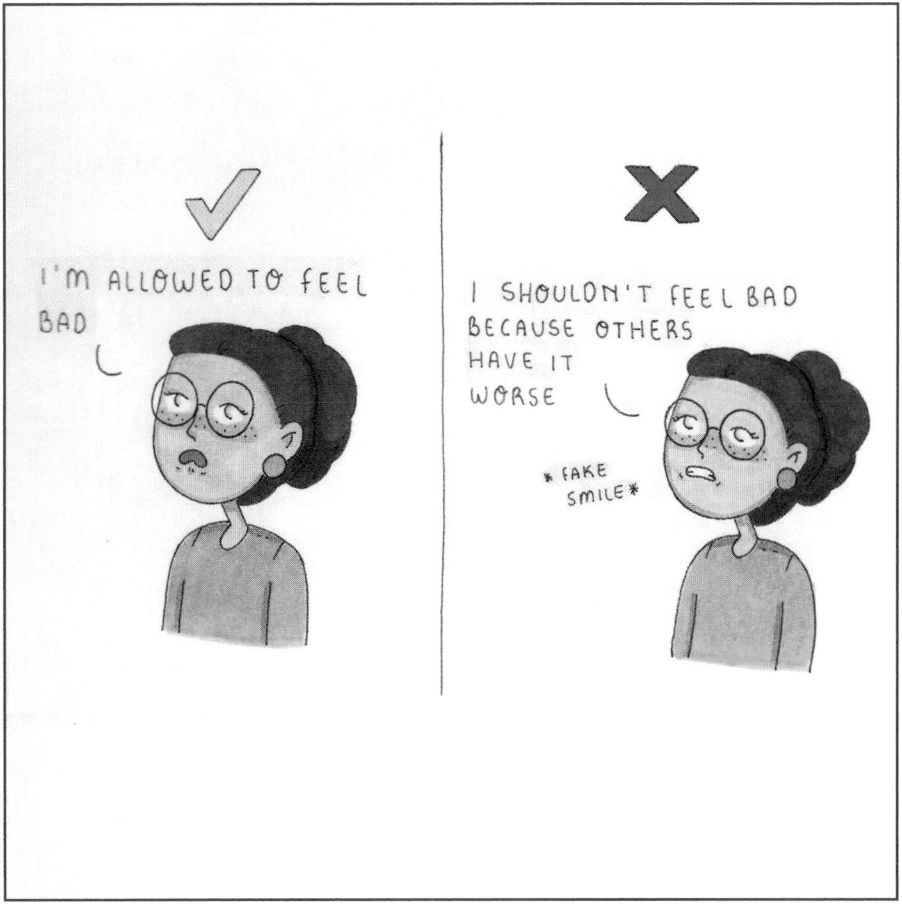
I'M ALLOWED TO FEEL BAD
I SHOULDN'T FEEL BAD BECAUSE OTHERS HAVE IT WORSE
FAKE SMILE

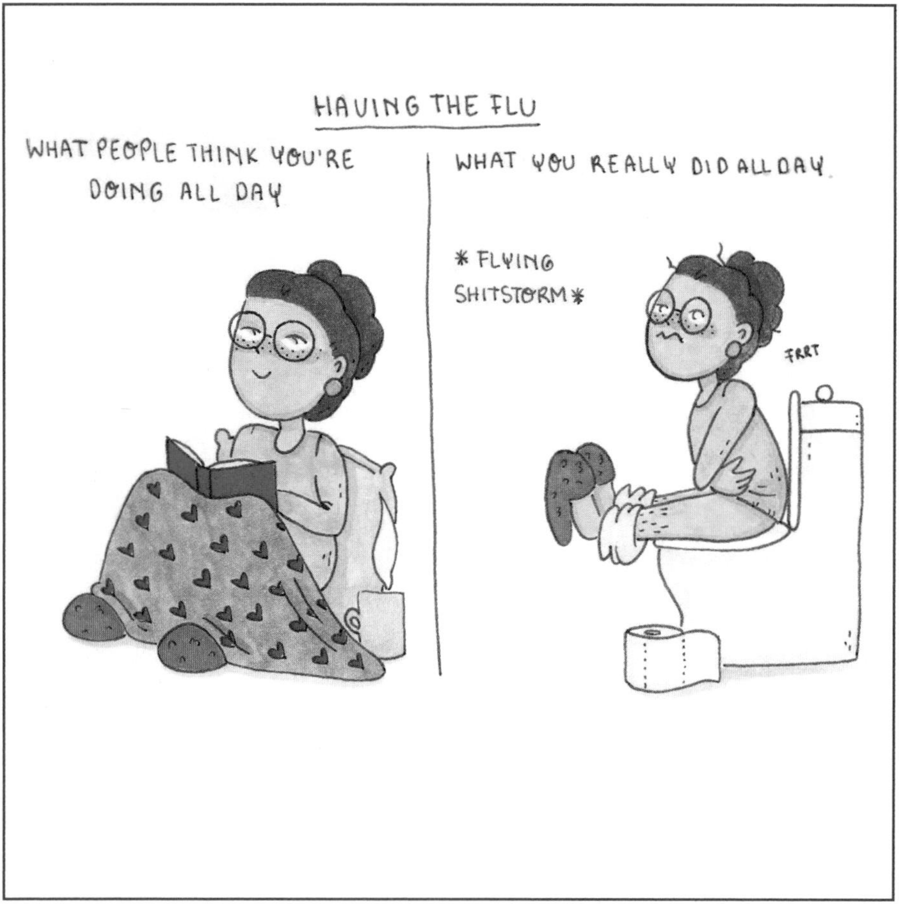
HAVING THE FLU
WHAT PEOPLE THINK YOU'RE DOING ALL DAY
WHAT YOU REALLY DID ALL DAY.
* FLYING SHITSTORM *
FRRT

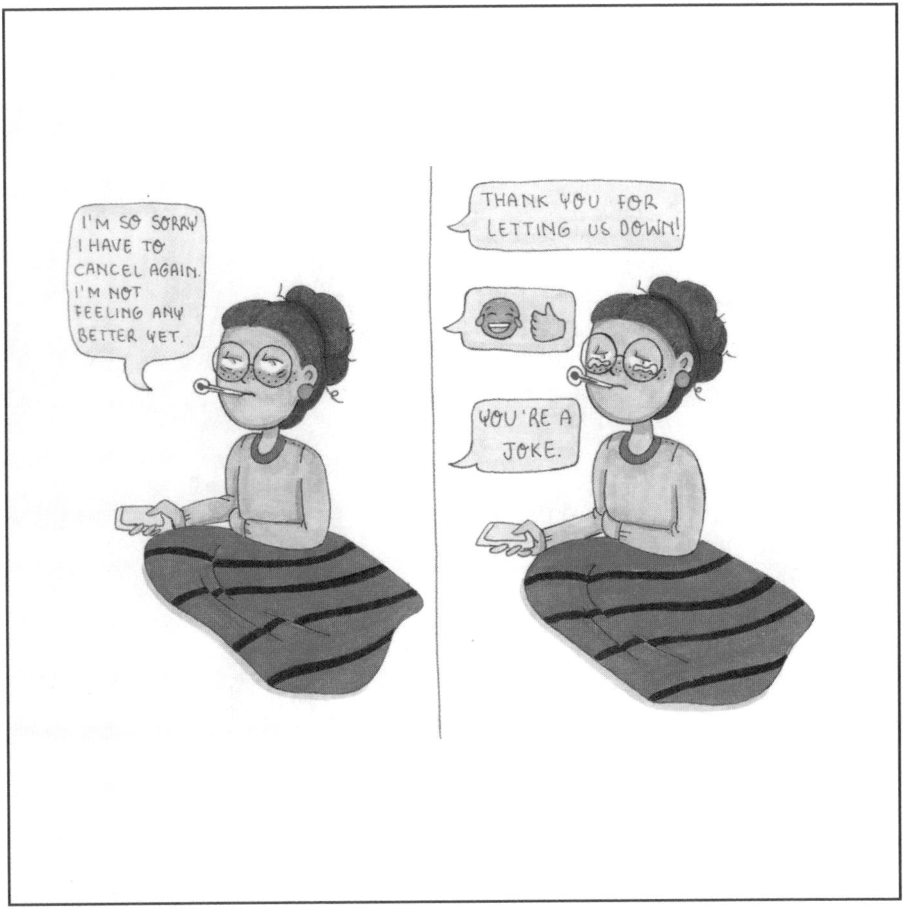
I'M SO SORRY I HAVE TO CANCEL AGAIN. I'M NOT FEELING ANY BETTER YET.
THANK YOU FOR LETTING US DOWN!
YOU'RE A JOKE.

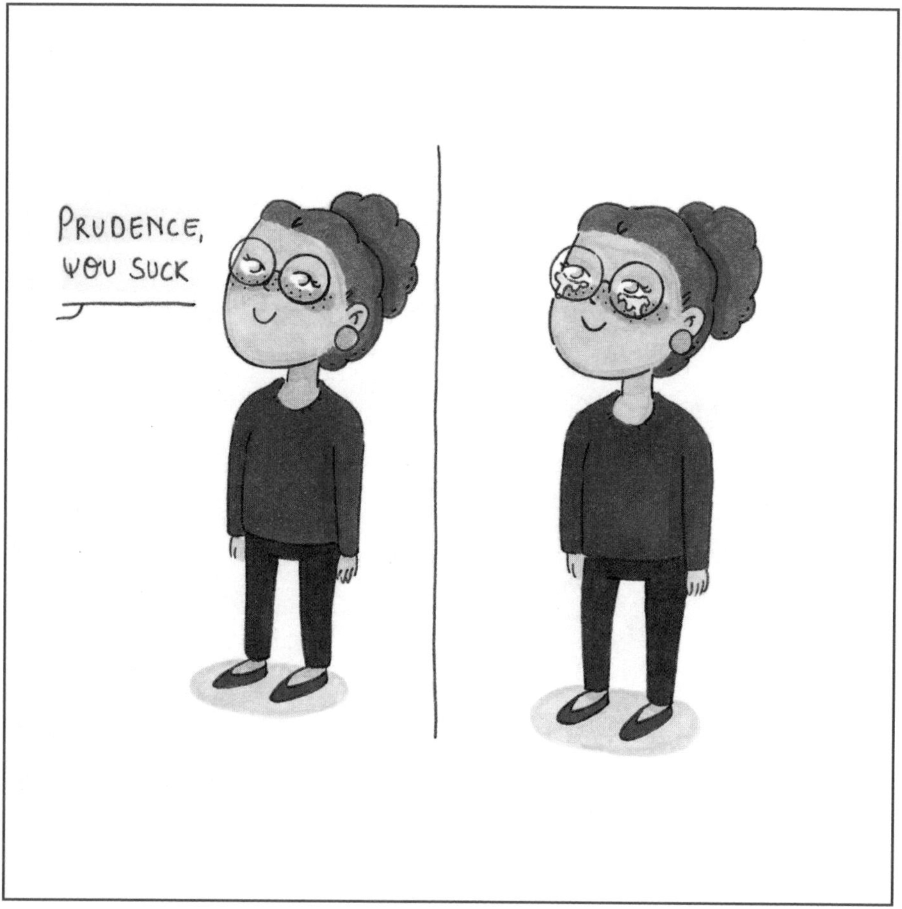
PRUDENCE,
YOU SUCK

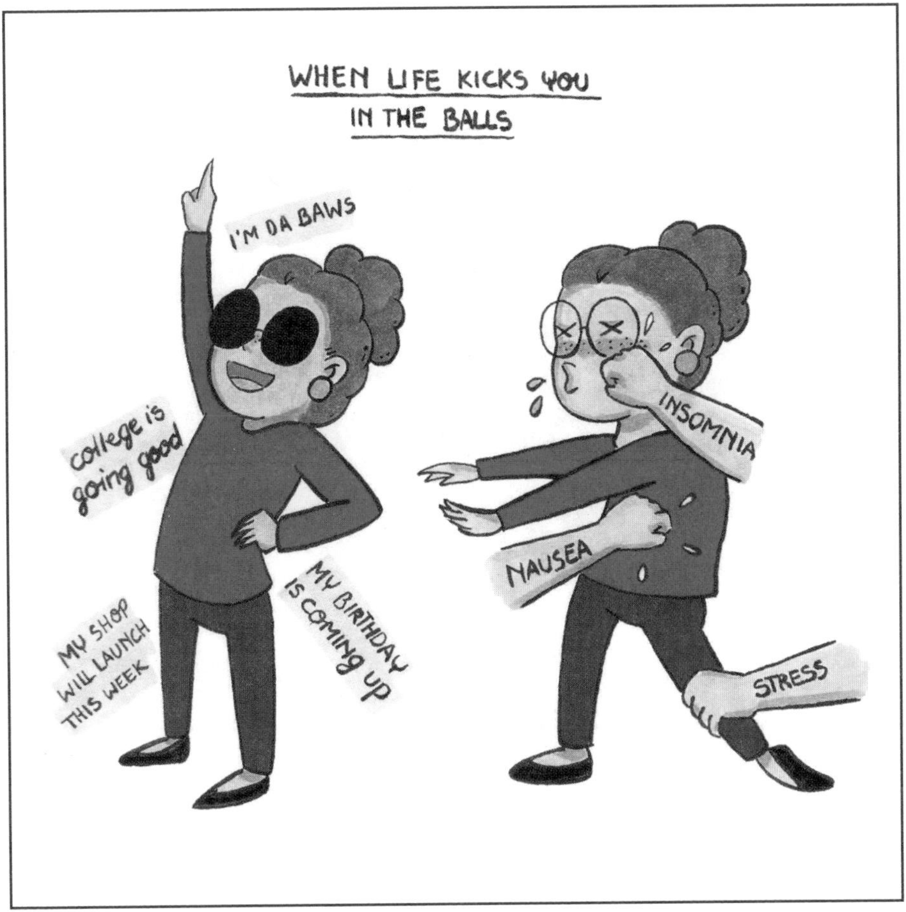

WHEN LIFE KICKS YOU IN THE BALLS
I'M DA BAWS
college is going good
MY SHOP WILL LAUNCH THIS WEEK
MY BIRTHDAY IS COMING UP
INSOMNIA
NAUSEA
STRESS

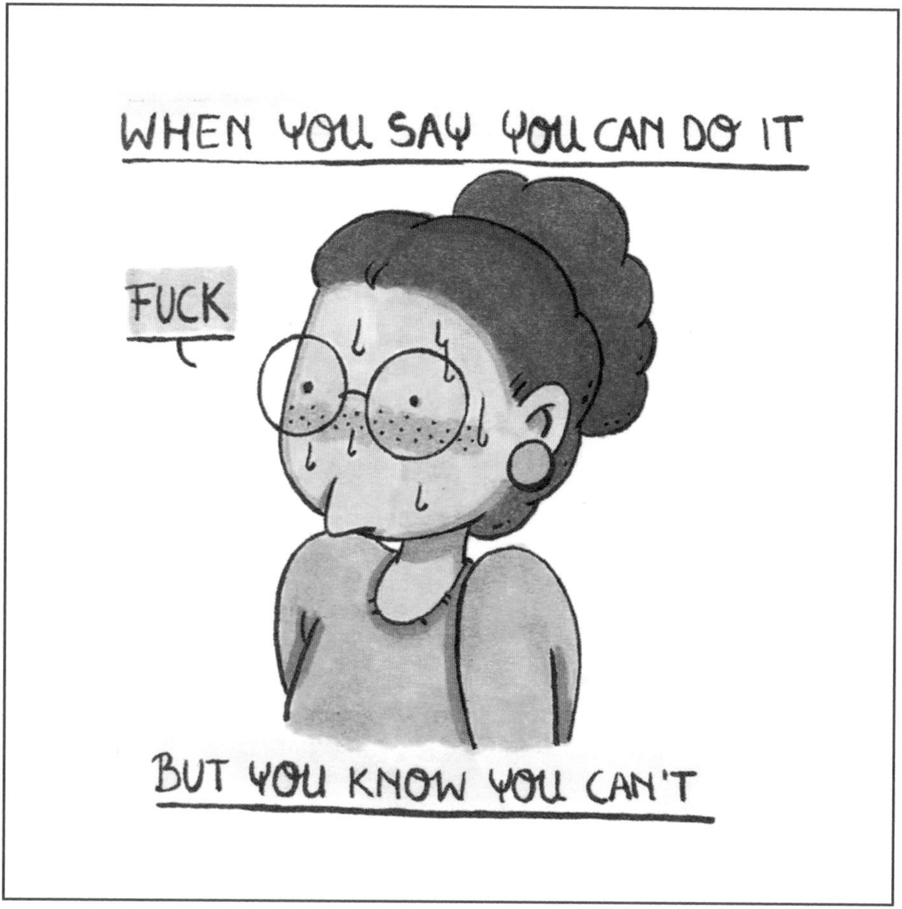
WHEN YOU SAY YOU CAN DO IT
FUCK
BUT YOU KNOW YOU CAN'T

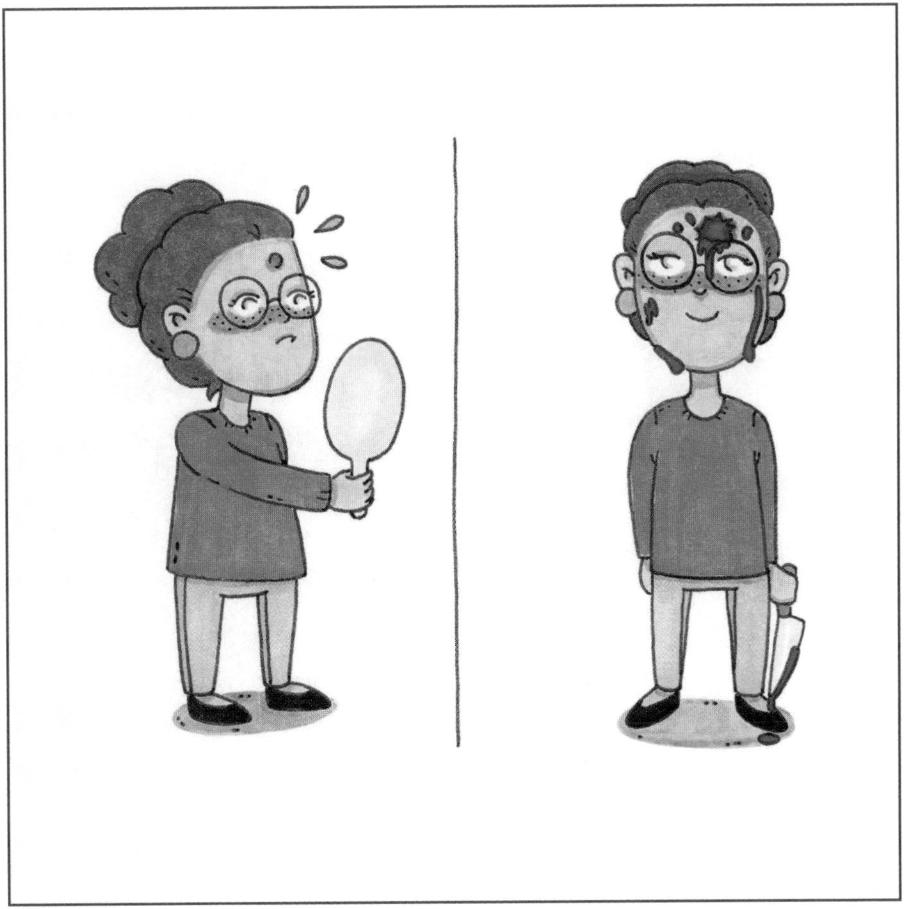

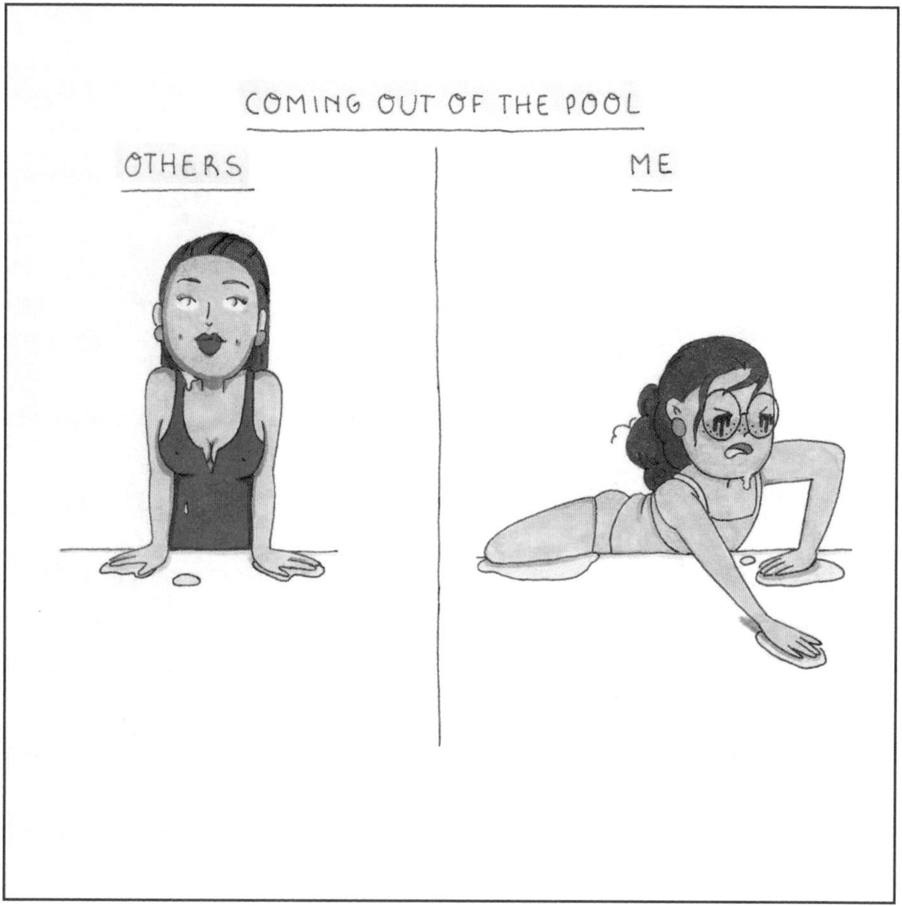
COMING OUT OF THE POOL
OTHERS
ME

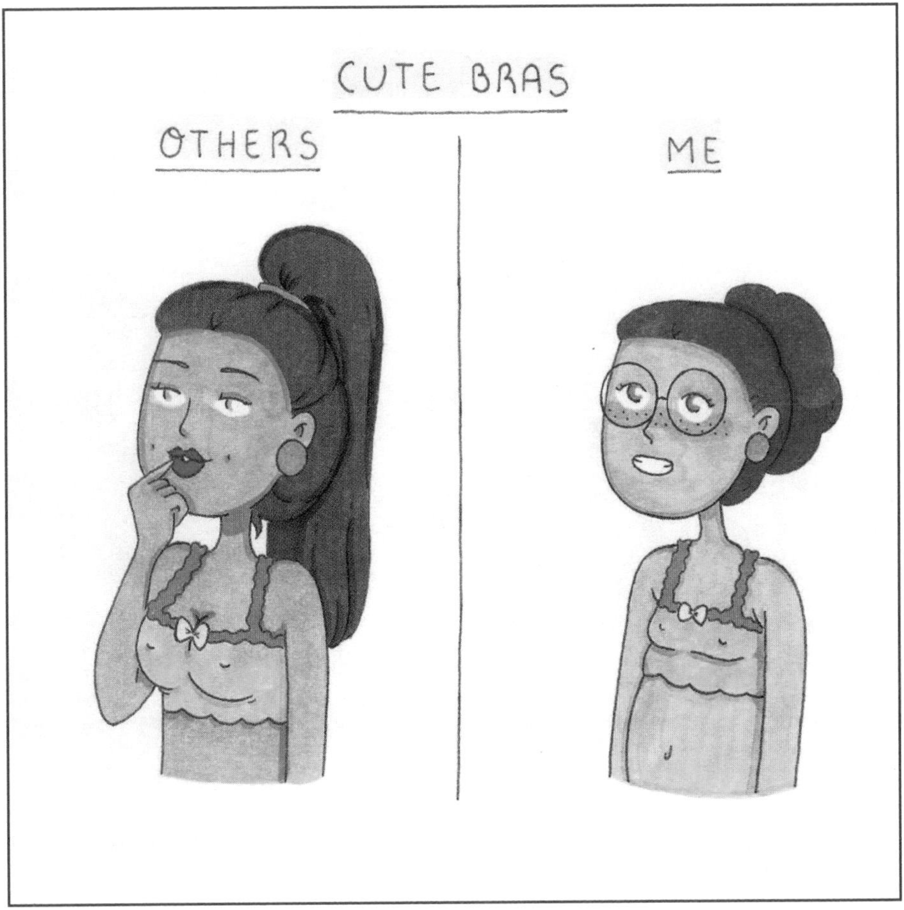
CUTE BRAS
OTHERS
ME

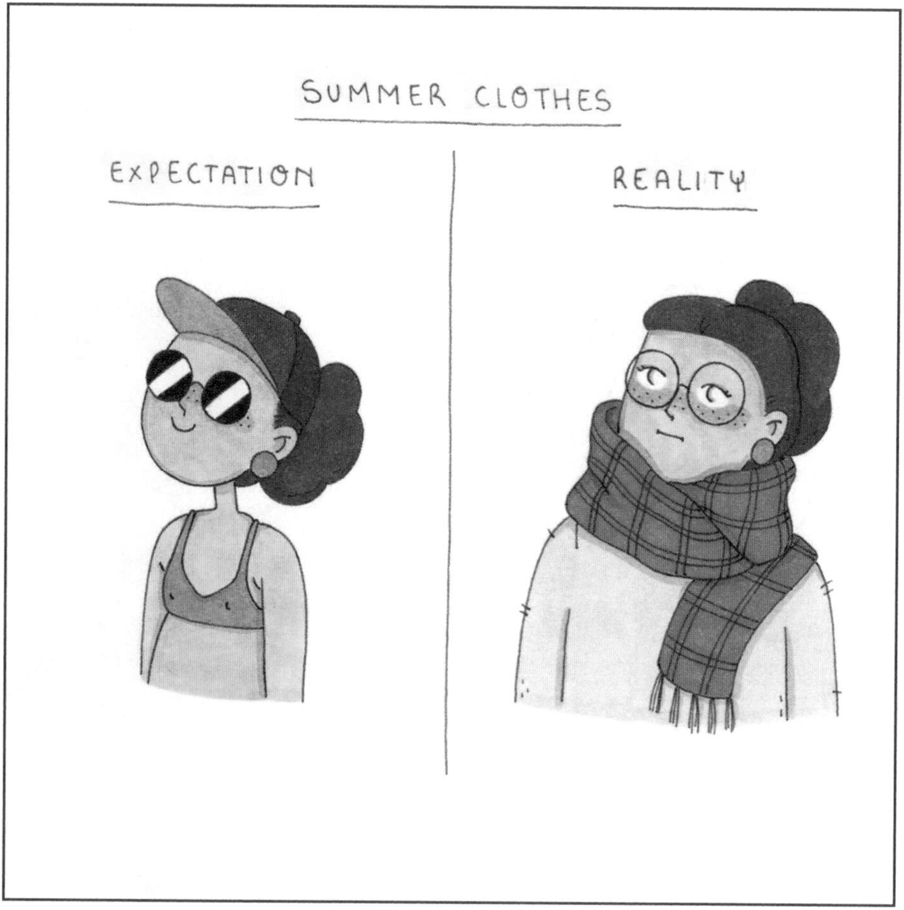
SUMMER CLOTHES
EXPECTATION
REALITY

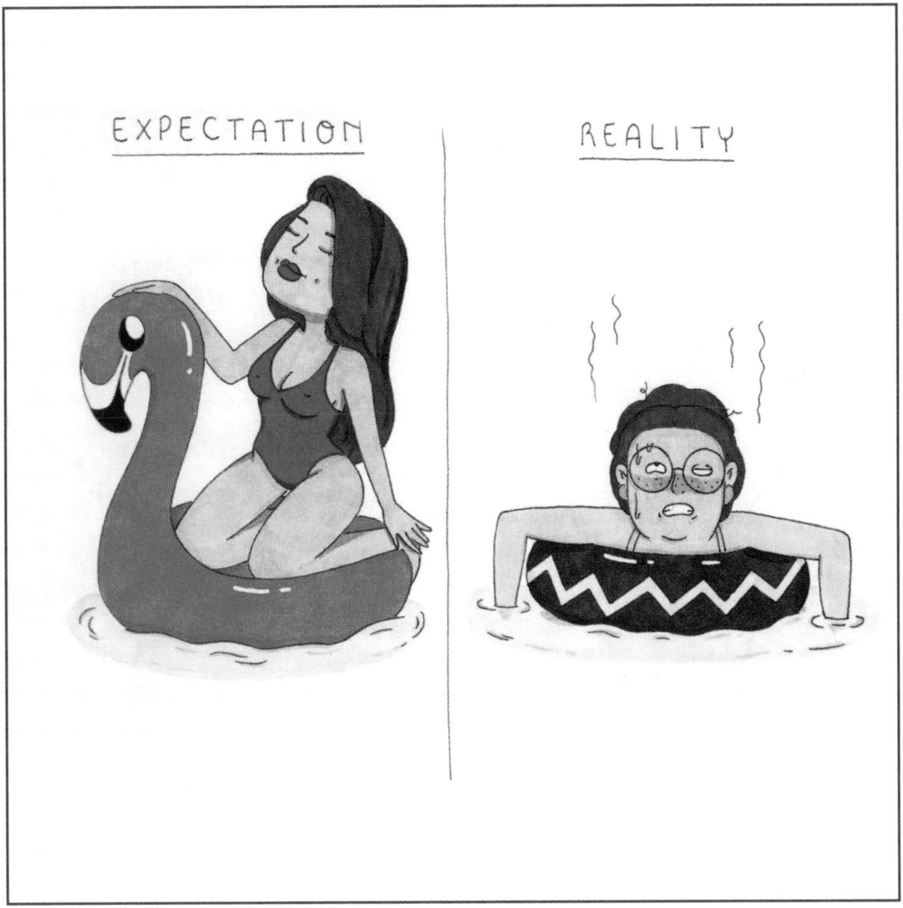
EXPECTATION
REALITY

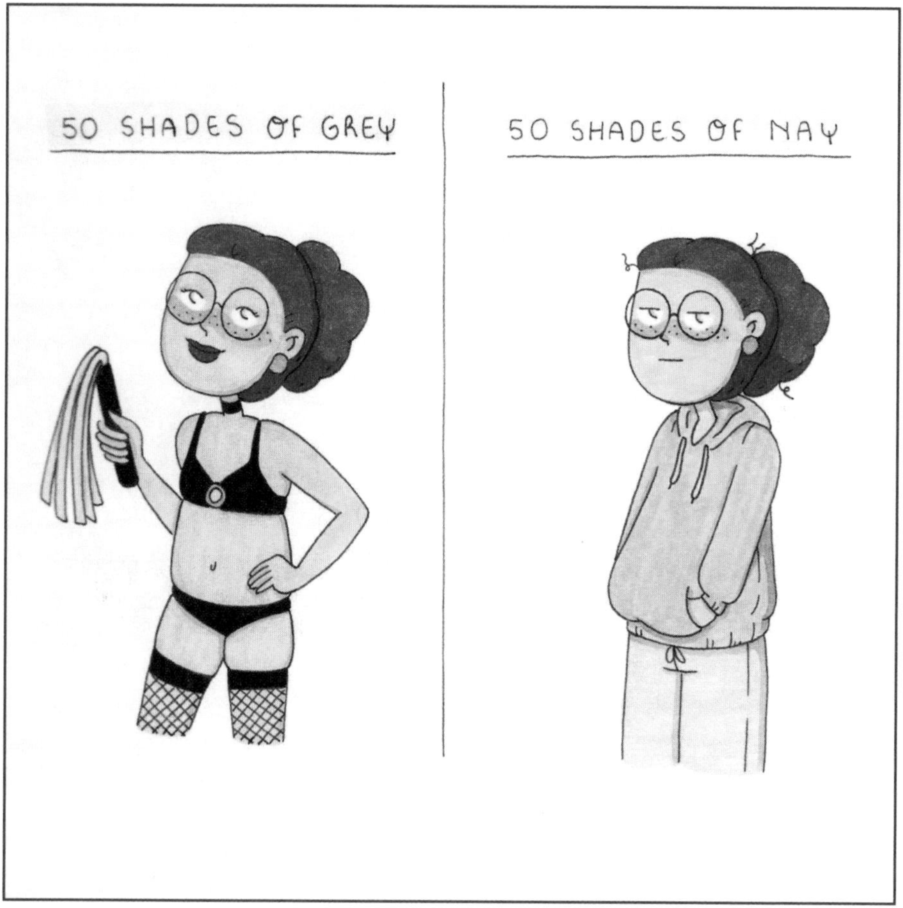
50 SHADES OF GREY
50 SHADES OF NAY

Finding the Strength

My health has been a pain in the ass for the last year. I've been sick, diagnosed, recovered, got sick again, went crazy, got happy, then crazy again, and eventually everything turned out okay. I'll just say, I'm very much able to live with it. To this day, many people write me encouraging messages and many of them can relate, as they were battling their own demons at the time. It surprised me how many people went through or are going through the same thing. Strength is something we really need in times like these, and I pull strength out of the lovely messages and support. I also want to support every person who is going through an illness. You are never alone.

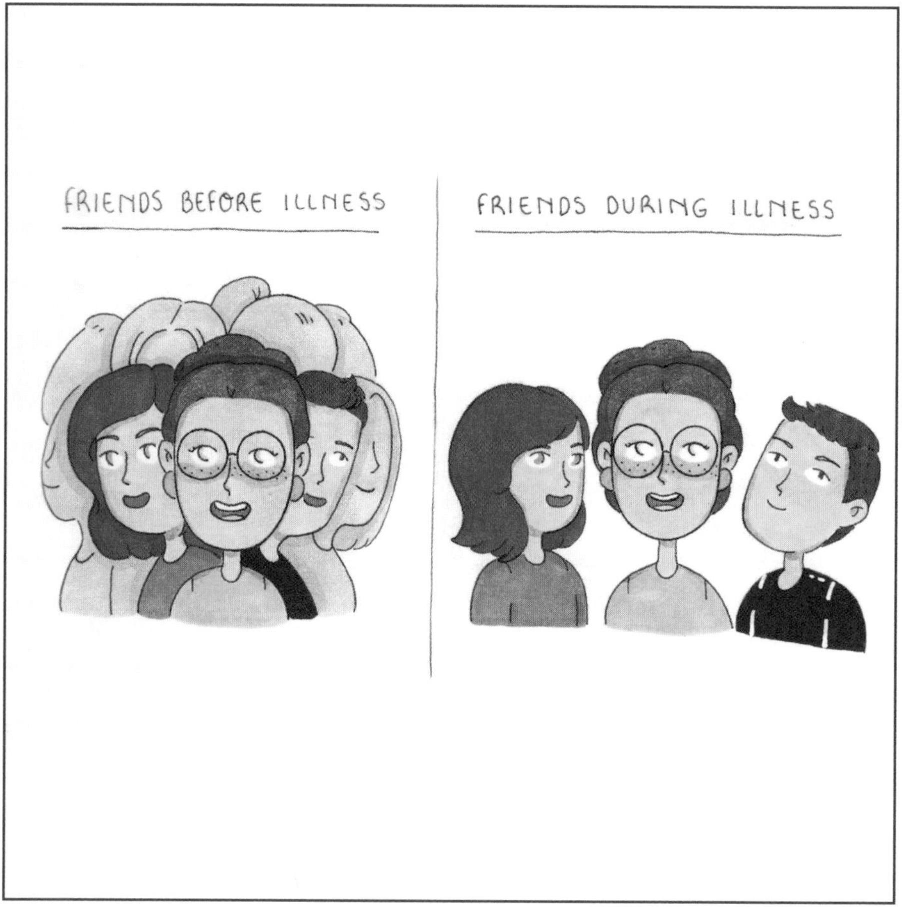
FRIENDS BEFORE ILLNESS
FRIENDS DURING ILLNESS

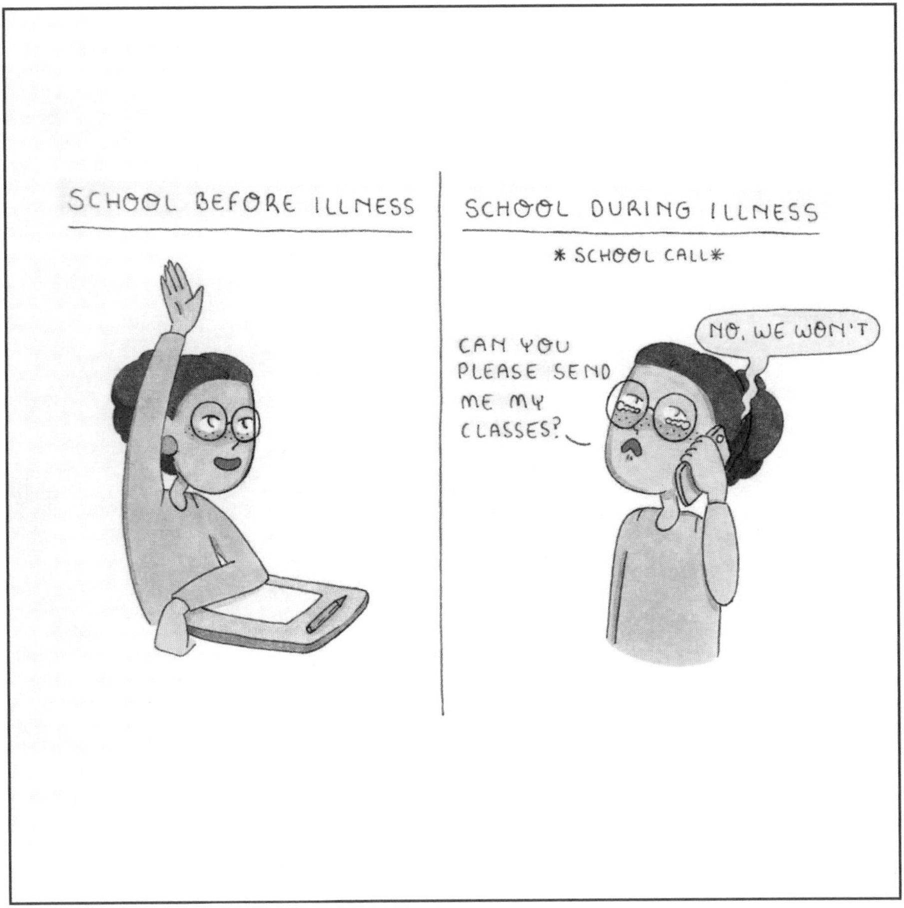
SCHOOL BEFORE ILLNESS
SCHOOL DURING ILLNESS
* SCHOOL CALL *
CAN YOU PLEASE SEND ME MY CLASSES?
NO, WE WON'T

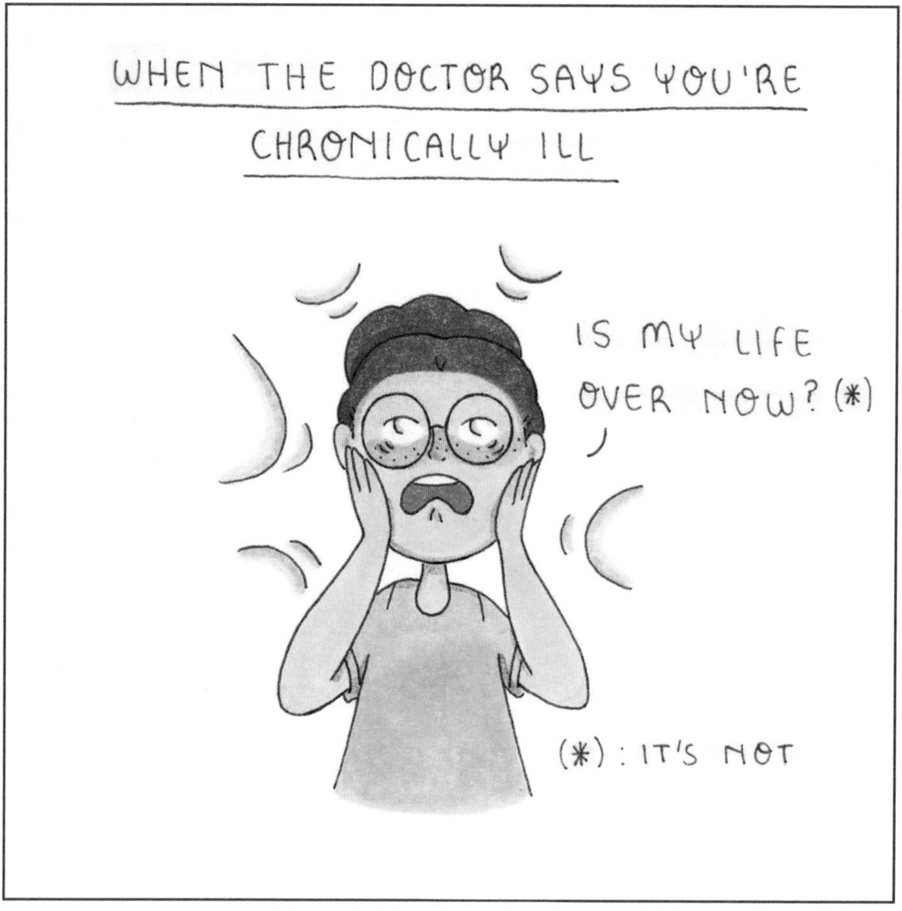
WHEN THE DOCTOR SAYS YOU'RE CHRONICALLY ILL
IS MY LIFE OVER NOW? (*)
(*) : IT'S NOT

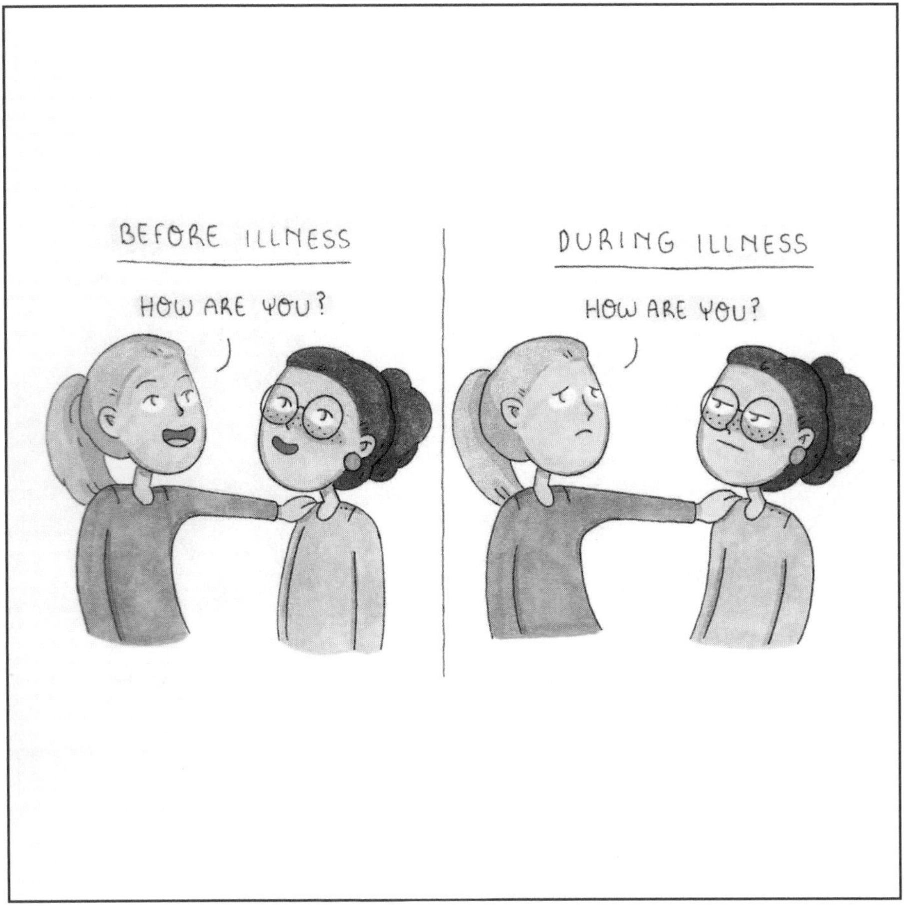
BEFORE ILLNESS
HOW ARE YOU?
DURING ILLNESS
HOW ARE YOU?

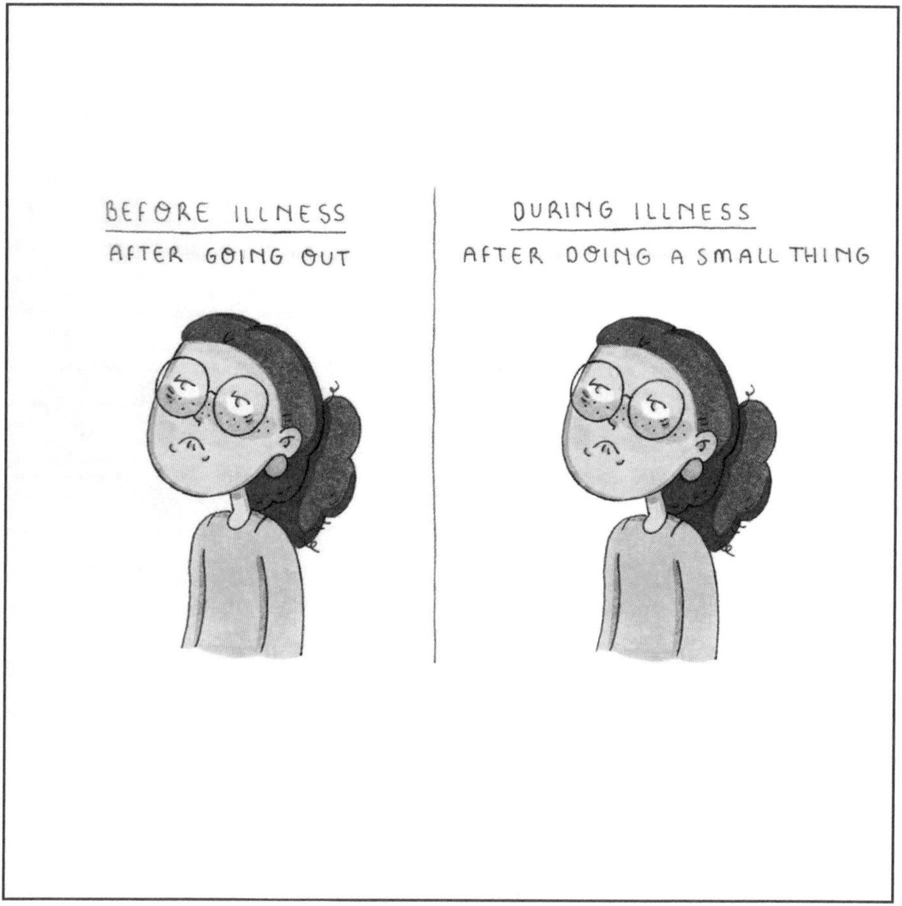
BEFORE ILLNESS
AFTER GOING OUT
DURING ILLNESS
AFTER DOING A SMALL THING

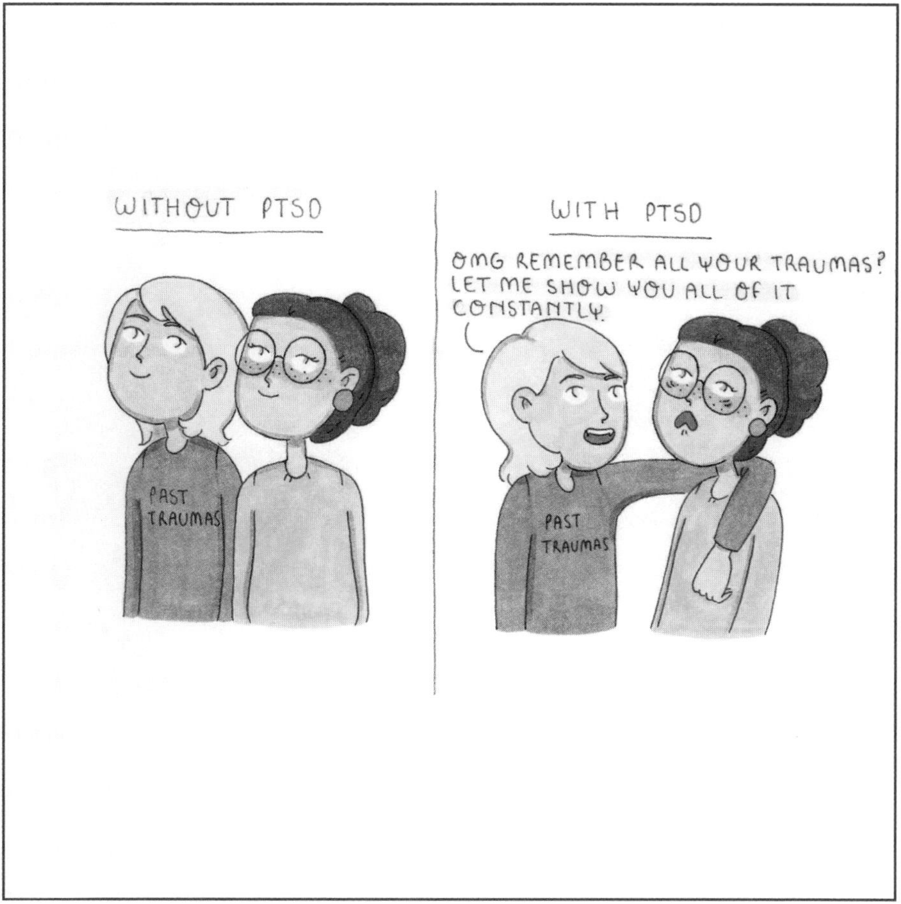
WITHOUT PTSD
PAST TRAUMAS
WITH PTSD
OMG REMEMBER ALL YOUR TRAUMAS? LET ME SHOW YOU ALL OF IT CONSTANTLY.
PAST TRAUMAS

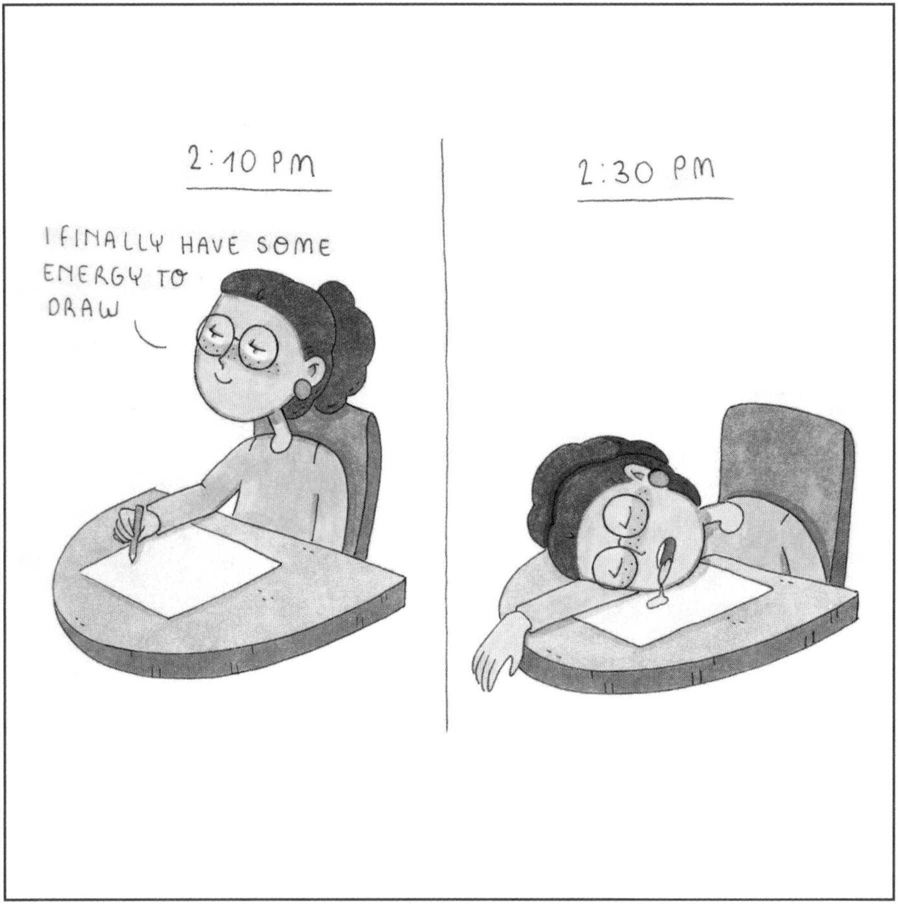
2:10 PM
I FINALLY HAVE SOME ENERGY TO DRAW
2:30 PM

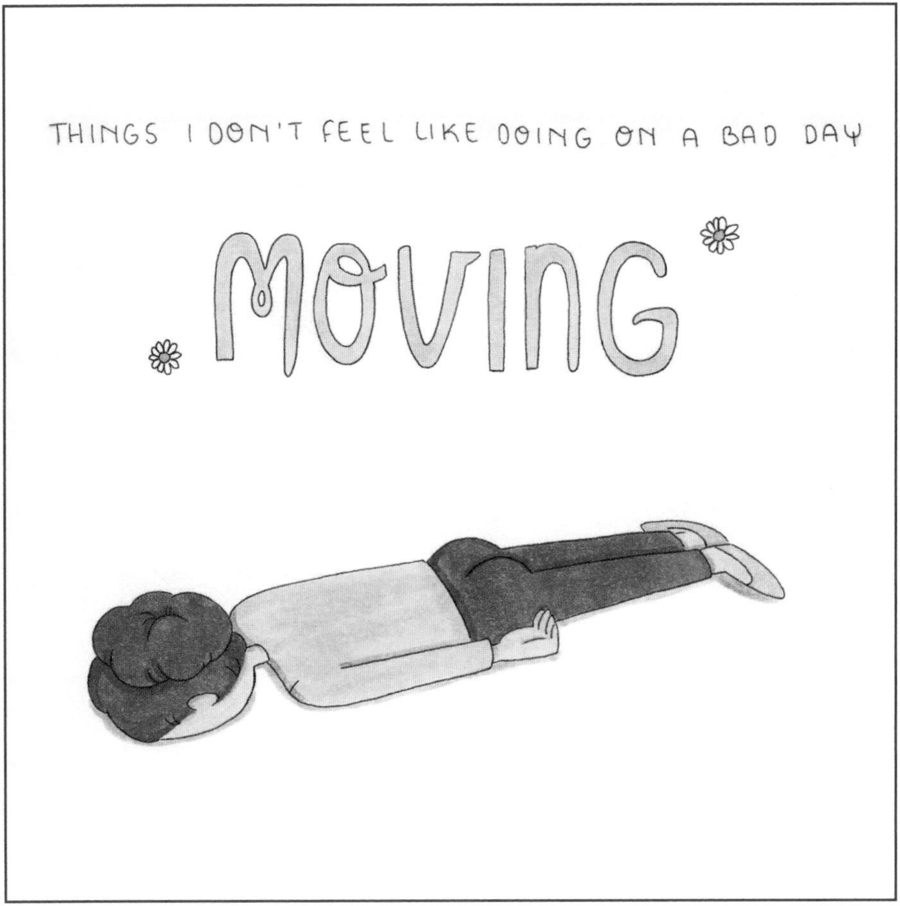
THINGS I DON'T FEEL LIKE DOING ON A BAD DAY
MOVING

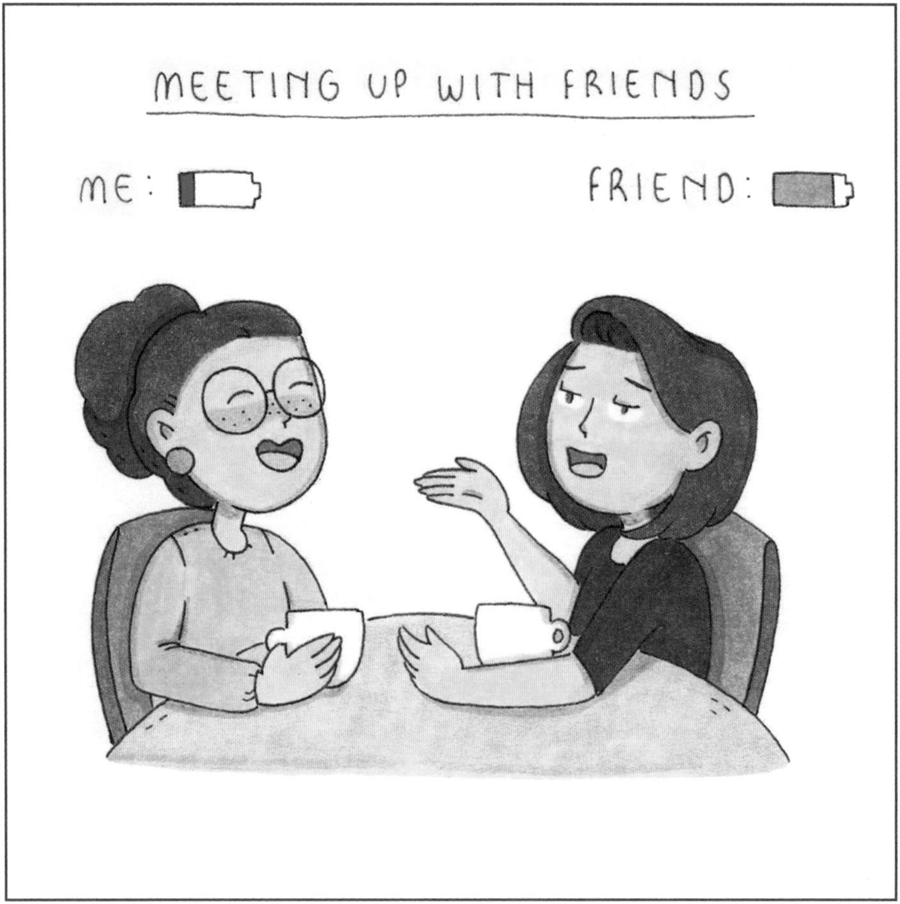
MEETING UP WITH FRIENDS
ME:
FRIEND:

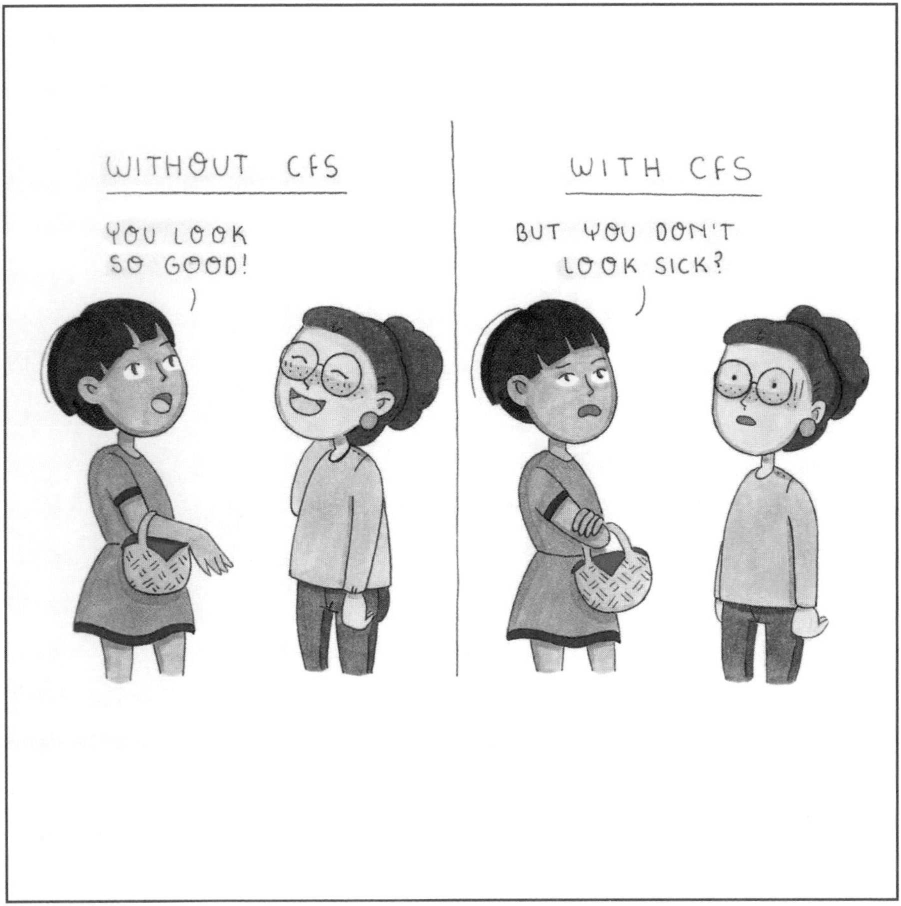
WITHOUT CFS
YOU LOOK SO GOOD!
WITH CFS
BUT YOU DON'T LOOK SICK?

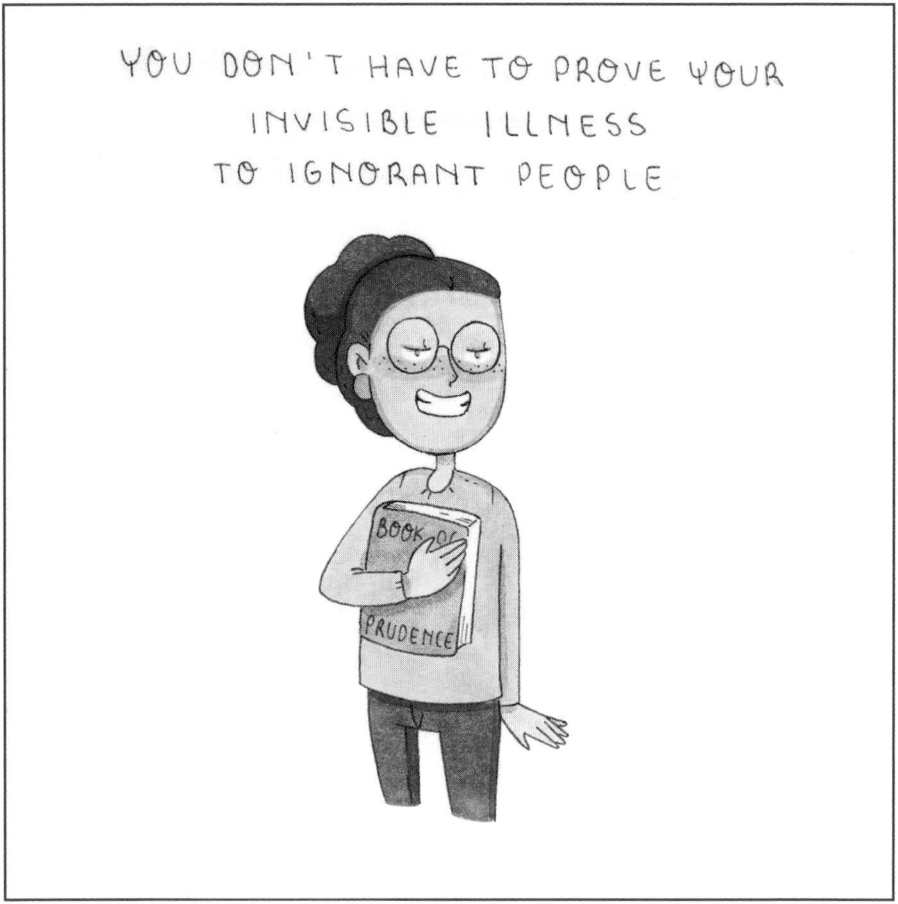
YOU DON'T HAVE TO PROVE YOUR
INVISIBLE ILLNESS
TO IGNORANT PEOPLE
BOOK OF
PRUDENCE

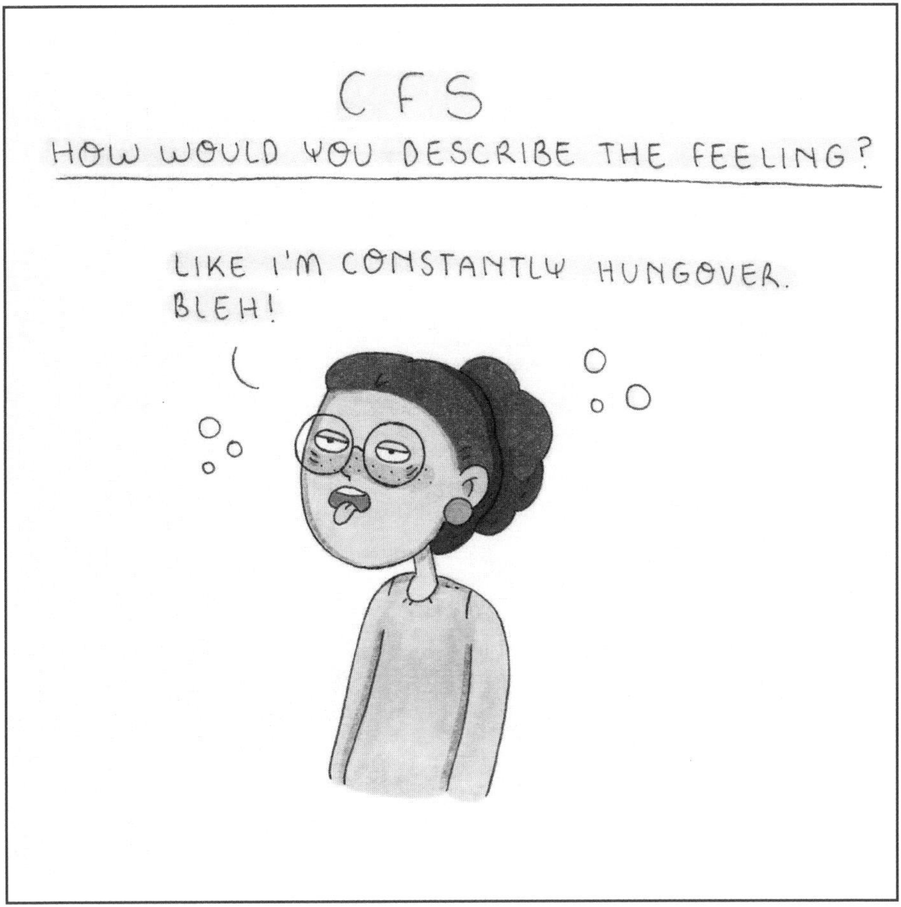
CFS
HOW WOULD YOU DESCRIBE THE FEELING?
LIKE I'M CONSTANTLY HUNGOVER. BLEH!

Millennial and Proud of It

Online shopping, auto-correct, ads disturbing our peace, and watching cat videos. It's all present in our daily lives as a millennial. I'm proud to be a millennial, though. I think we do pretty well, fighting for our rights and what we believe in. I think our generation is changing the world and if we continue doing so, we're definitely going places.

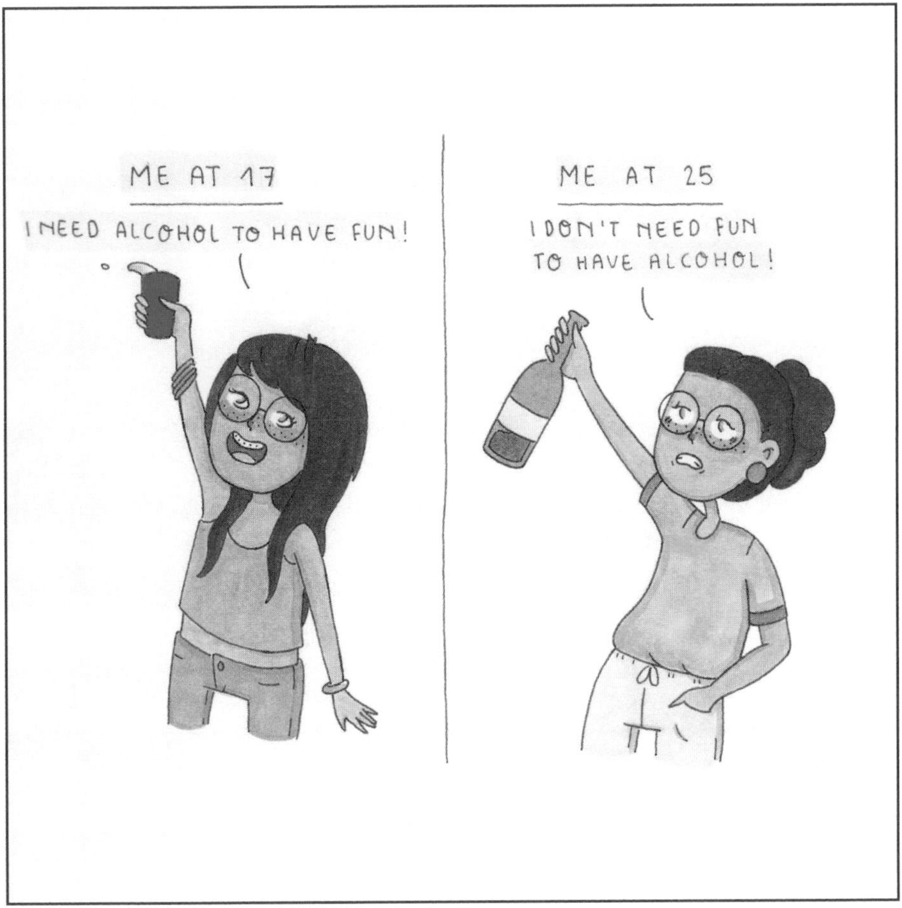
ME AT 17
I NEED ALCOHOL TO HAVE FUN!
ME AT 25
I DON'T NEED FUN TO HAVE ALCOHOL!

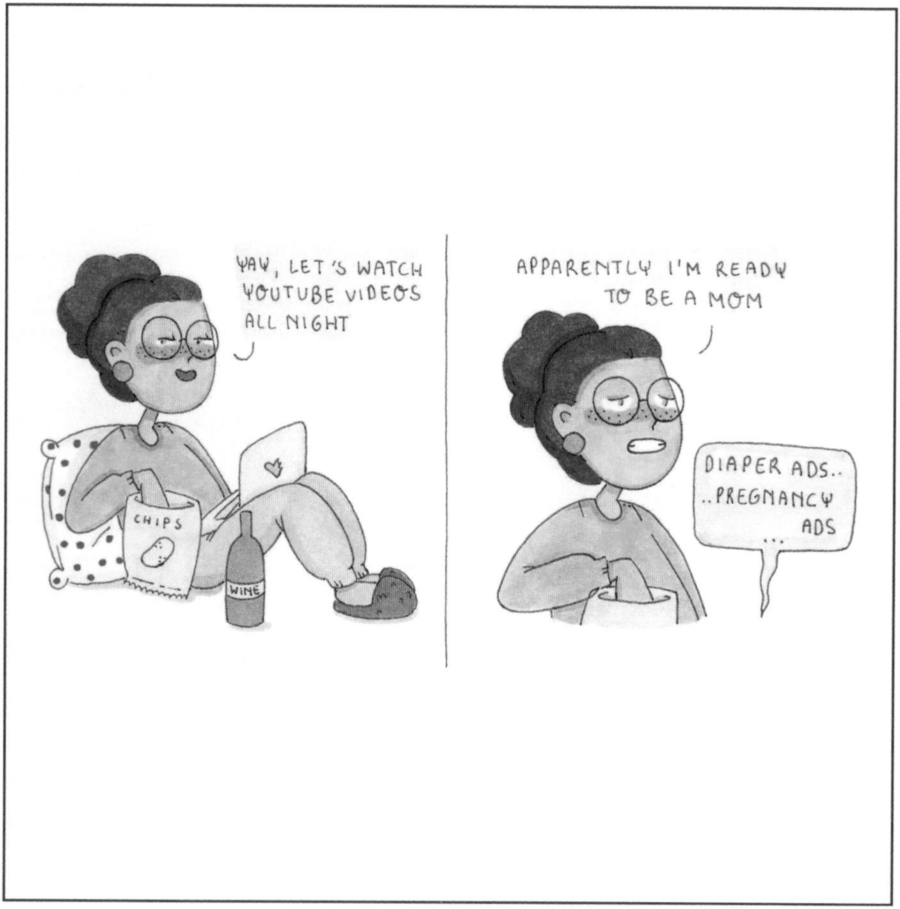
YAY, LET'S WATCH YOUTUBE VIDEOS ALL NIGHT
CHIPS
WINE
APPARENTLY I'M READY TO BE A MOM
DIAPER ADS.. ..PREGNANCY ADS ...

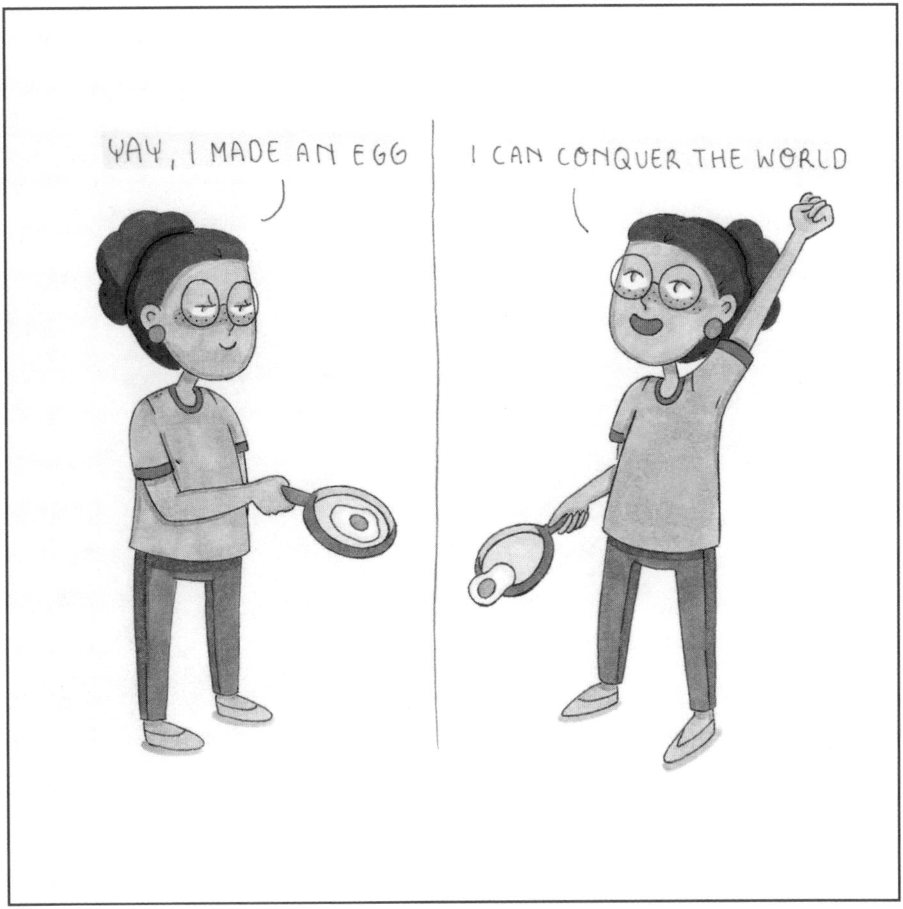
YAY, I MADE AN EGG
I CAN CONQUER THE WORLD

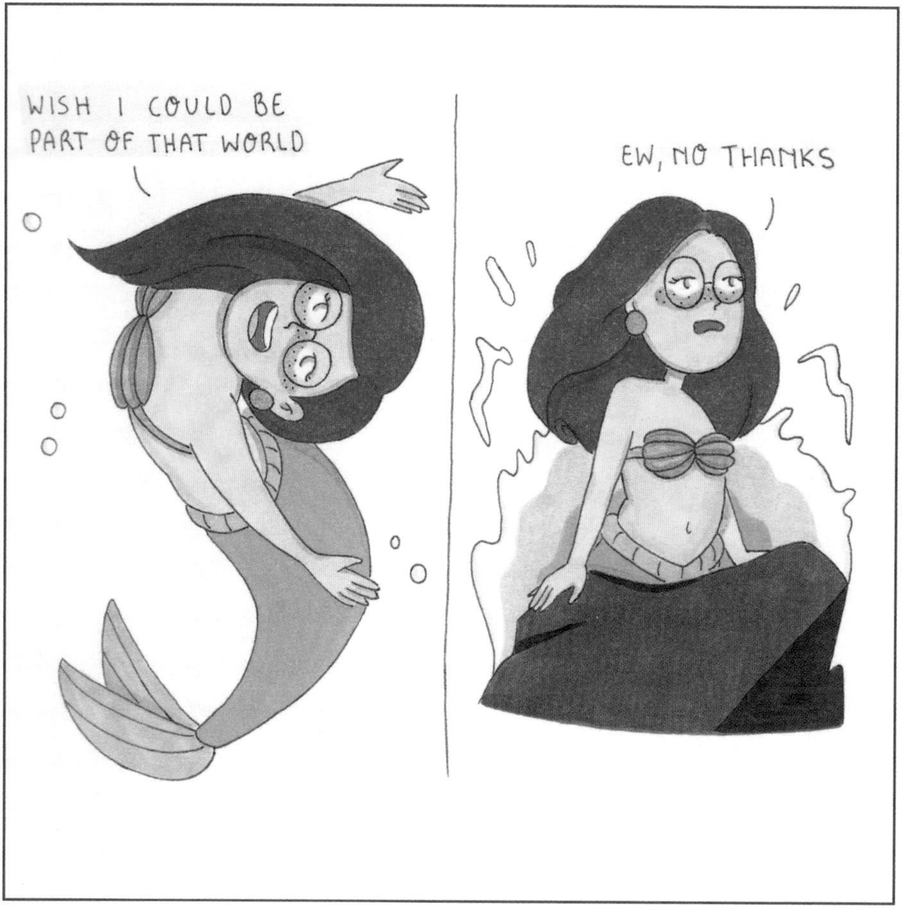
WISH I COULD BE PART OF THAT WORLD
EW, NO THANKS

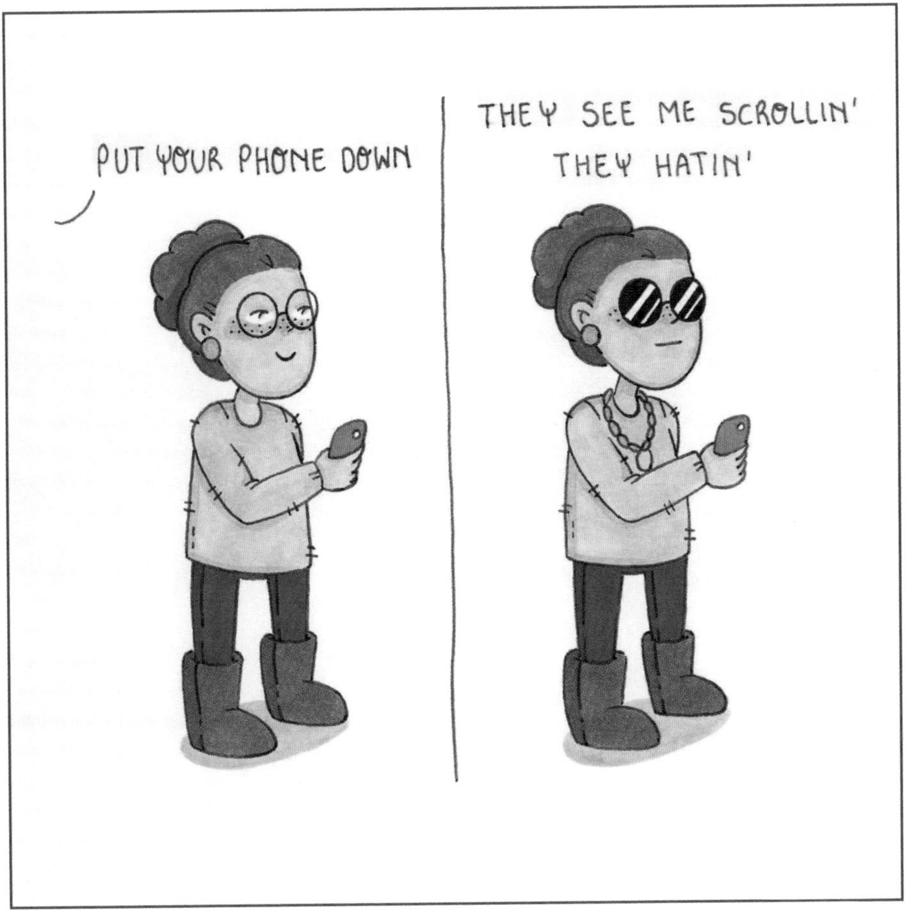
PUT YOUR PHONE DOWN
THEY SEE ME SCROLLIN'
THEY HATIN'

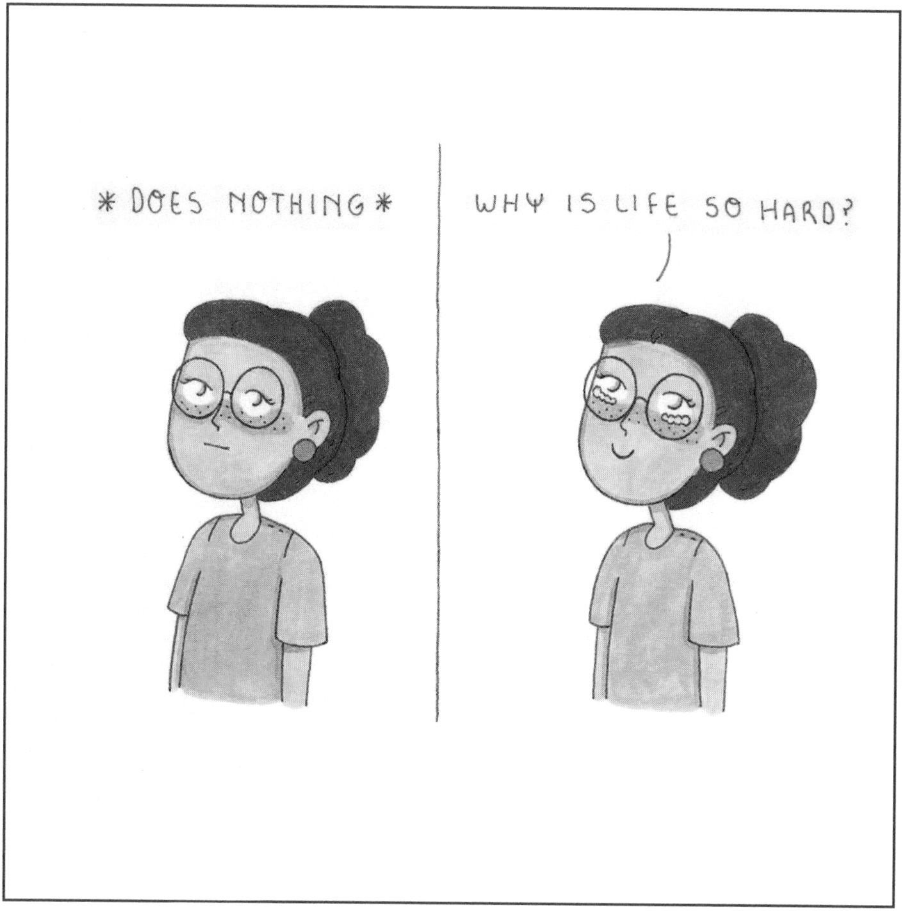
DOES NOTHING
WHY IS LIFE SO HARD?

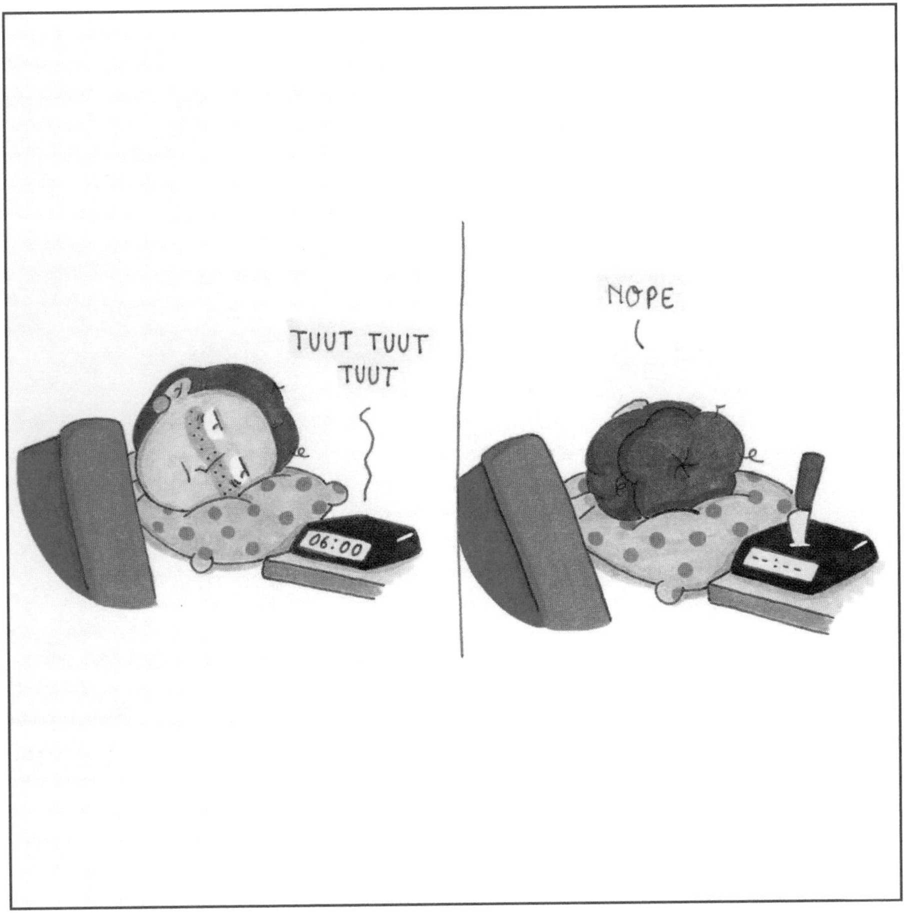
TUUT TUUT
TUUT
06:00
NOPE

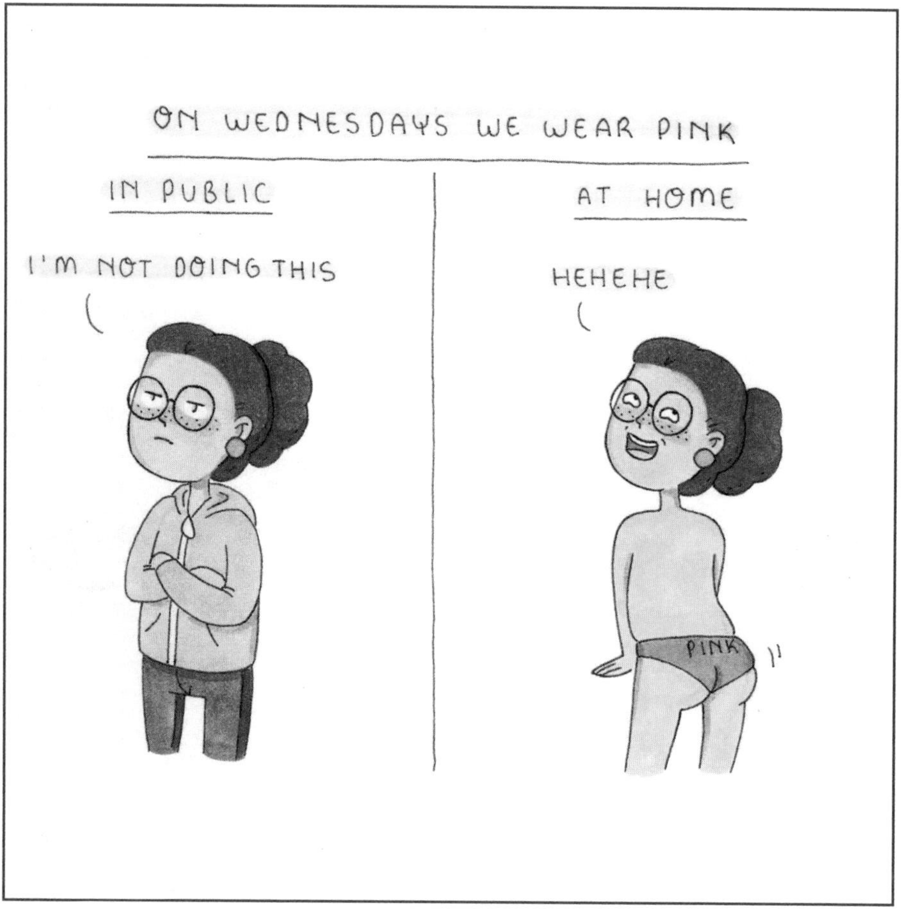

ON WEDNESDAYS WE WEAR PINK
IN PUBLIC
AT HOME
I'M NOT DOING THIS
HEHEHE
PINK

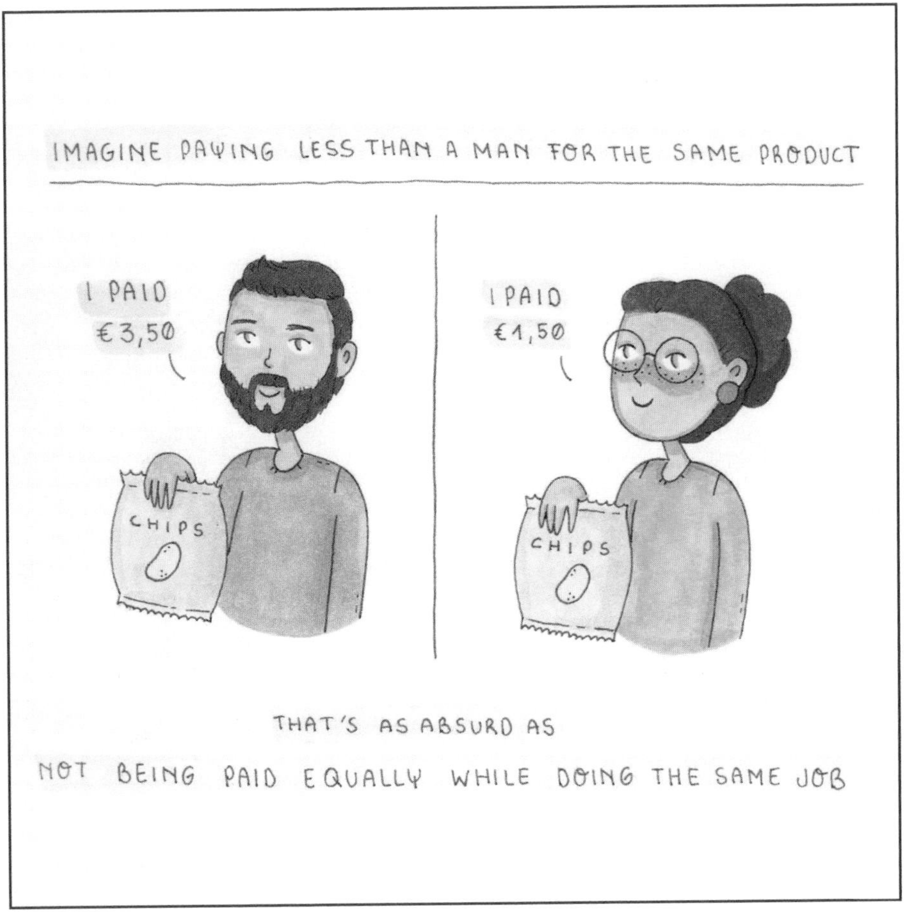
IMAGINE PAYING LESS THAN A MAN FOR THE SAME PRODUCT
I PAID €3,50
CHIPS
I PAID €1,50
CHIPS
THAT'S AS ABSURD AS
NOT BEING PAID EQUALLY WHILE DOING THE SAME JOB

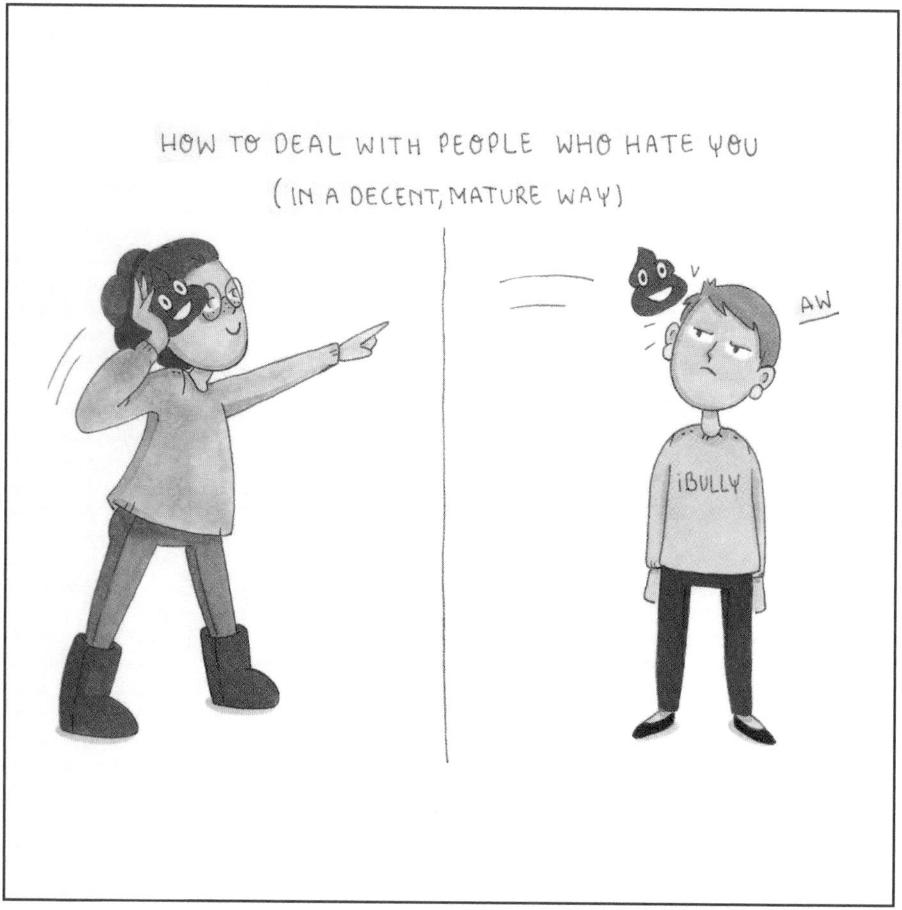
HOW TO DEAL WITH PEOPLE WHO HATE YOU
(IN A DECENT, MATURE WAY)
AW
iBULLY

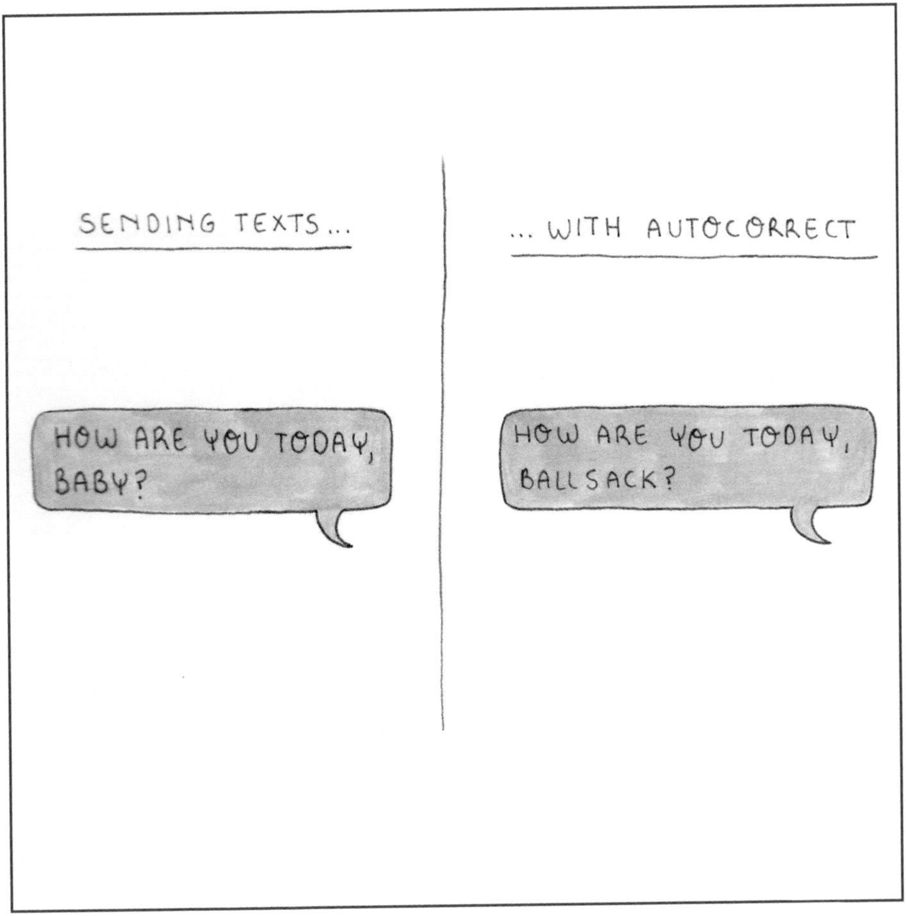
SENDING TEXTS...
HOW ARE YOU TODAY, BABY?
... WITH AUTOCORRECT
HOW ARE YOU TODAY, BALLSACK?

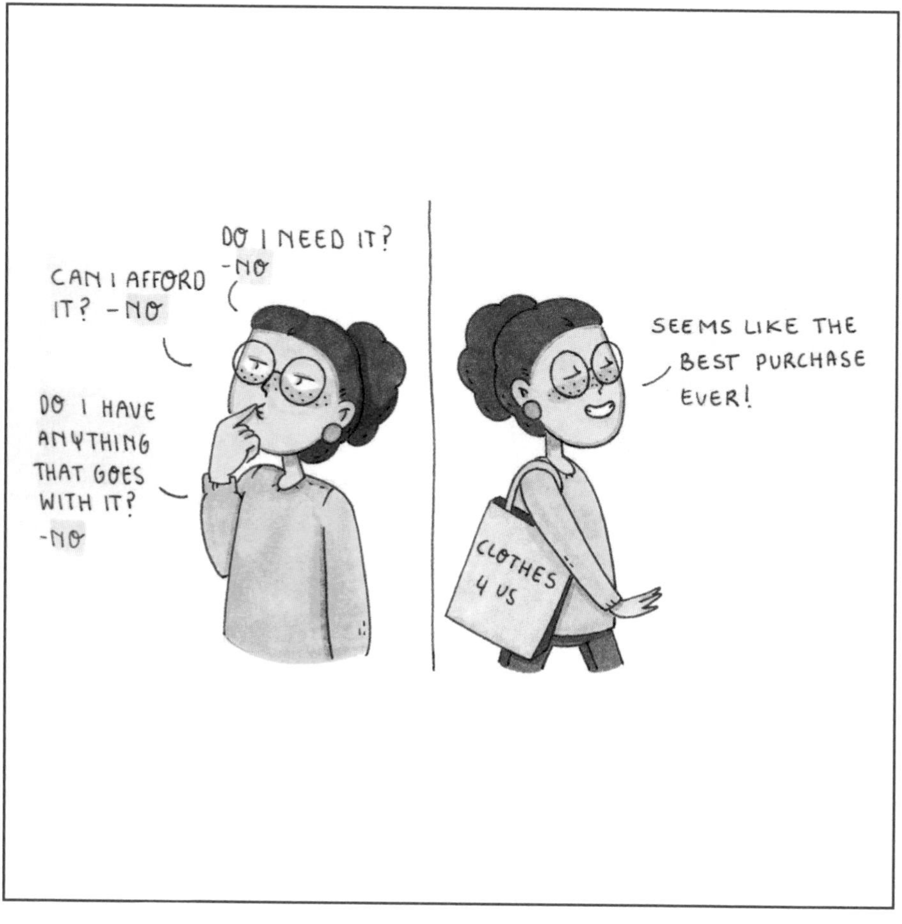
DO I NEED IT? -NO
CAN I AFFORD IT? -NO
DO I HAVE ANYTHING THAT GOES WITH IT? -NO
SEEMS LIKE THE BEST PURCHASE EVER!
CLOTHES 4 US

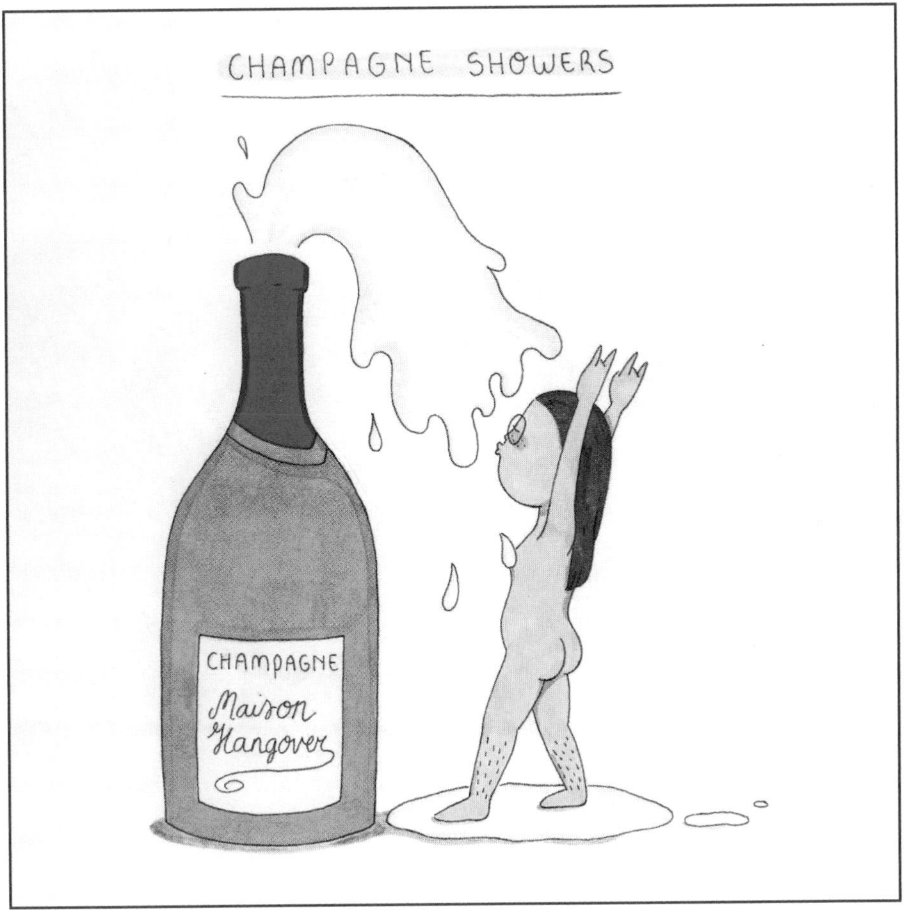
CHAMPAGNE SHOWERS
CHAMPAGNE
Maison
Hangover

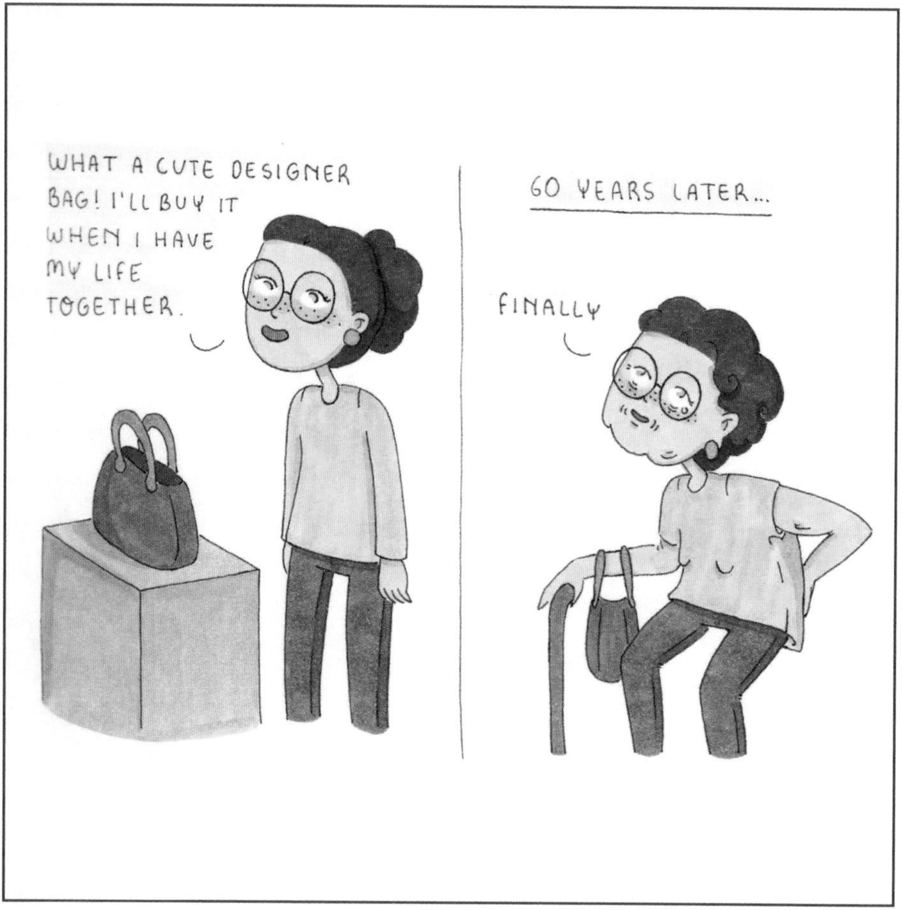
WHAT A CUTE DESIGNER BAG! I'LL BUY IT WHEN I HAVE MY LIFE TOGETHER.
60 YEARS LATER...
FINALLY

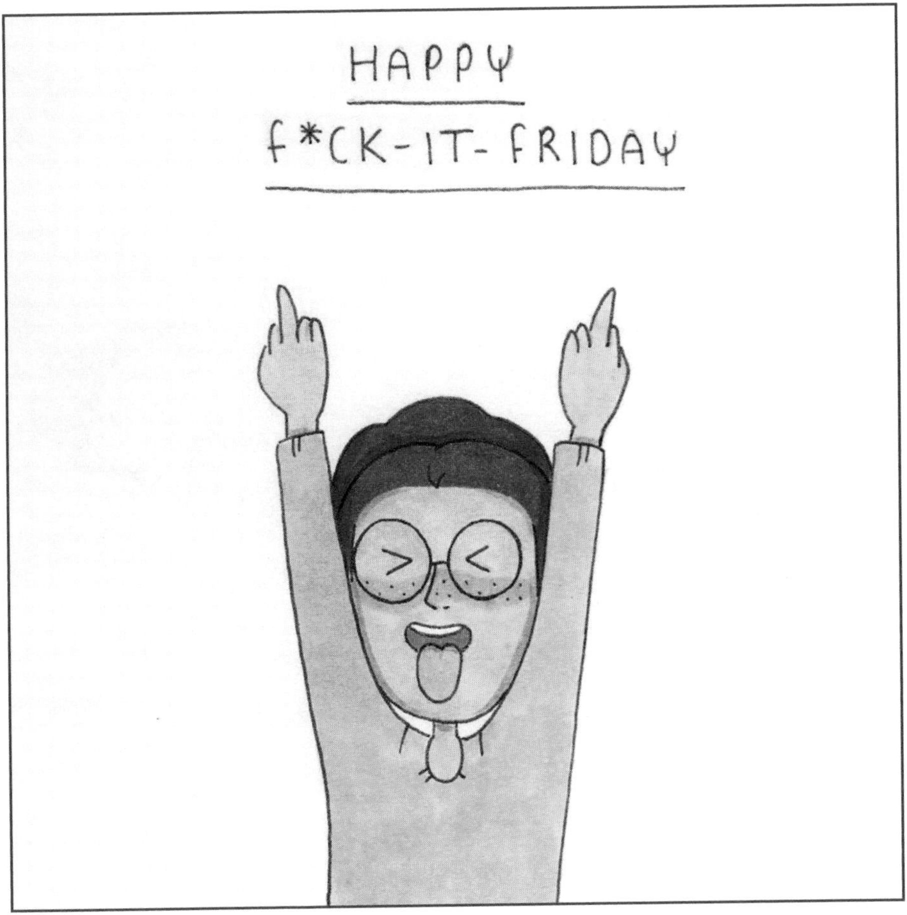
HAPPY
F*CK-IT-FRIDAY

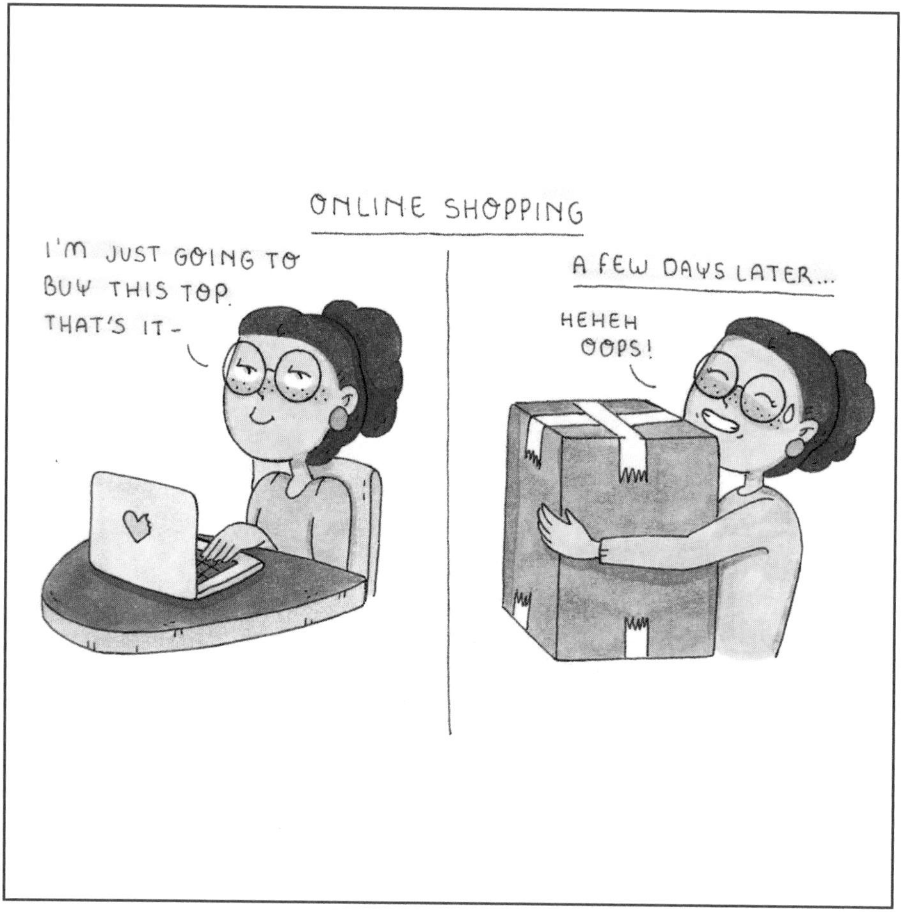
ONLINE SHOPPING
I'M JUST GOING TO BUY THIS TOP. THAT'S IT-
A FEW DAYS LATER...
HEHEH OOPS!

We are Female, Hear us Roar

Bloody hell. No, literally! I, myself, am going through hell each month! Mother Nature was not the best mother out there for me. Or perhaps I wasn't the best daughter. But anyway, she left me bleeding to death each month, with cramps and crankiness and everything I'd rather not have. But I battle through and so should you. As the saying goes, "What doesn't kill us, makes us stronger." And we women have gone through hell and back. From inequality and sexualization of our bodies to misrepresentation. But we continue to fight because we are not only mothers, daughters, and wives...we are human.

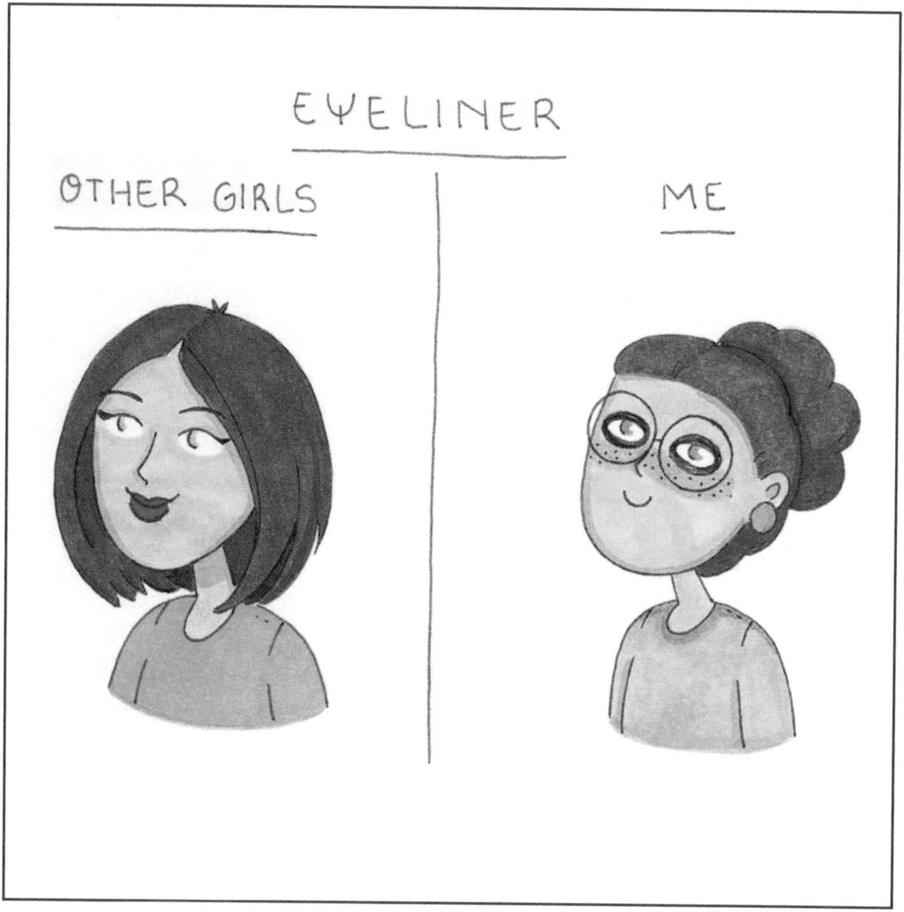
EYELINER
OTHER GIRLS
ME

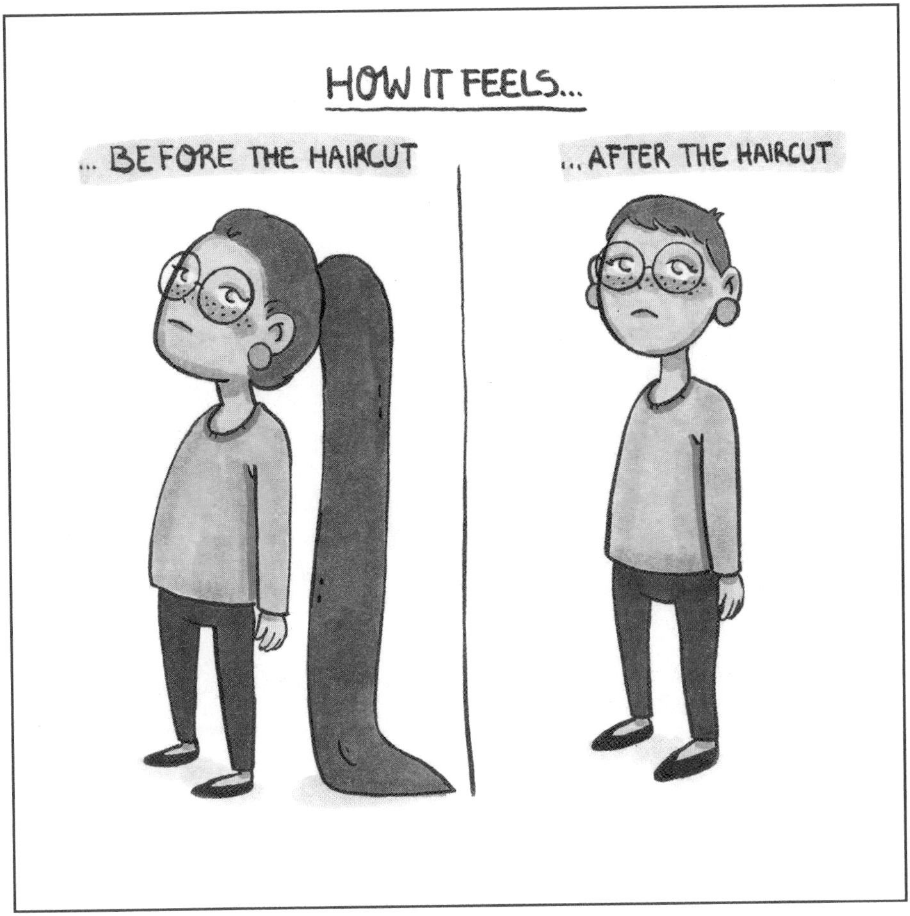
HOW IT FEELS...
... BEFORE THE HAIRCUT
... AFTER THE HAIRCUT

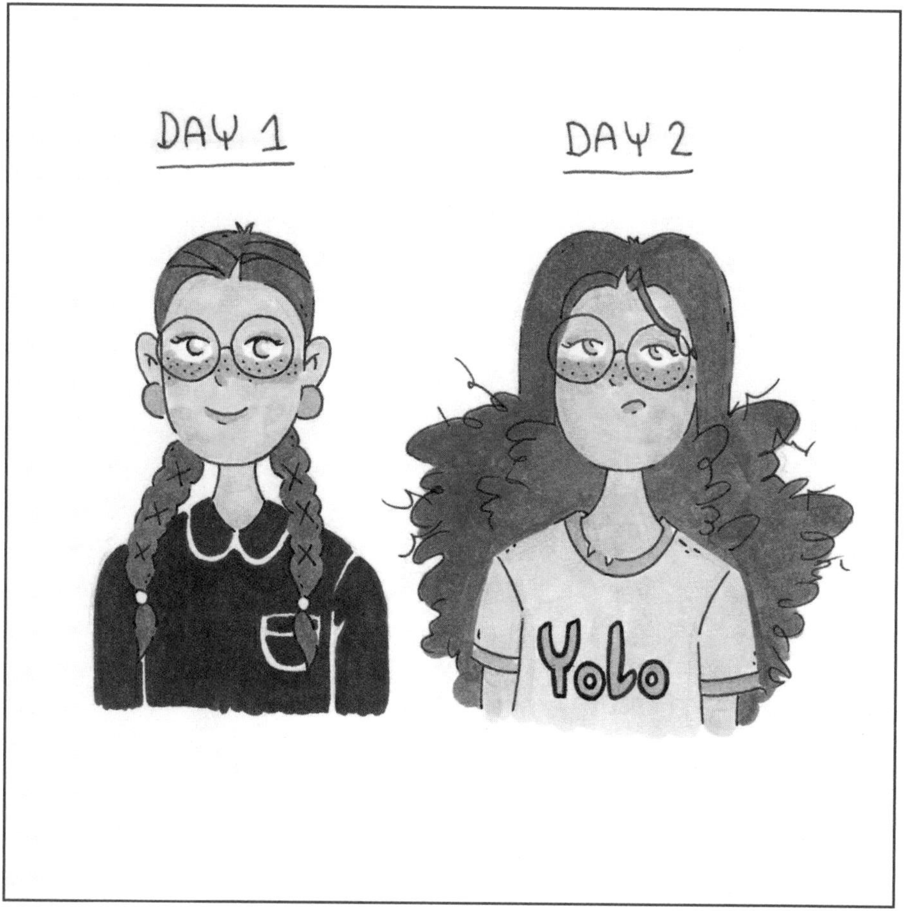
DAY 1
DAY 2
Yolo

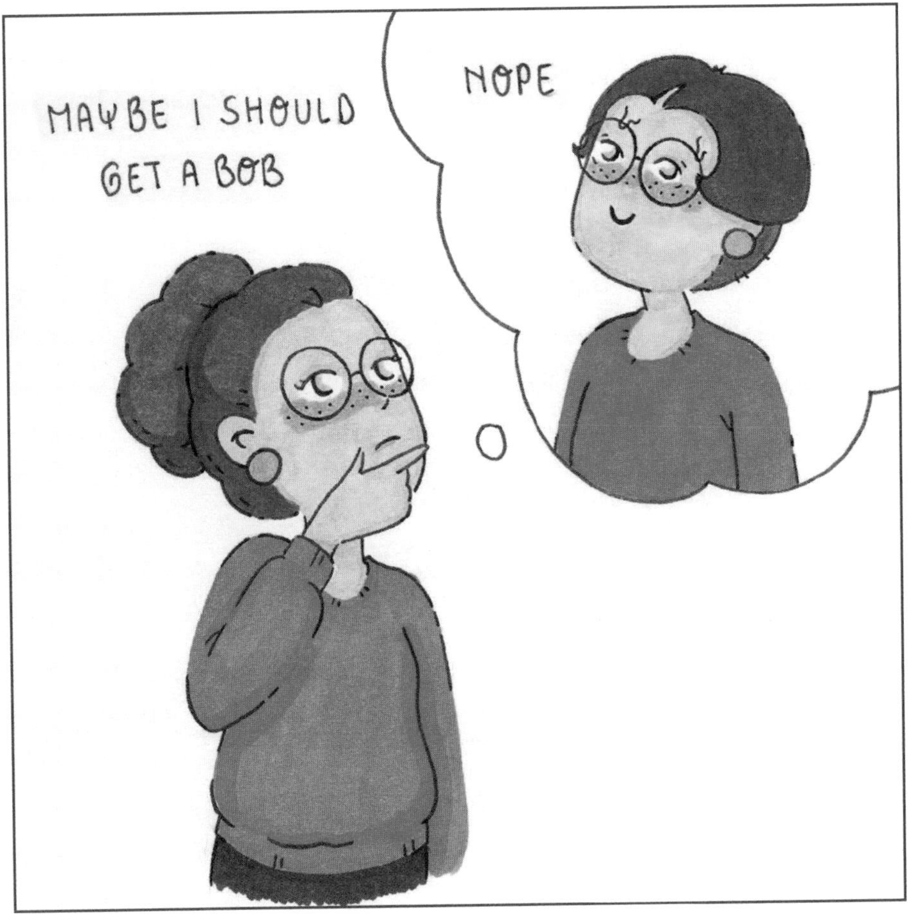
MAYBE I SHOULD
GET A BOB
NOPE

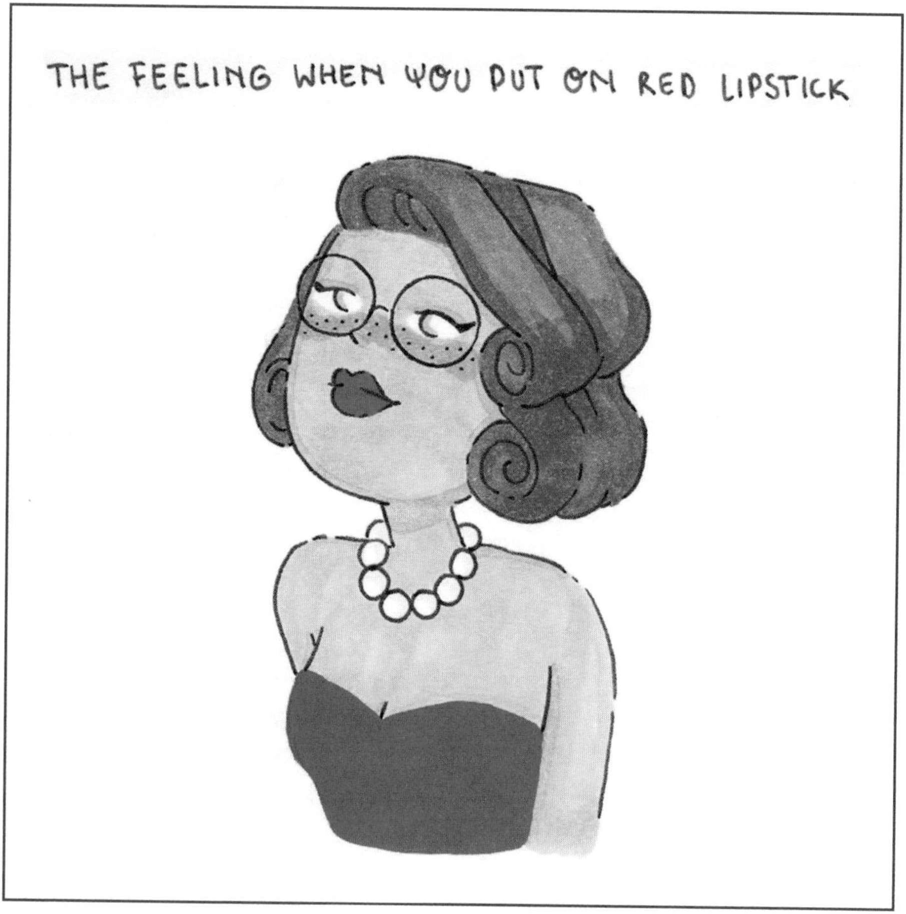
THE FEELING WHEN YOU PUT ON RED LIPSTICK

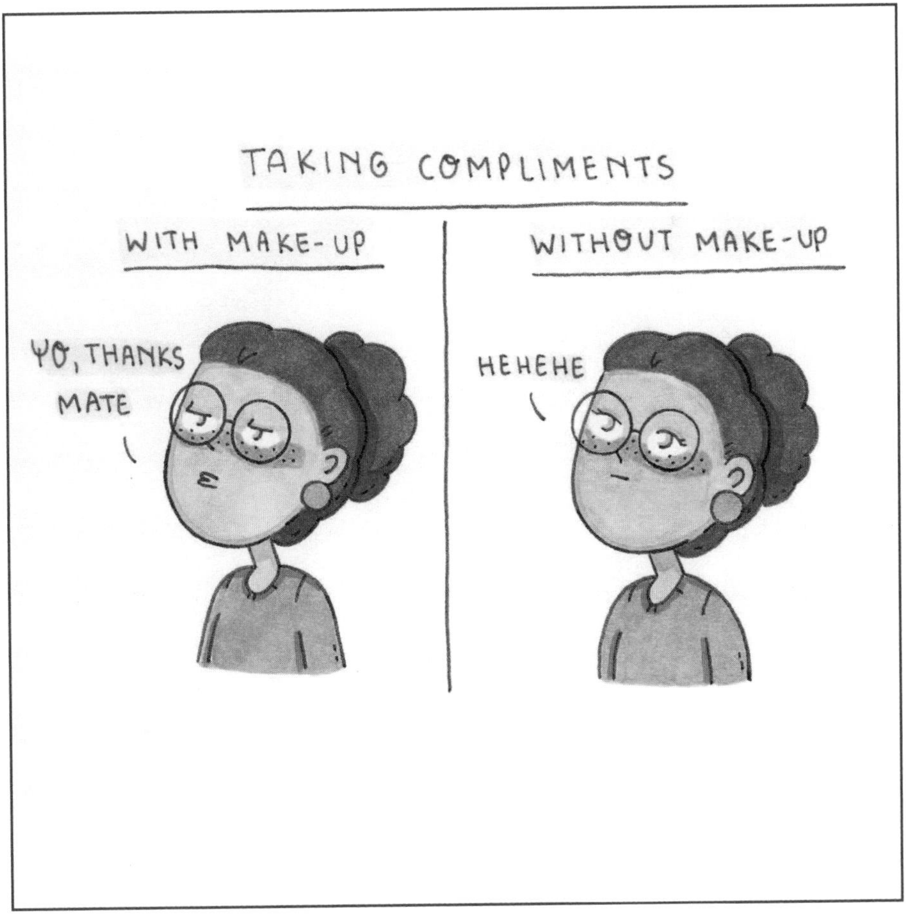
TAKING COMPLIMENTS
WITH MAKE-UP
WITHOUT MAKE-UP
YO, THANKS MATE
HEHEHE

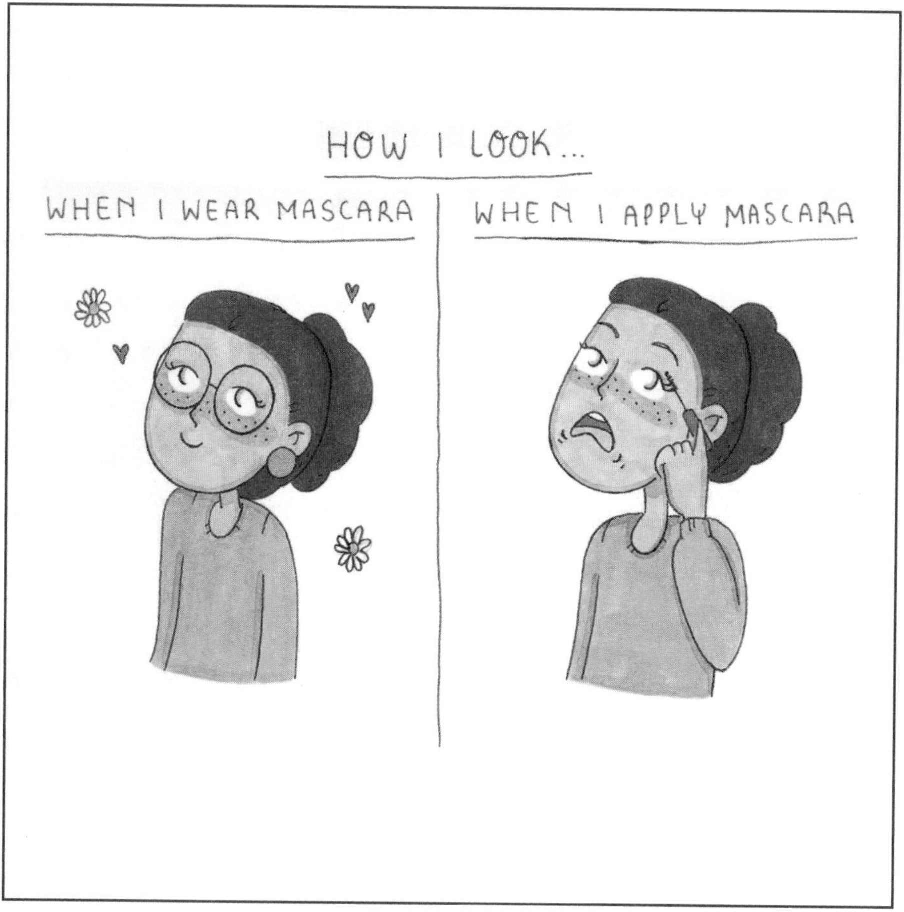
HOW I LOOK...
WHEN I WEAR MASCARA
WHEN I APPLY MASCARA

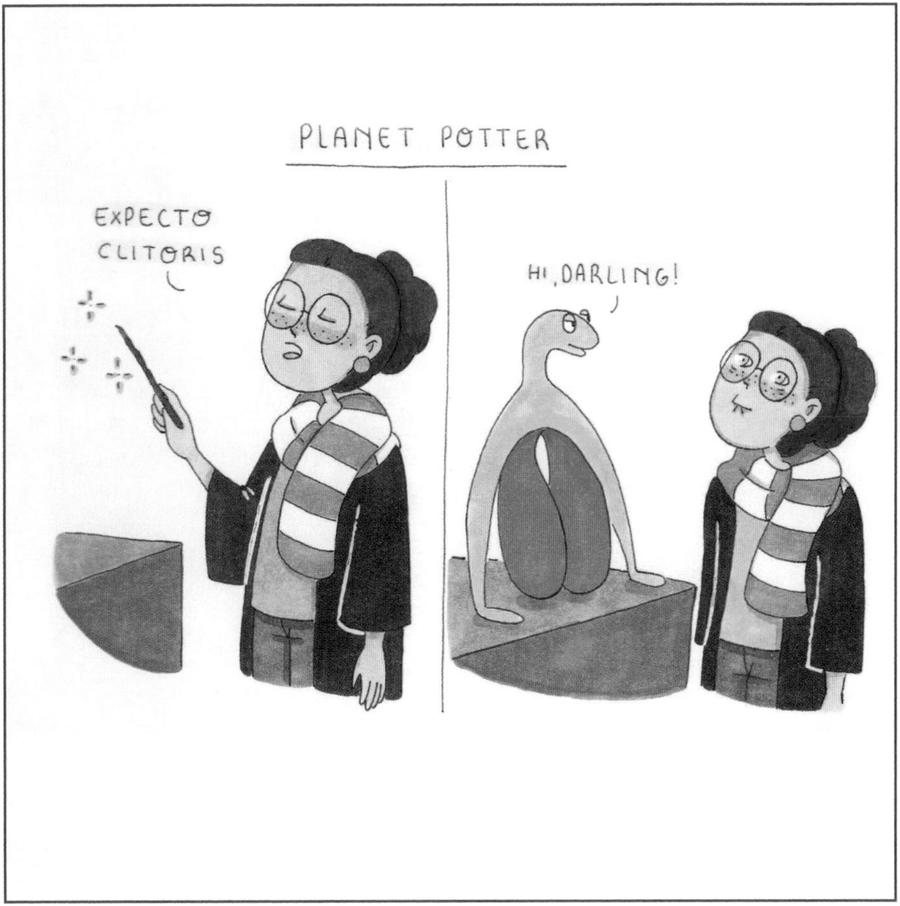
PLANET POTTER
EXPECTO CLITORIS
HI, DARLING!

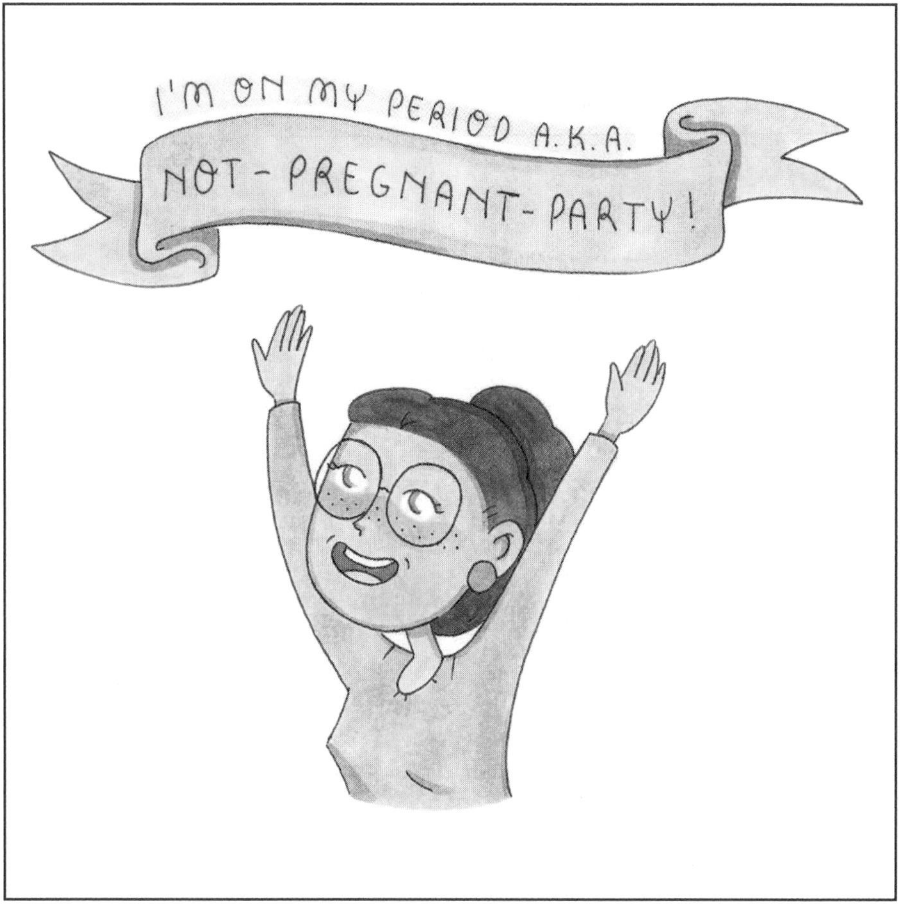
I'M ON MY PERIOD A.K.A.
NOT-PREGNANT-PARTY!

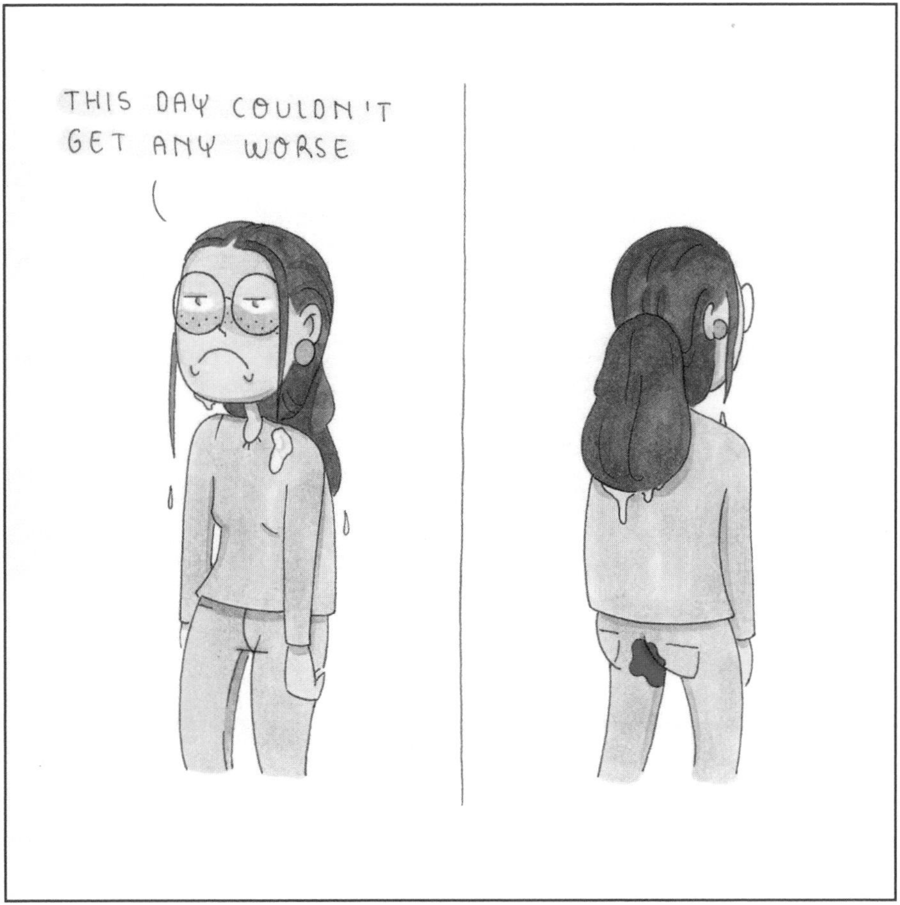
THIS DAY COULDN'T GET ANY WORSE

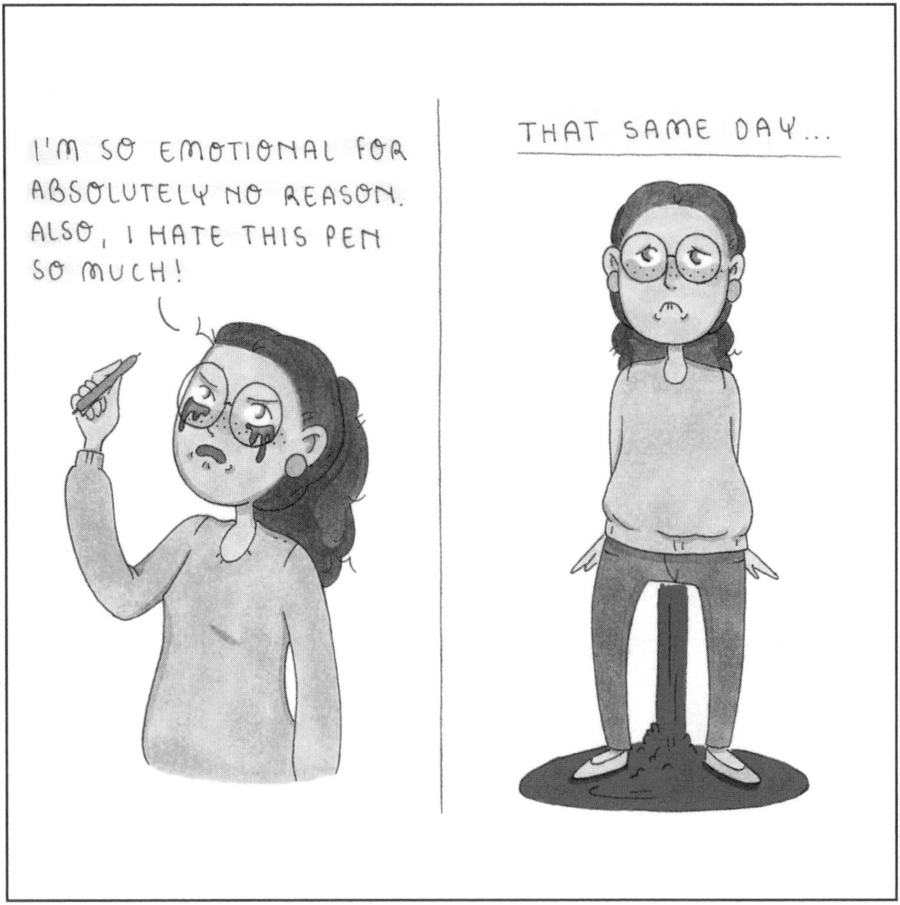
I'M SO EMOTIONAL FOR ABSOLUTELY NO REASON. ALSO, I HATE THIS PEN SO MUCH!
THAT SAME DAY...

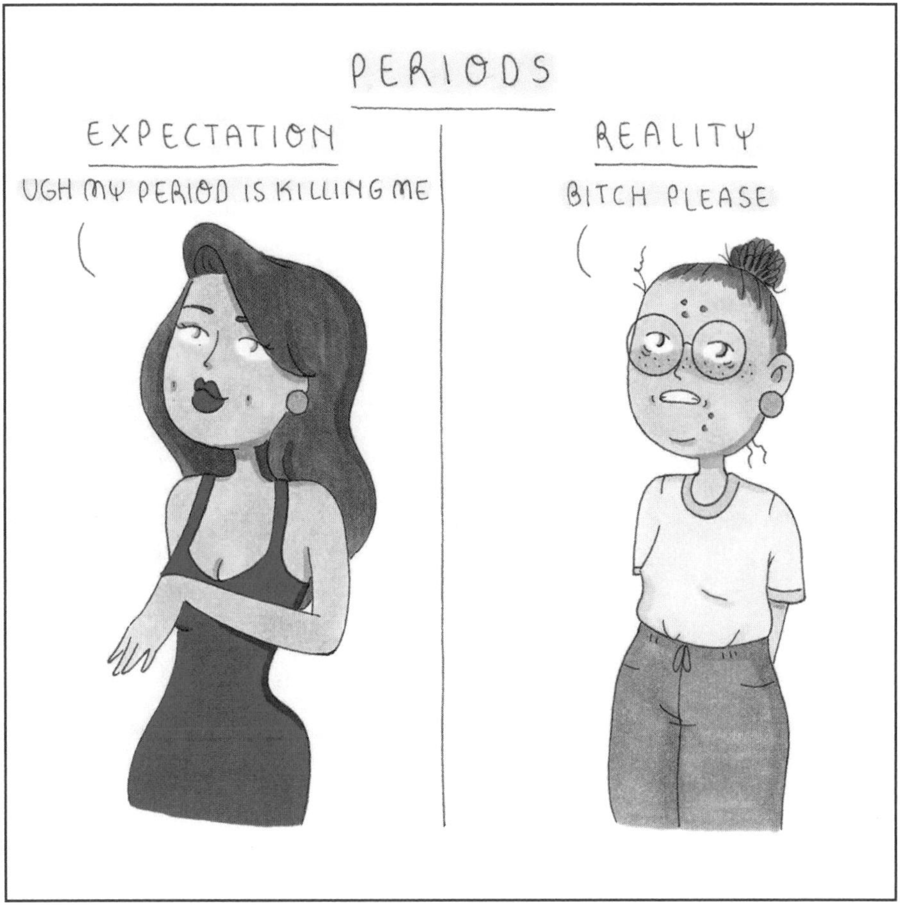
PERIODS
EXPECTATION
UGH MY PERIOD IS KILLING ME
REALITY
BITCH PLEASE

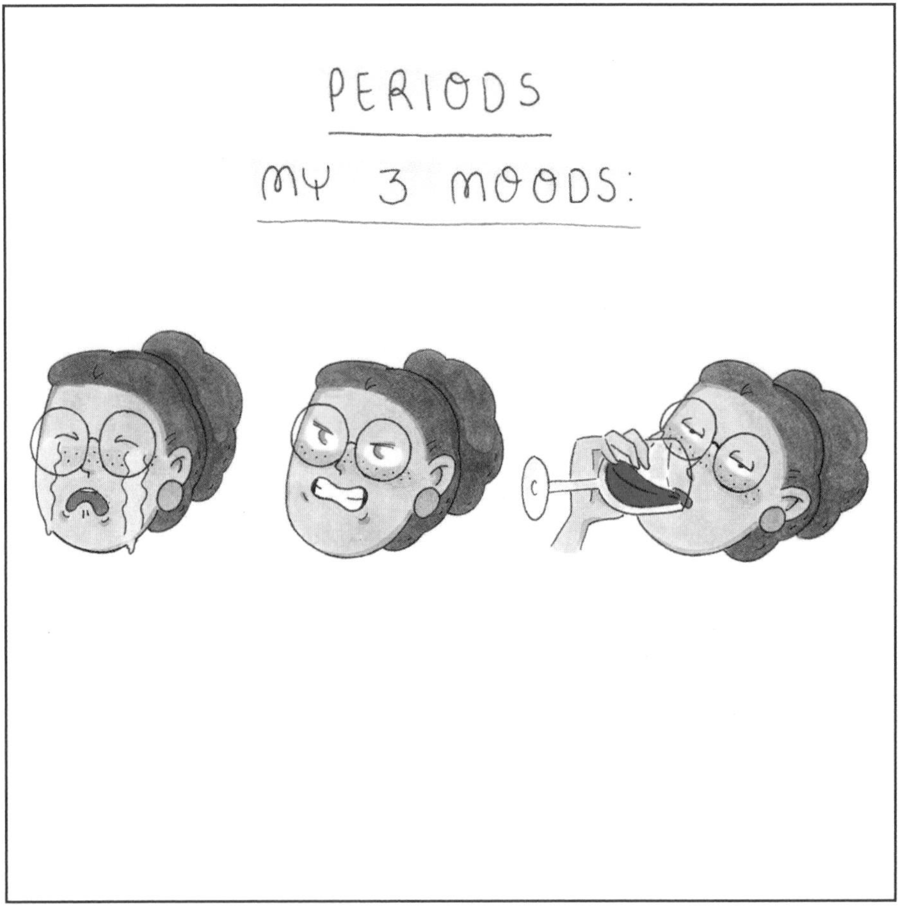
PERIODS
MY 3 MOODS:

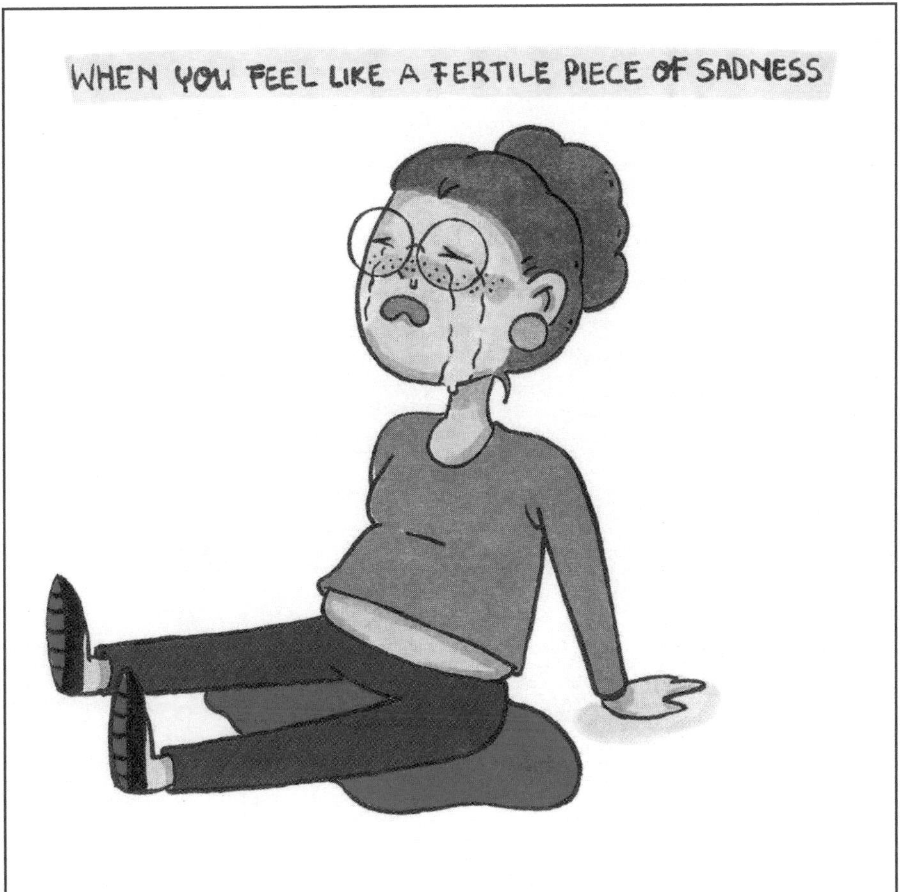
WHEN YOU FEEL LIKE A FERTILE PIECE OF SADNESS

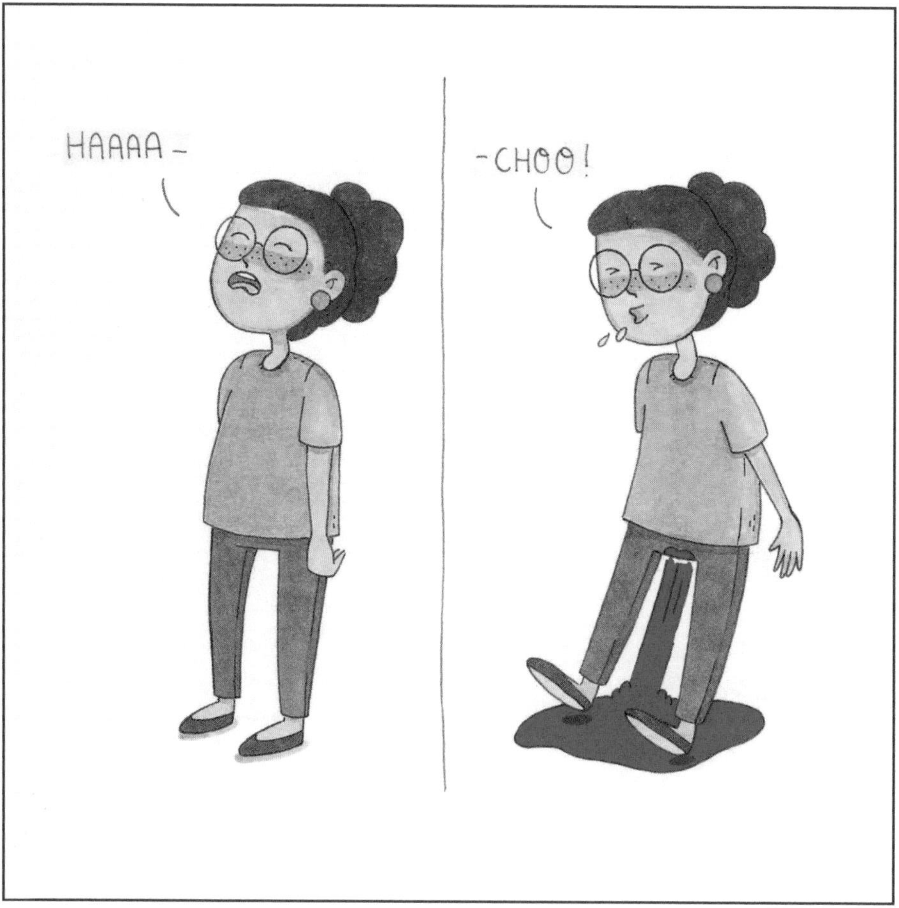
HAAAA –
–CHOO!

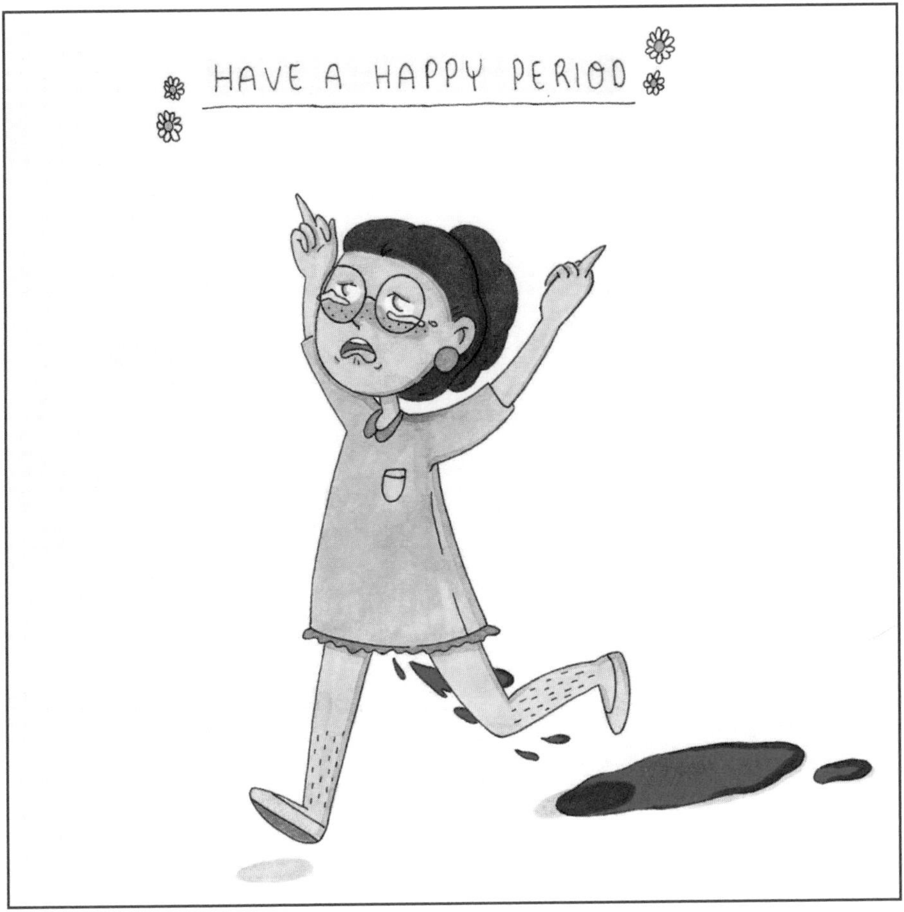
HAVE A HAPPY PERIOD

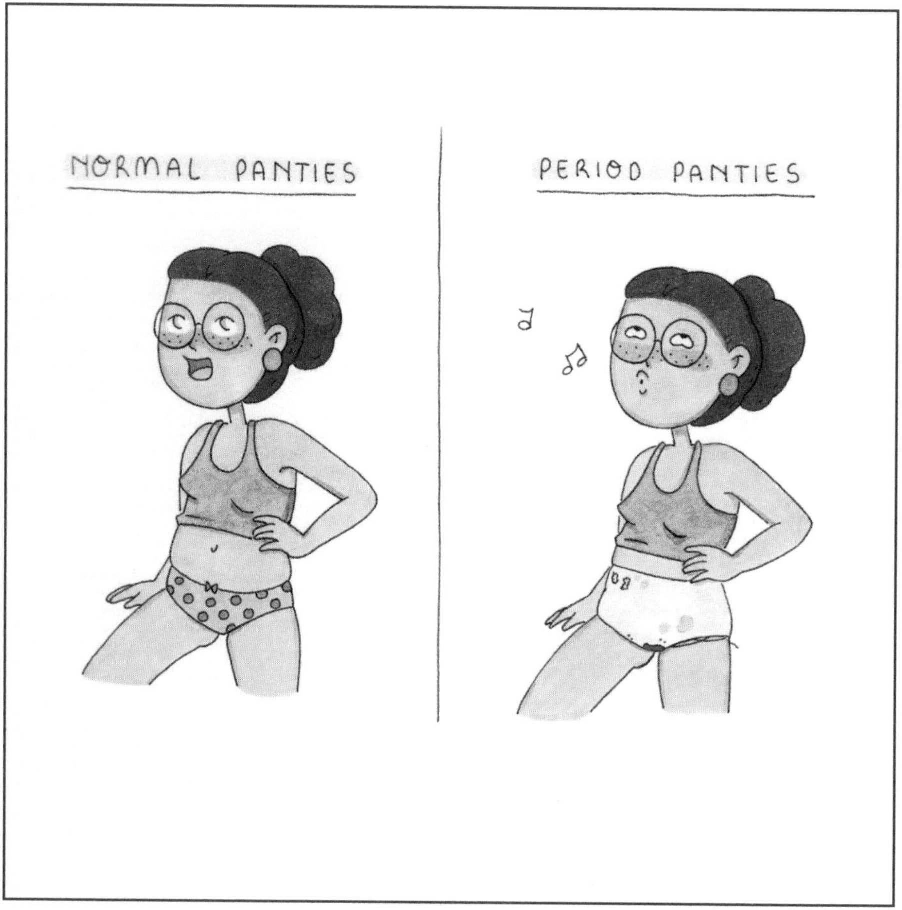
NORMAL PANTIES
PERIOD PANTIES

Best Friends Forever

She looks at me with her eyes wide—the look of eternal love for me—hugging me tight every day since I met her. My furball is the best friend I could have ever wished for. She's my rock. I'll always be there for her and I know she will always be there for me as well. Find yourself a best friend. Hold them tight and love them unconditionally, because they'll love you the same.

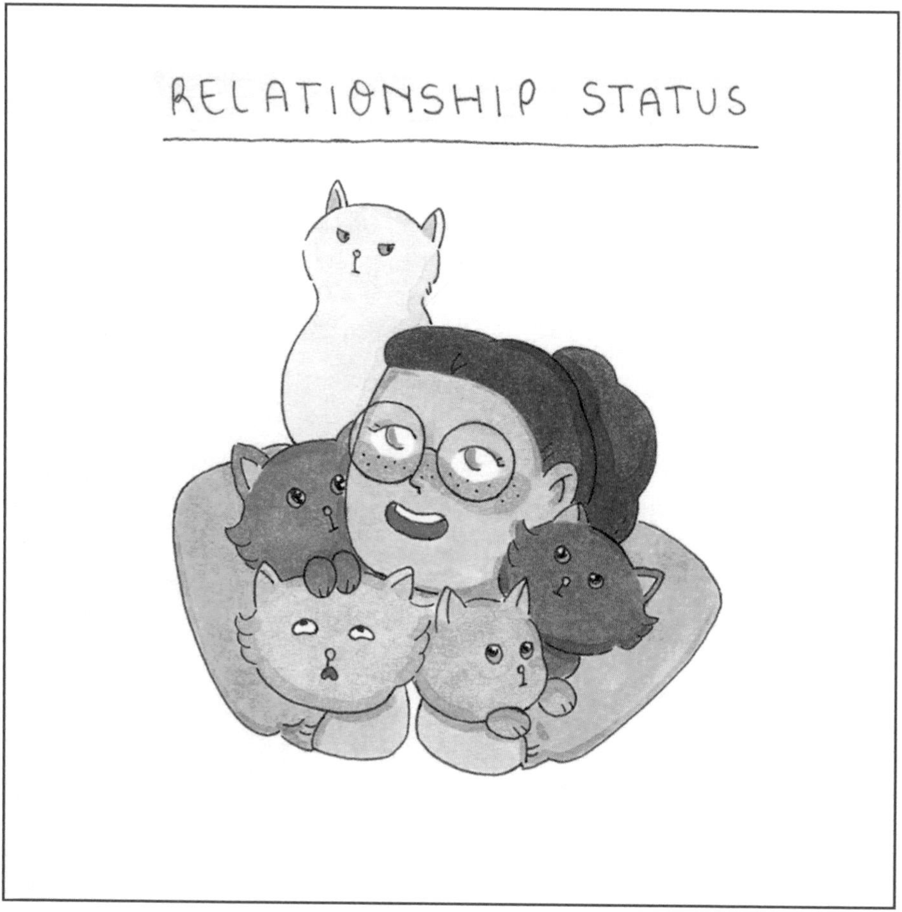
RELATIONSHIP STATUS

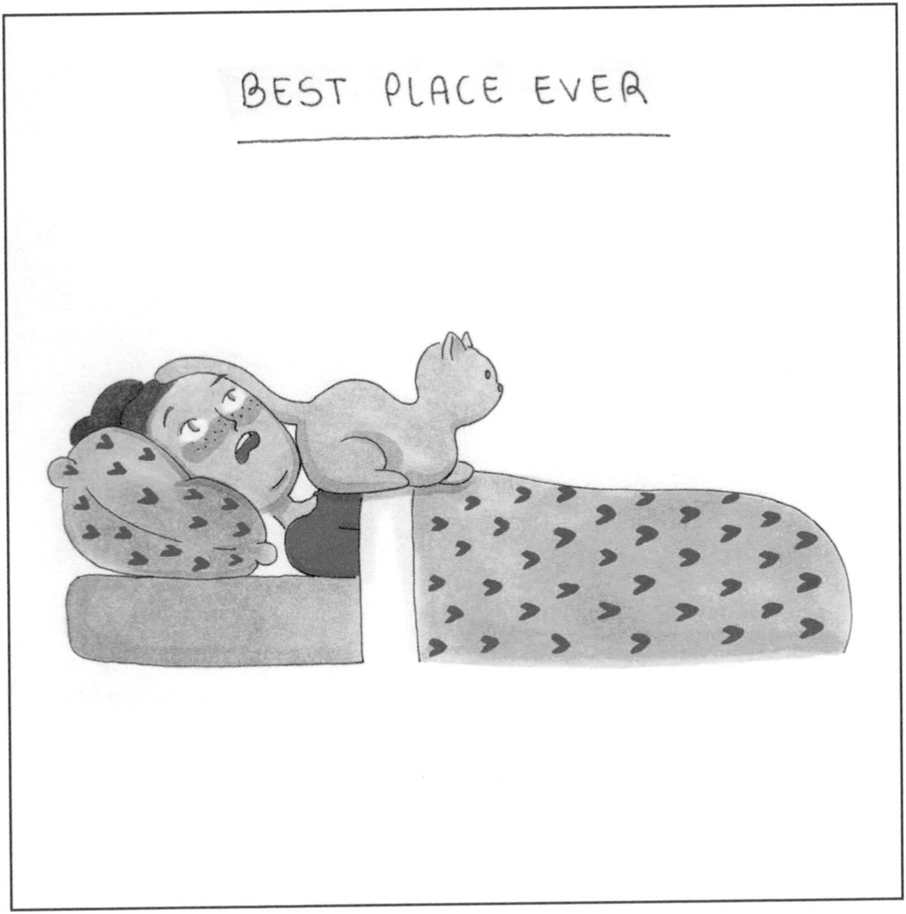
BEST PLACE EVER

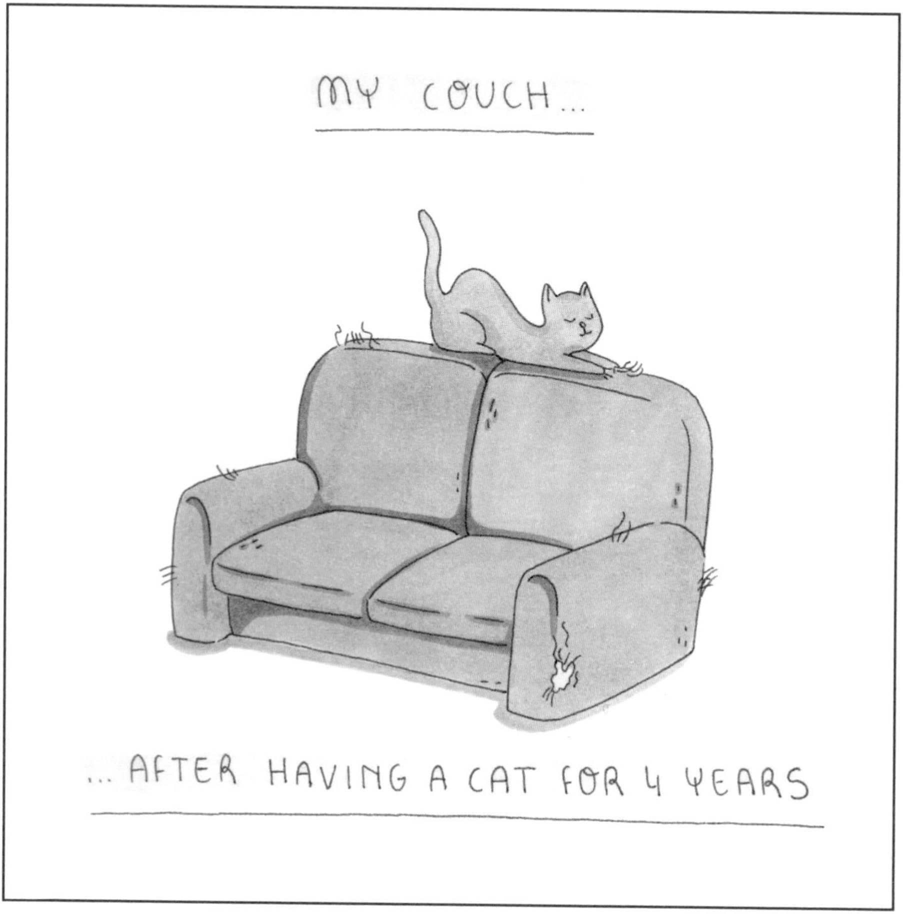
MY COUCH...
...AFTER HAVING A CAT FOR 4 YEARS

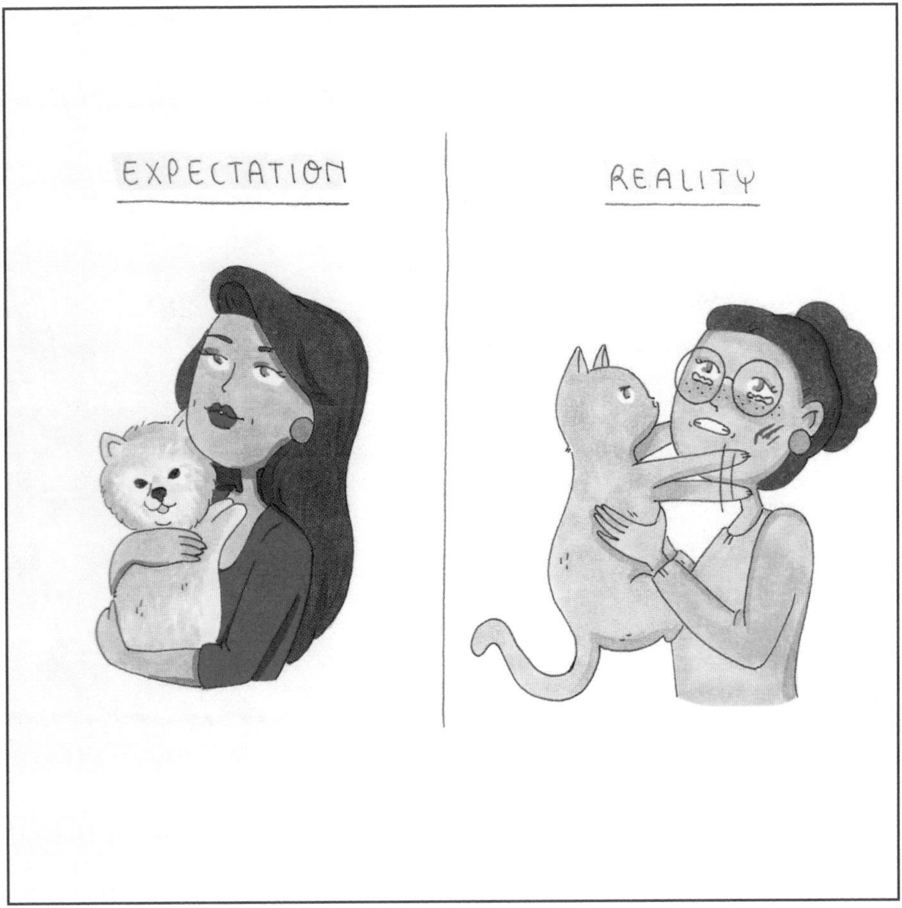
EXPECTATION
REALITY

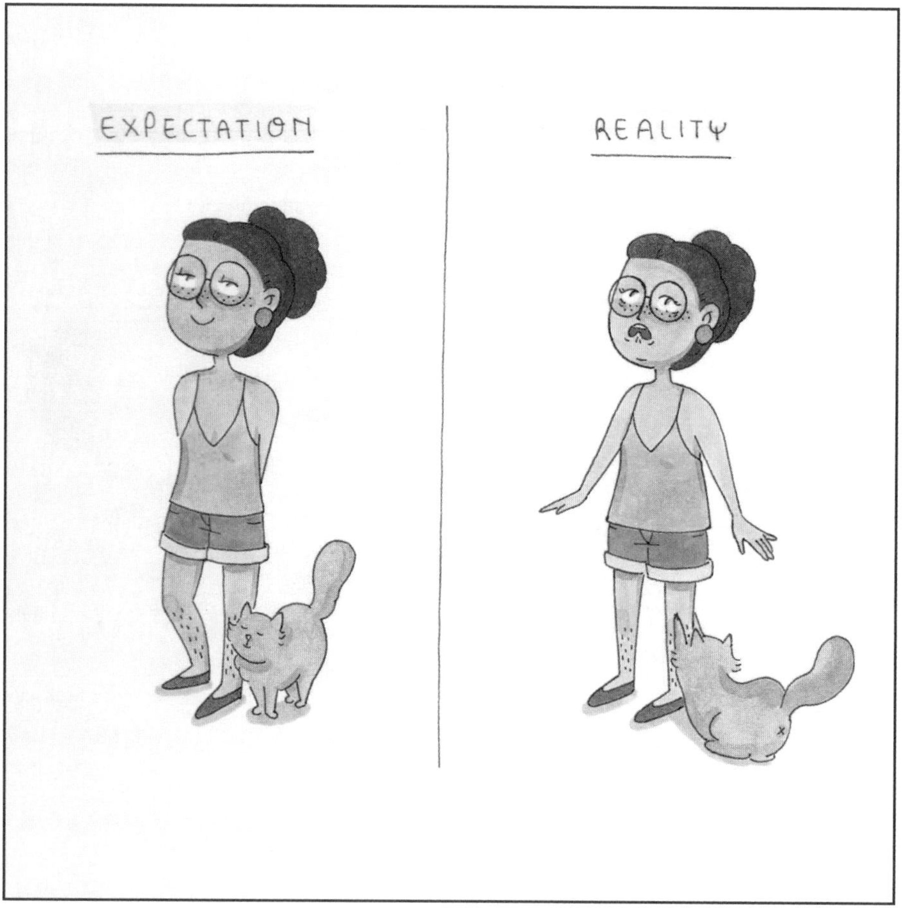
EXPECTATION
REALITY

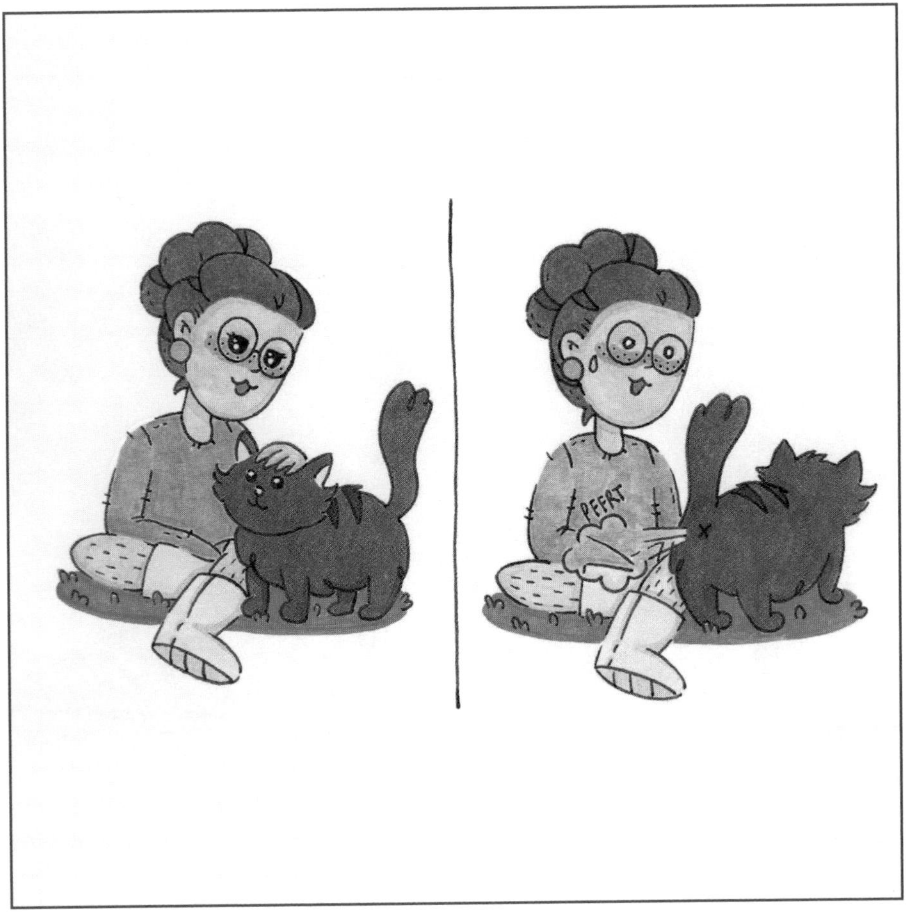
PFFRT

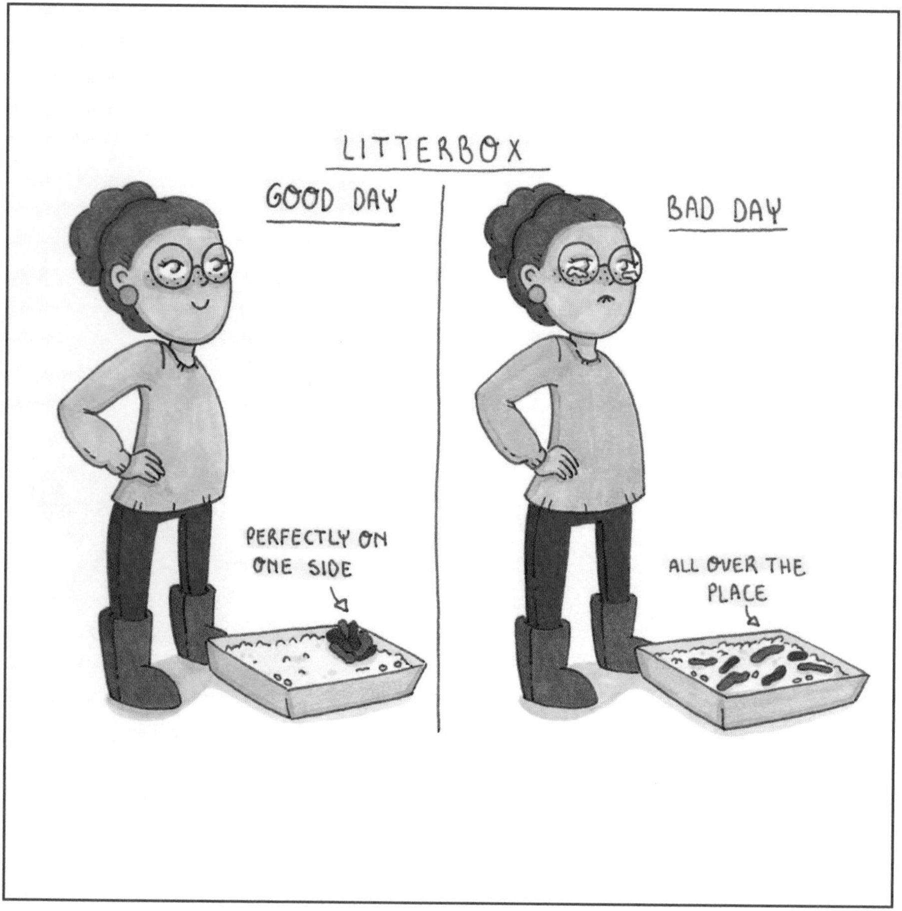
LITTERBOX
GOOD DAY
BAD DAY
PERFECTLY ON ONE SIDE
ALL OVER THE PLACE

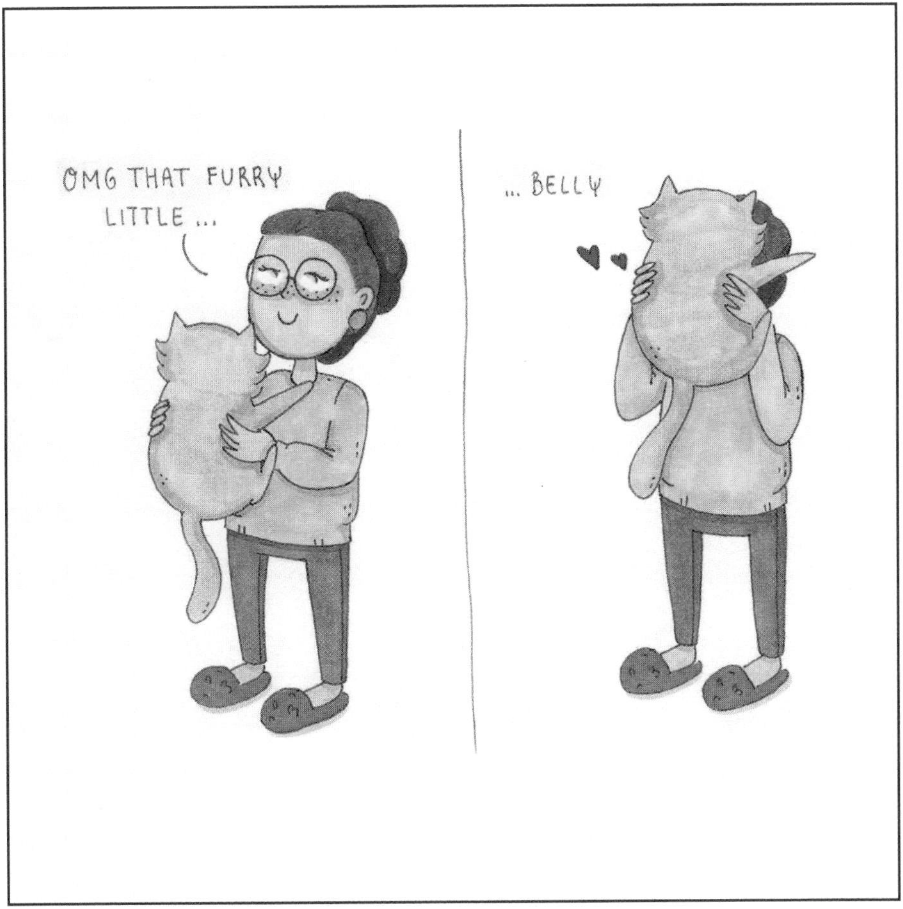
OMG THAT FURRY LITTLE ...
... BELLY

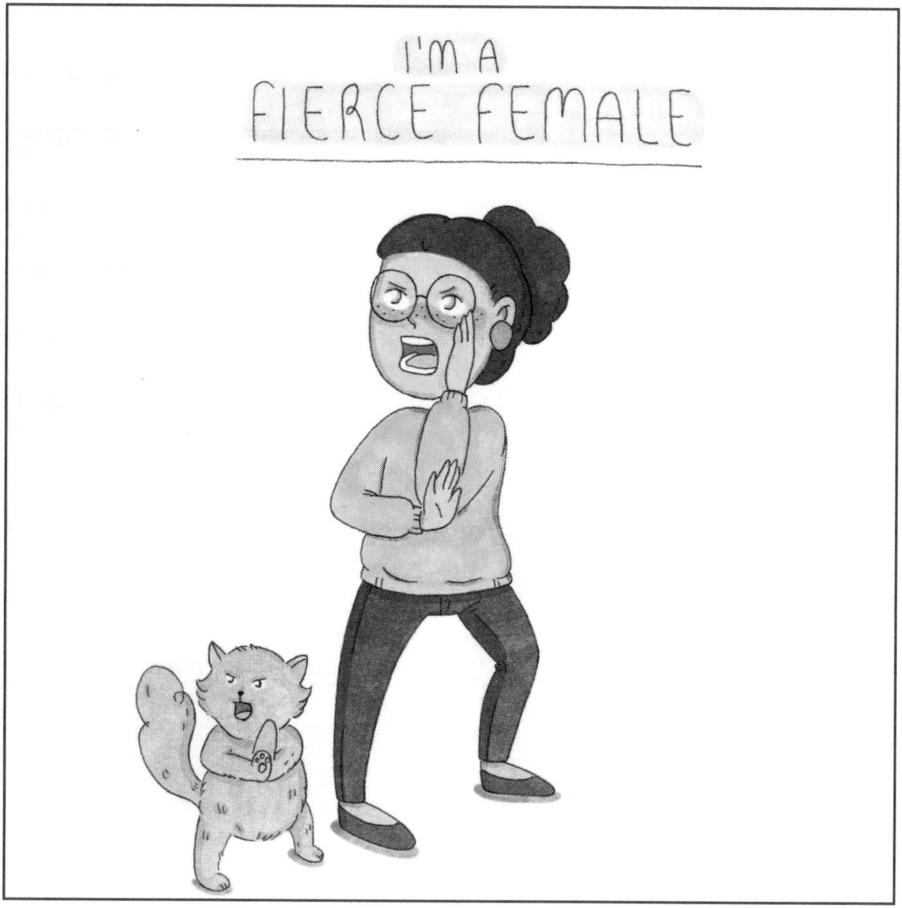
I'M A
FIERCE FEMALE

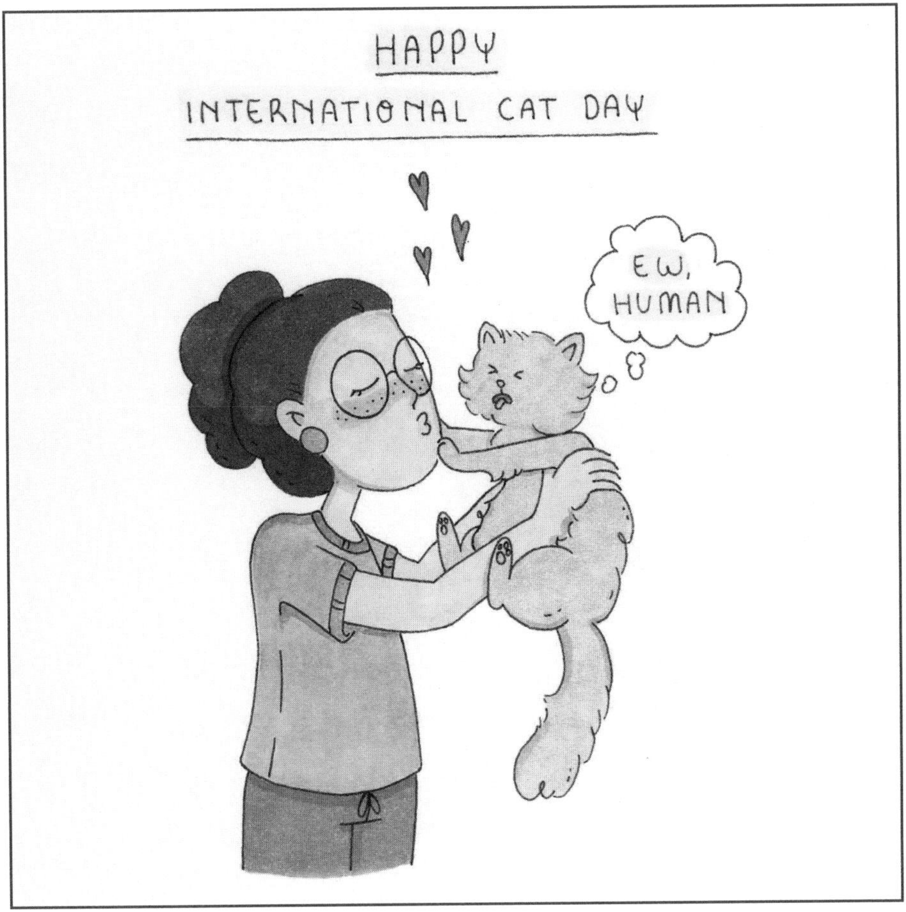
HAPPY
INTERNATIONAL CAT DAY
EW, HUMAN

Love Letters

We all fall in love at least once in our lives, and we're the luckiest people if our love is answered. You know that feeling you get when butterflies start living in your stomach, when eating gets hard, when pooping starts to become a hobby, when you think about him 24/7, and you start to smile more often with stars in your eyes? Yeah, that kind of love is awesome.

BAE ♥

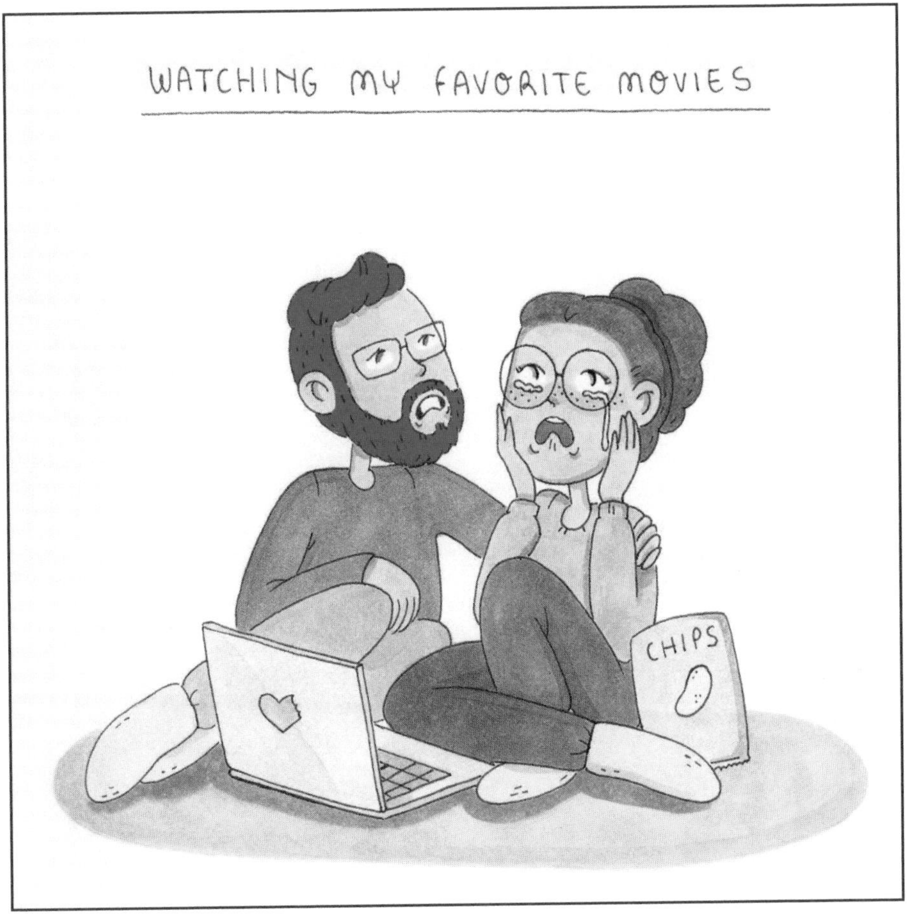
WATCHING MY FAVORITE MOVIES
CHIPS

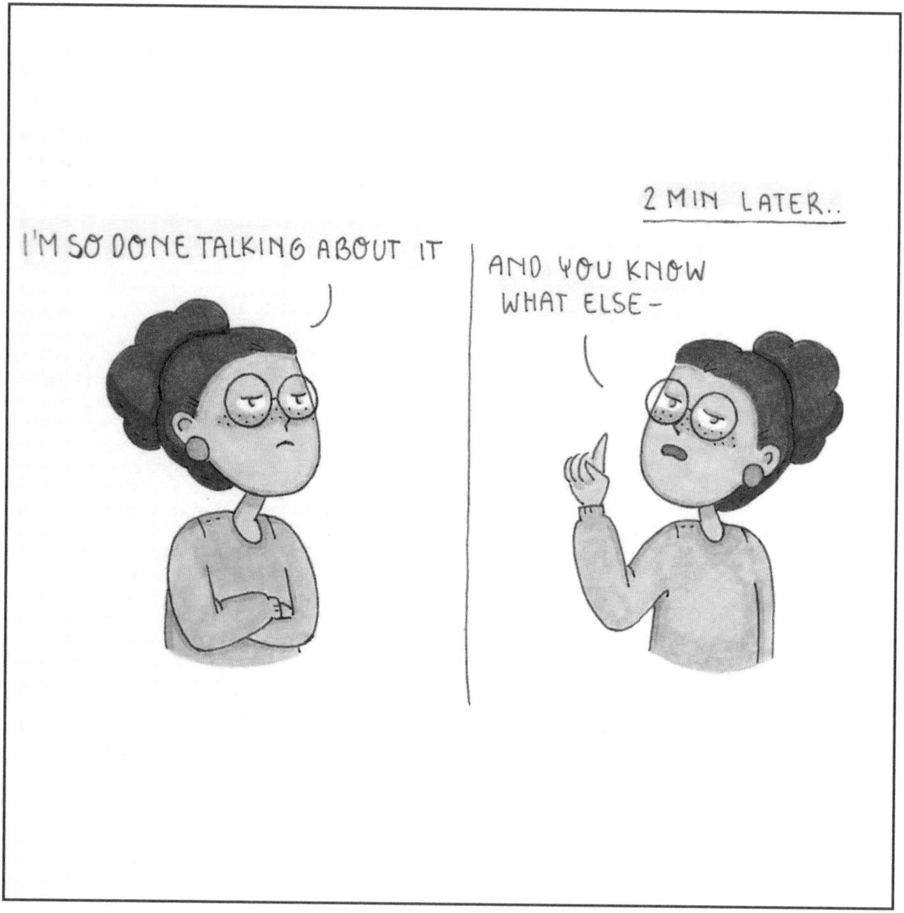
I'M SO DONE TALKING ABOUT IT
2 MIN LATER..
AND YOU KNOW
WHAT ELSE-

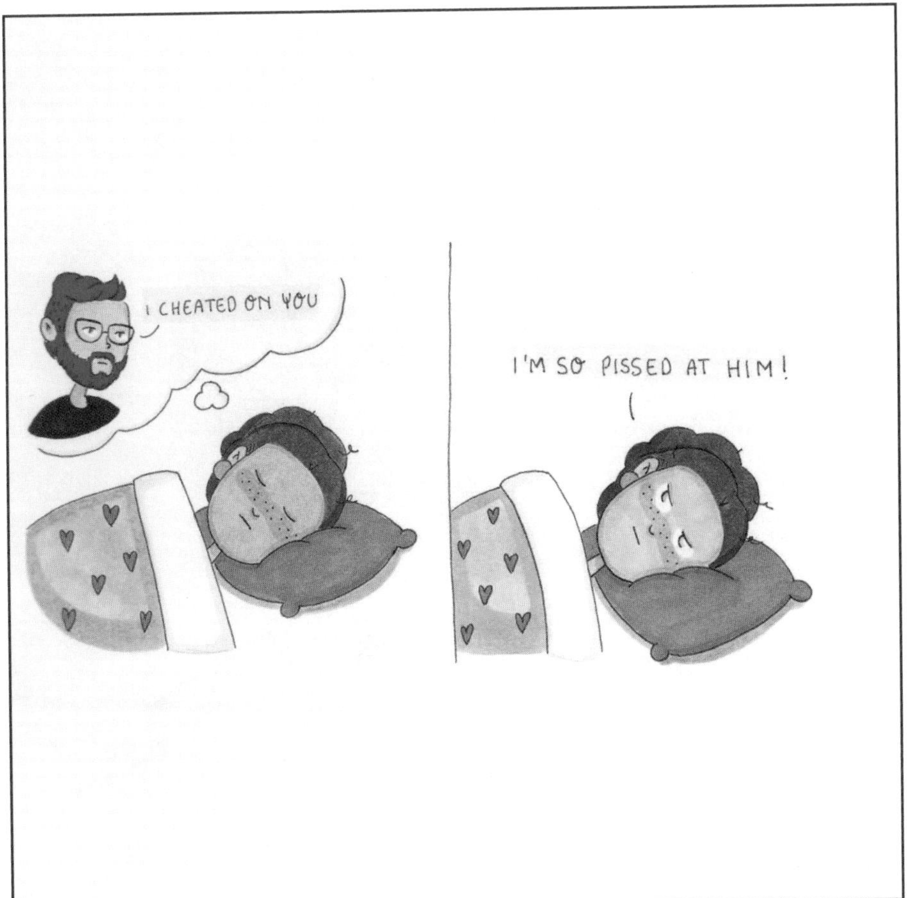
I CHEATED ON YOU
I'M SO PISSED AT HIM!

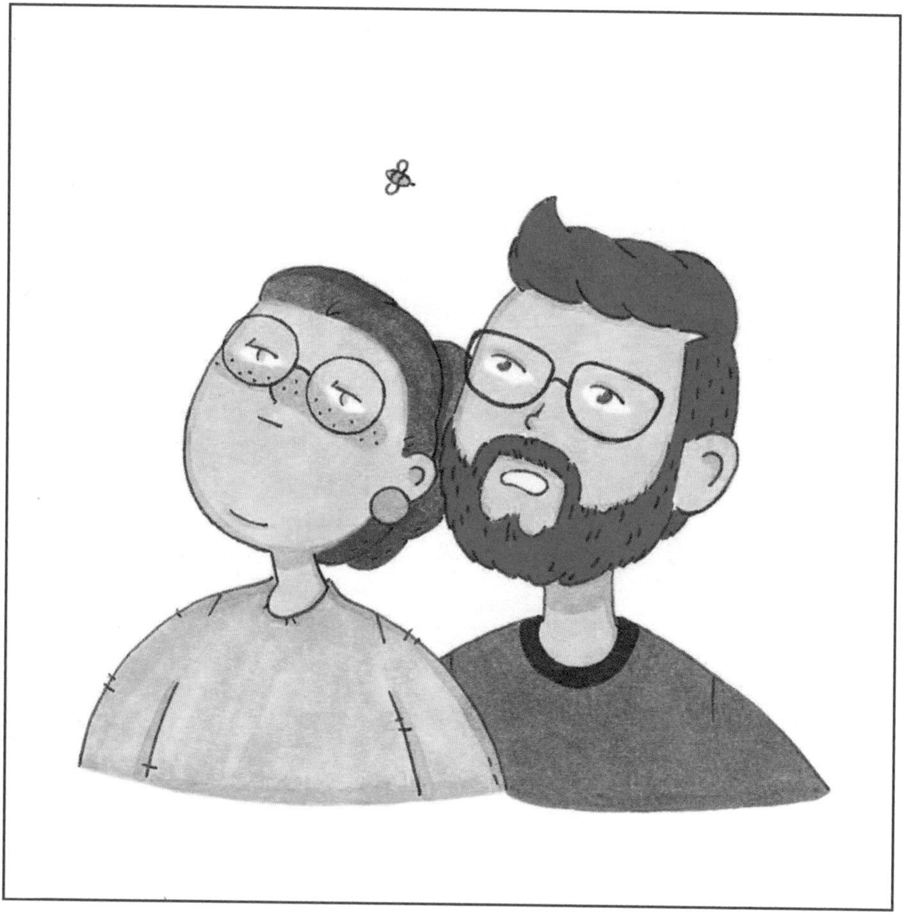

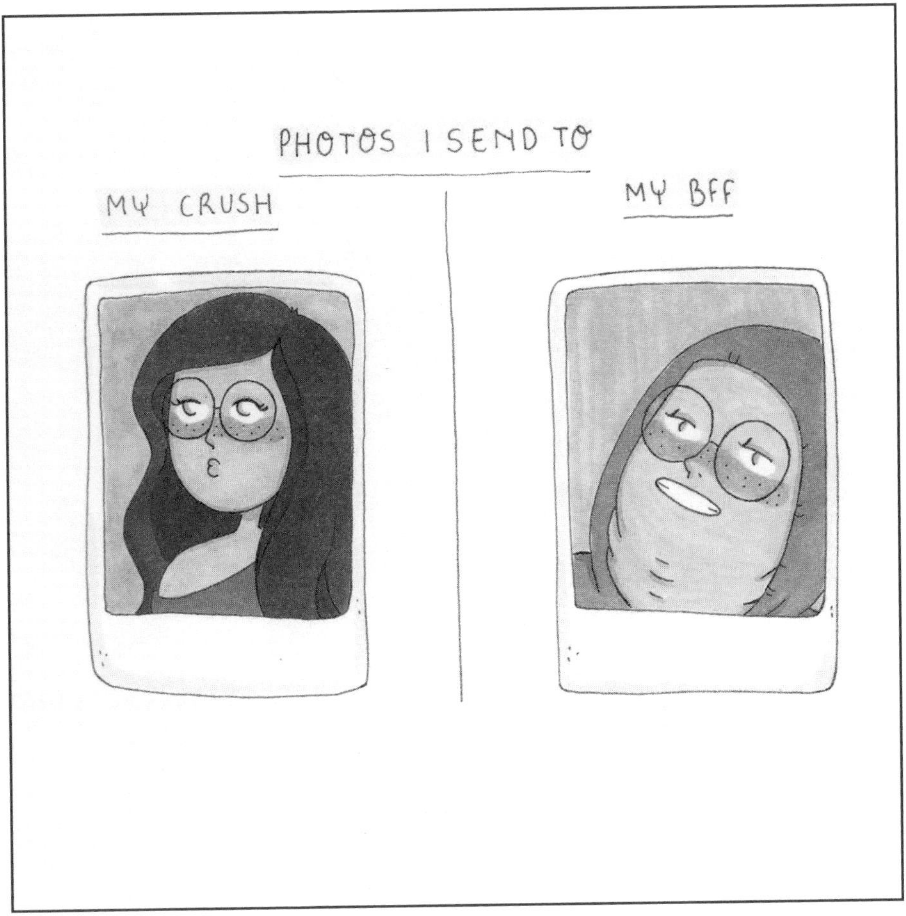
PHOTOS I SEND TO
MY CRUSH
MY BFF

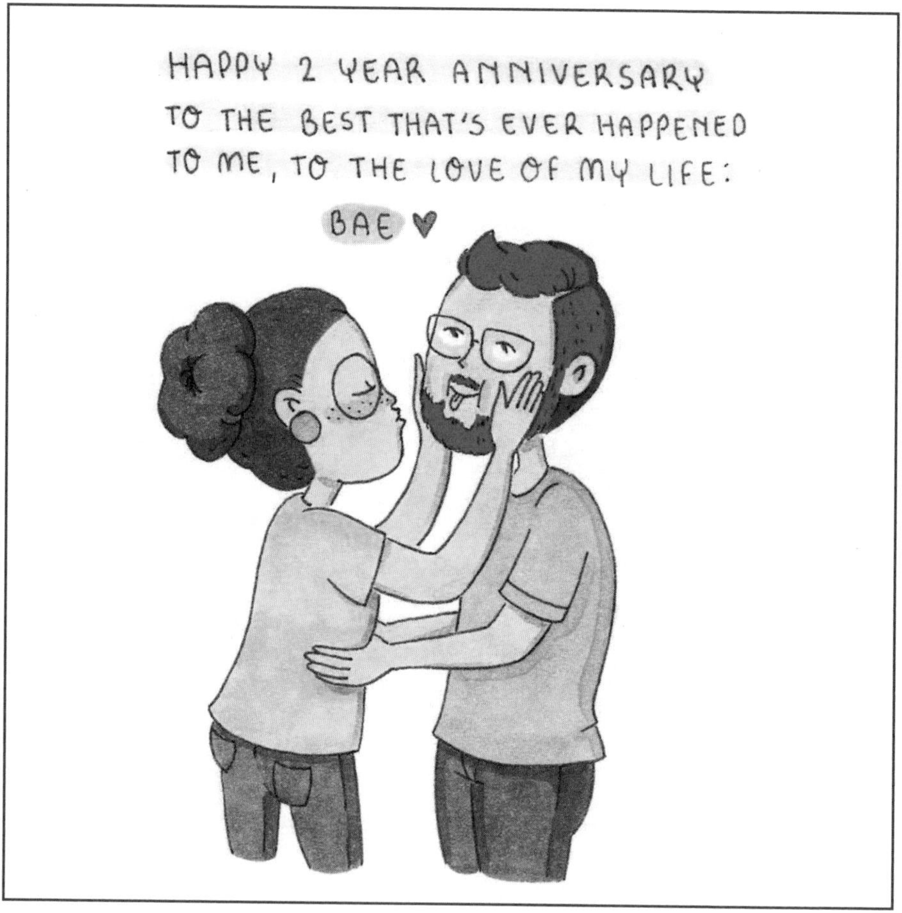
HAPPY 2 YEAR ANNIVERSARY
TO THE BEST THAT'S EVER HAPPENED
TO ME, TO THE LOVE OF MY LIFE:
BAE ♥

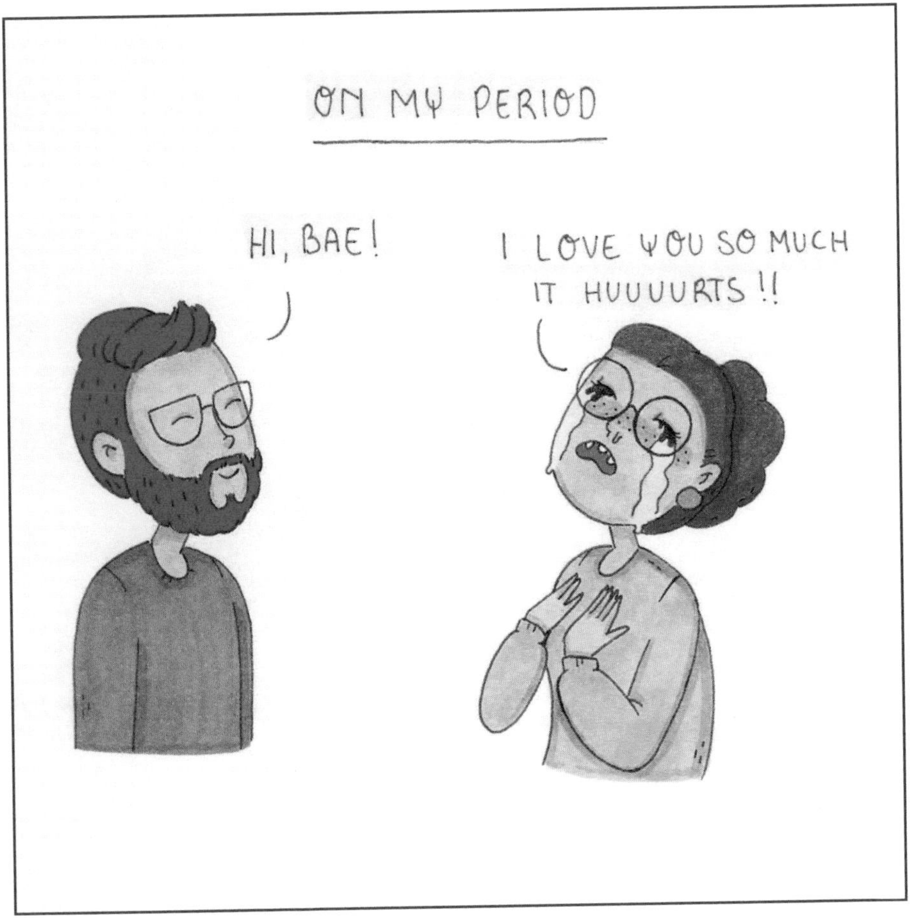
ON MY PERIOD
HI, BAE!
I LOVE YOU SO MUCH IT HUUUURTS !!

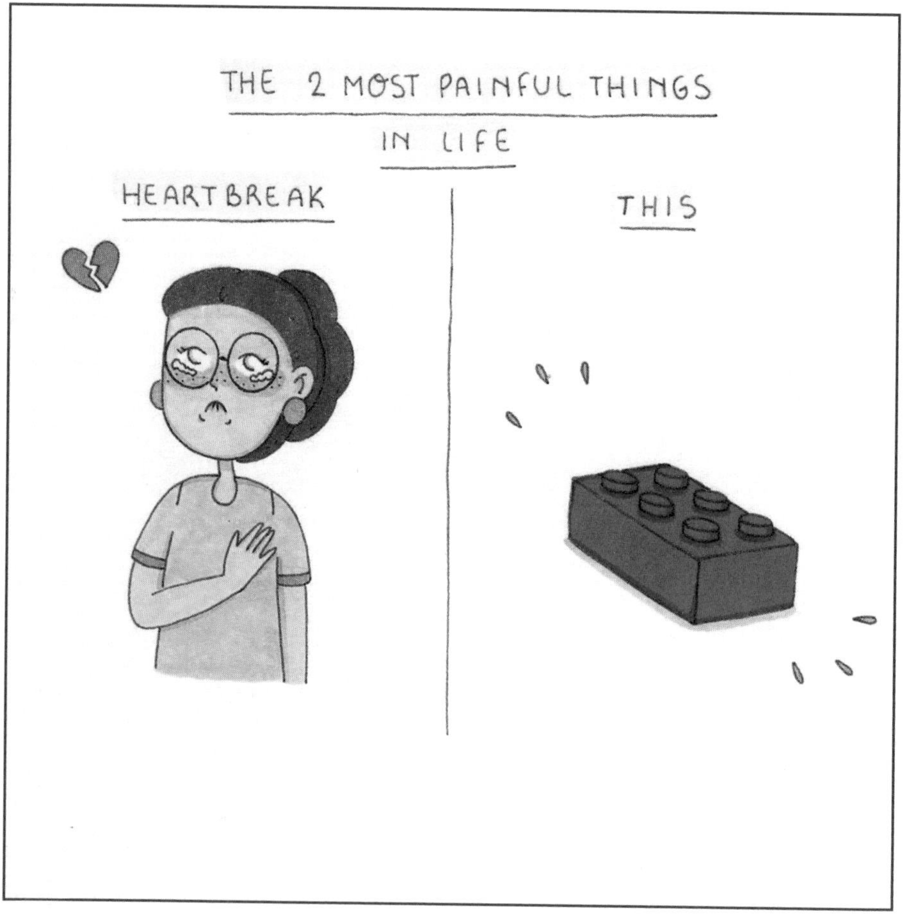
THE 2 MOST PAINFUL THINGS IN LIFE
HEARTBREAK
THIS

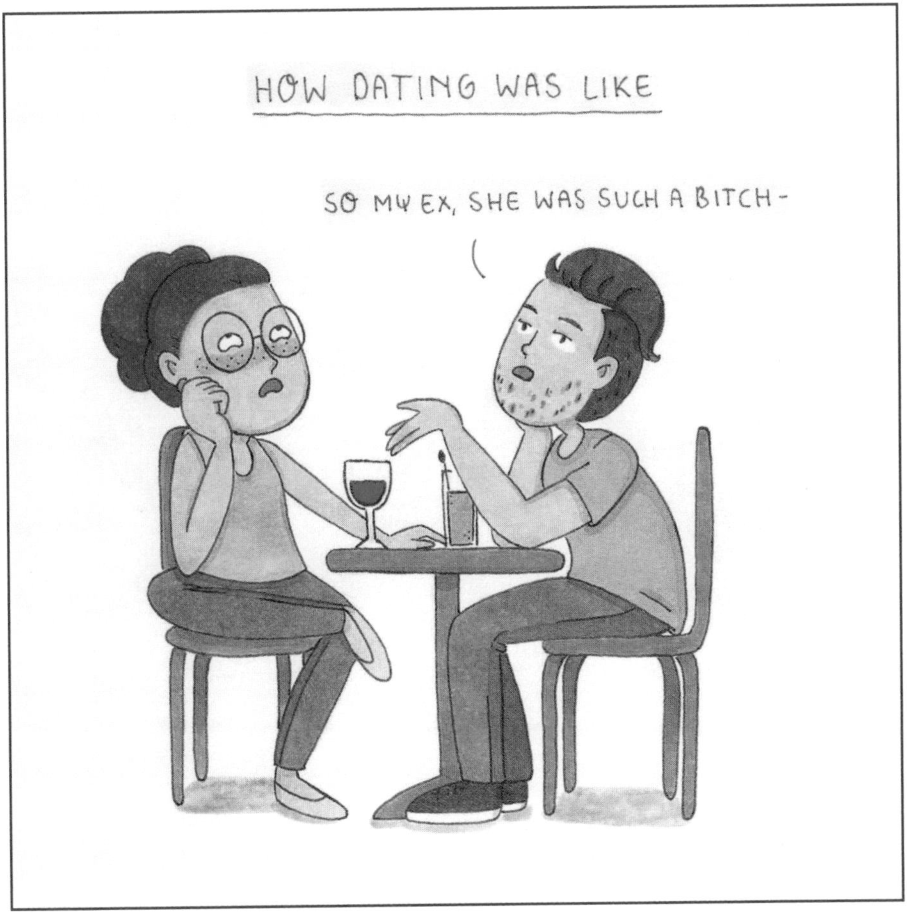
HOW DATING WAS LIKE
SO MY EX, SHE WAS SUCH A BITCH-

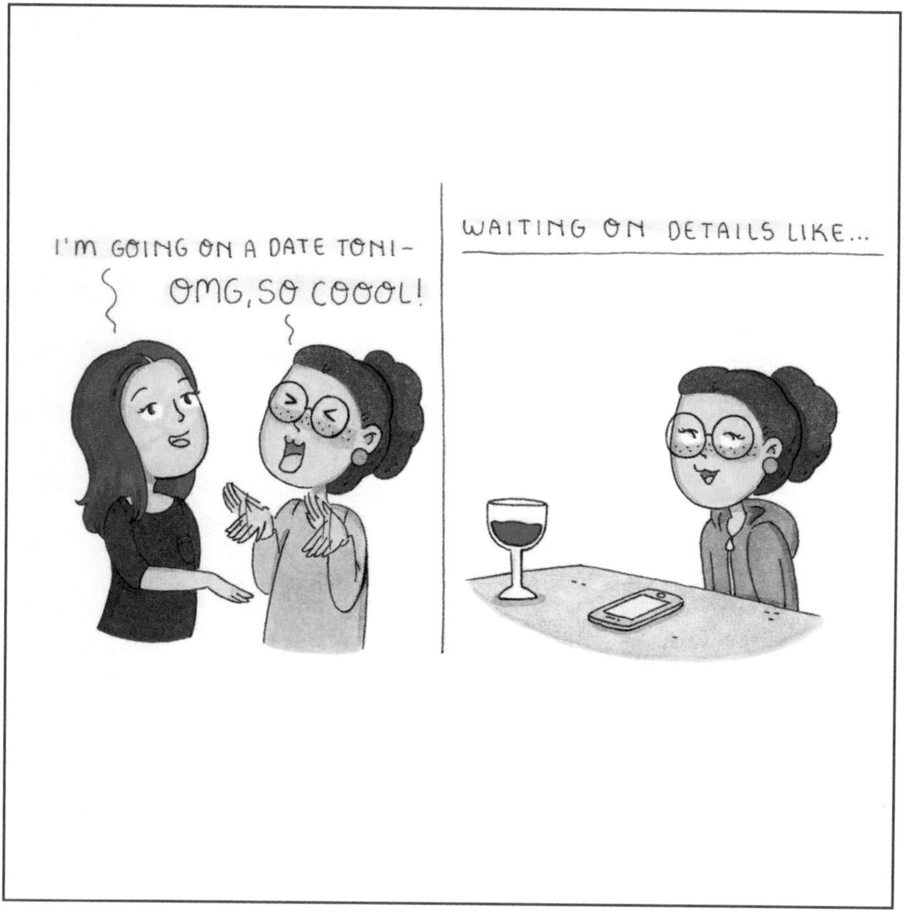
I'M GOING ON A DATE TONI-
OMG, SO COOOL!
WAITING ON DETAILS LIKE...

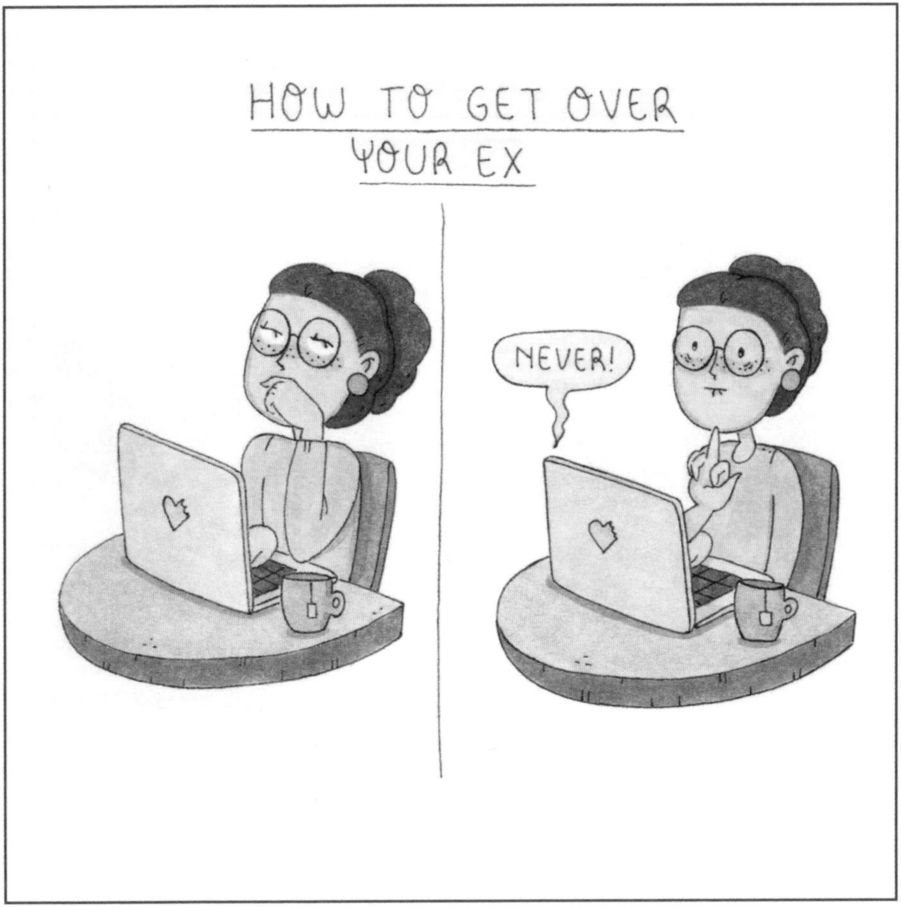
HOW TO GET OVER YOUR EX
NEVER!

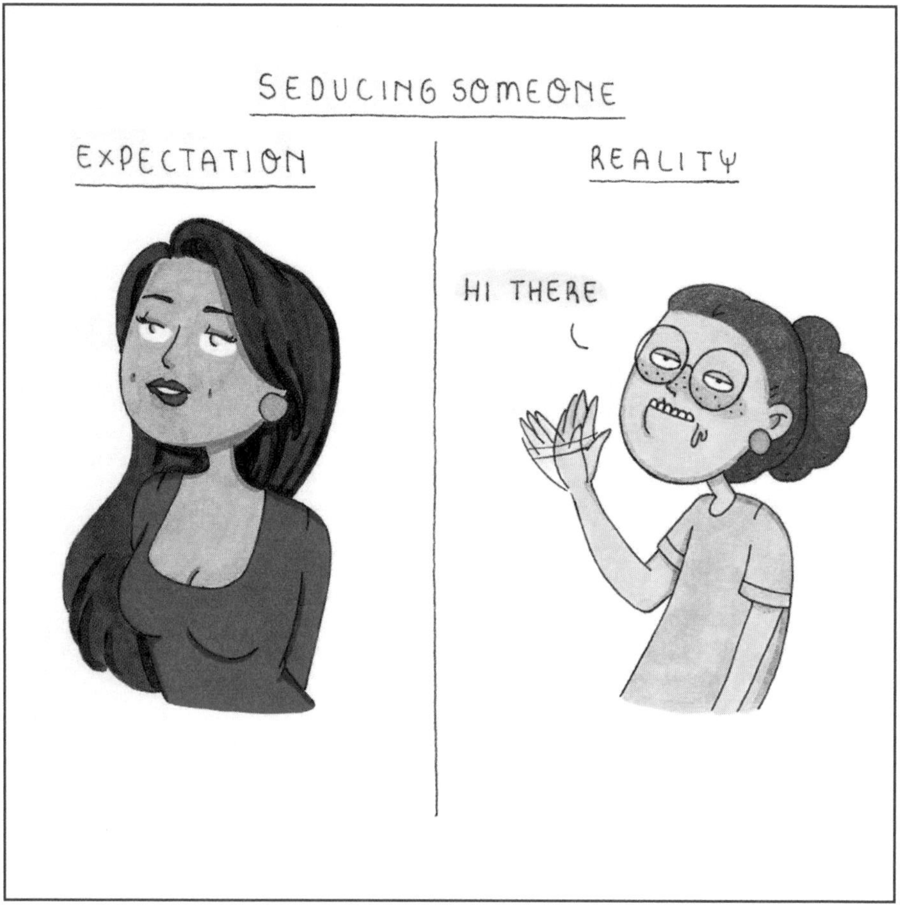
SEDUCING SOMEONE
EXPECTATION
REALITY
HI THERE

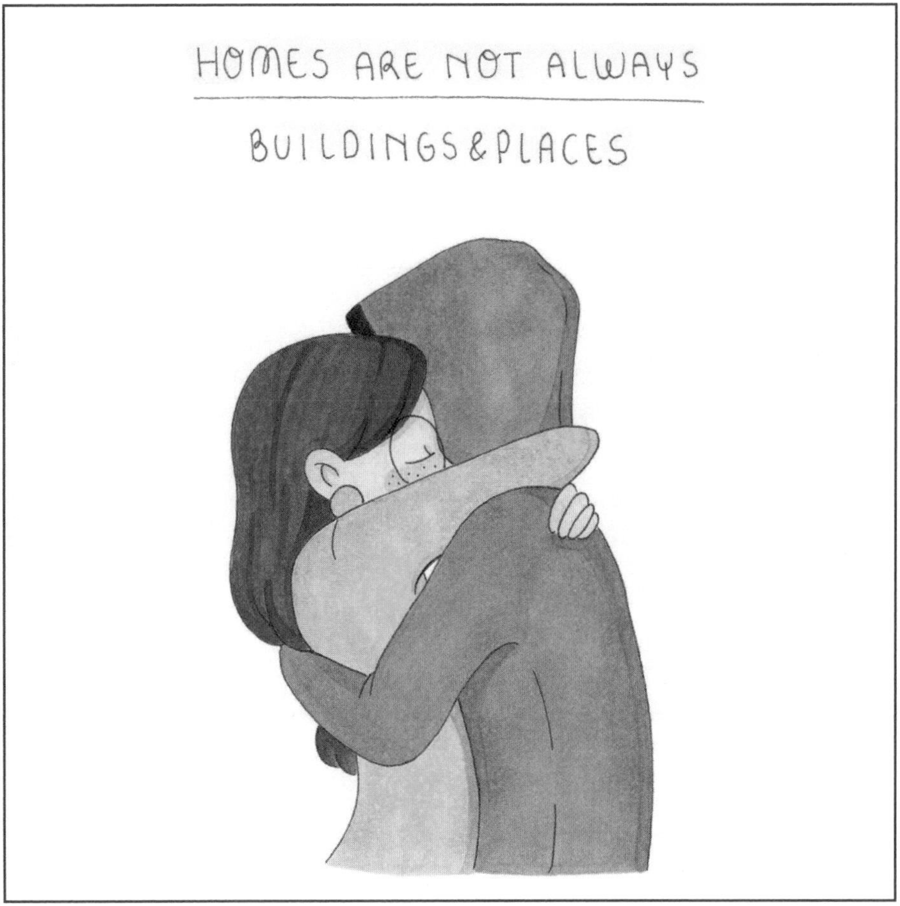
HOMES ARE NOT ALWAYS
BUILDINGS & PLACES

I Don't Want to Go

School and work are the kinds of things that we just have to accept in our lives. Since we spend more of our waking hours at work than we do at home, I've always told myself that I don't want to spend my life doing something I don't like. Although, honestly, I *did* spend some time doing jobs I didn't like, I knew I was just doing them to get where I wanted be.

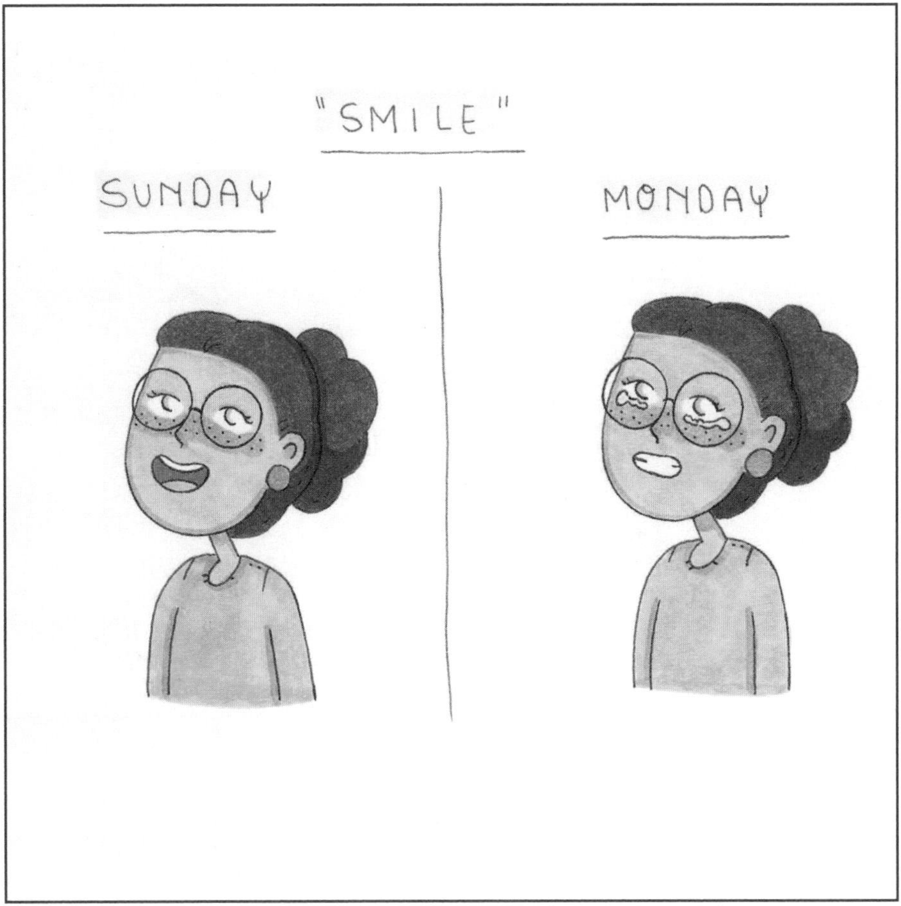
"SMILE"
SUNDAY
MONDAY

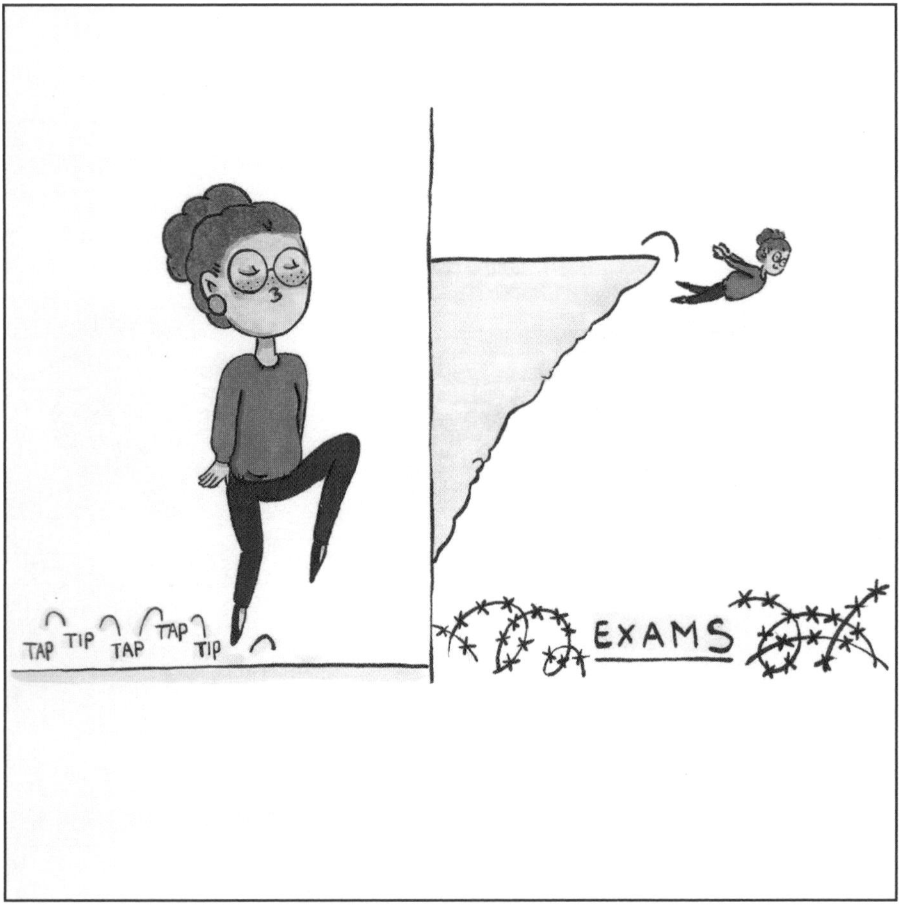
TAP TIP TAP TAP TIP
EXAMS

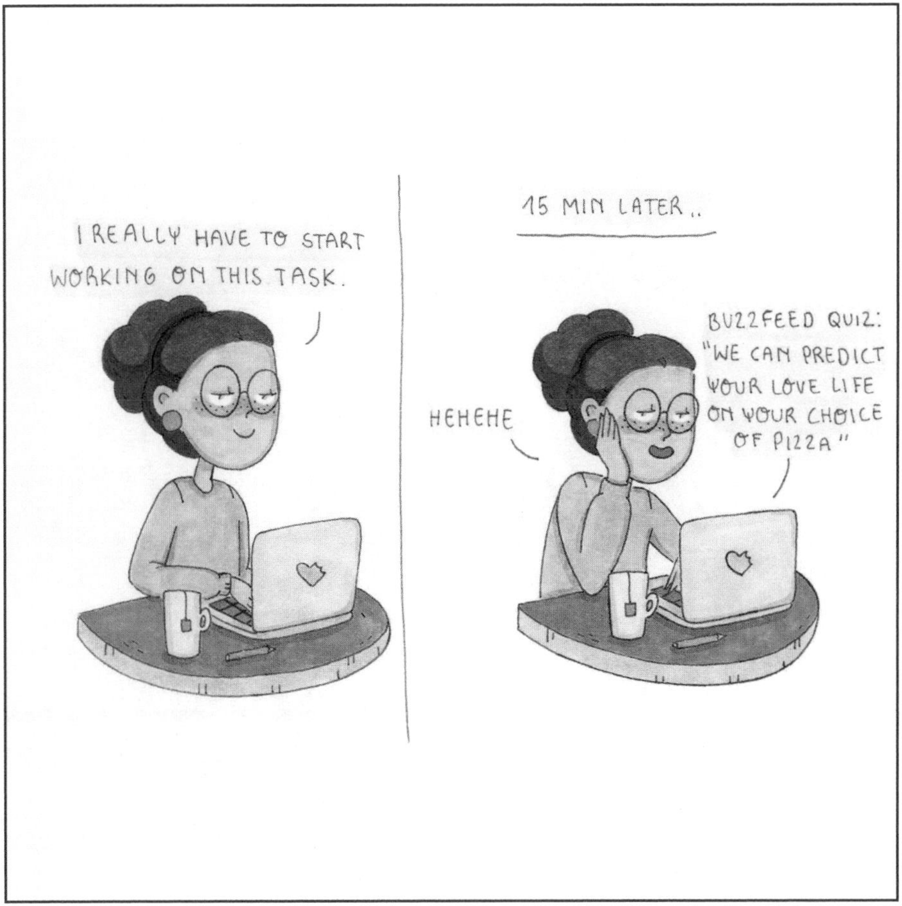
I REALLY HAVE TO START WORKING ON THIS TASK.
15 MIN LATER..
HEHEHE
BUZZFEED QUIZ: "WE CAN PREDICT YOUR LOVE LIFE ON YOUR CHOICE OF PIZZA"

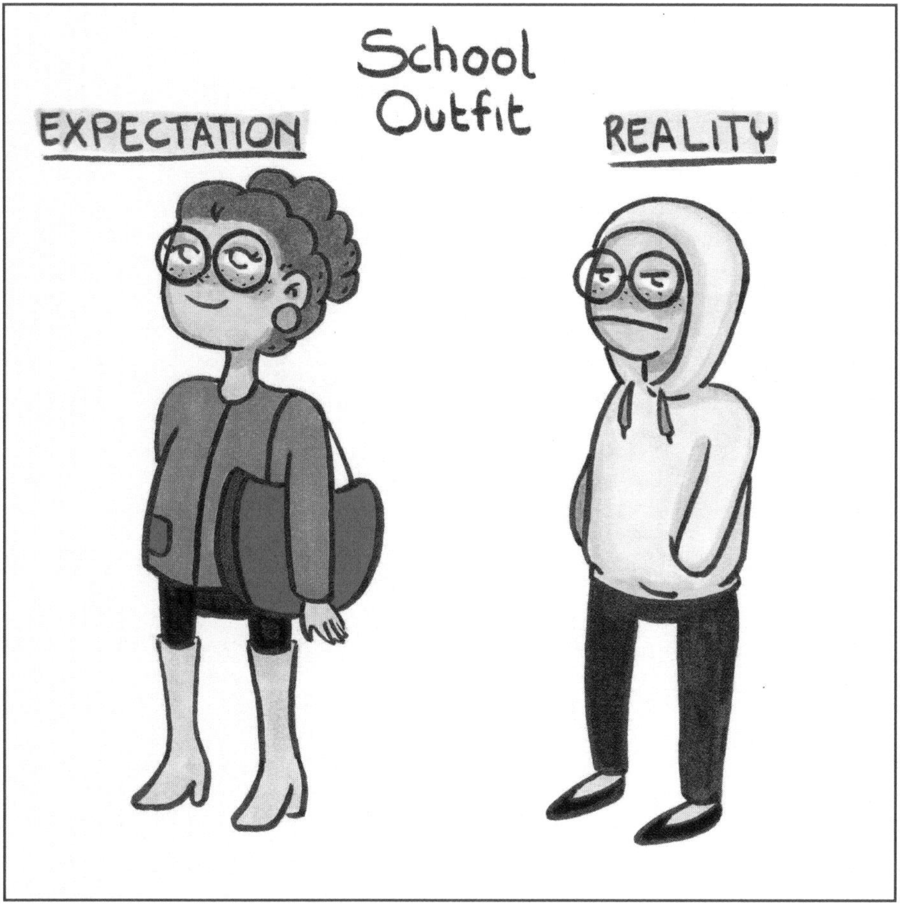
School Outfit
EXPECTATION
REALITY

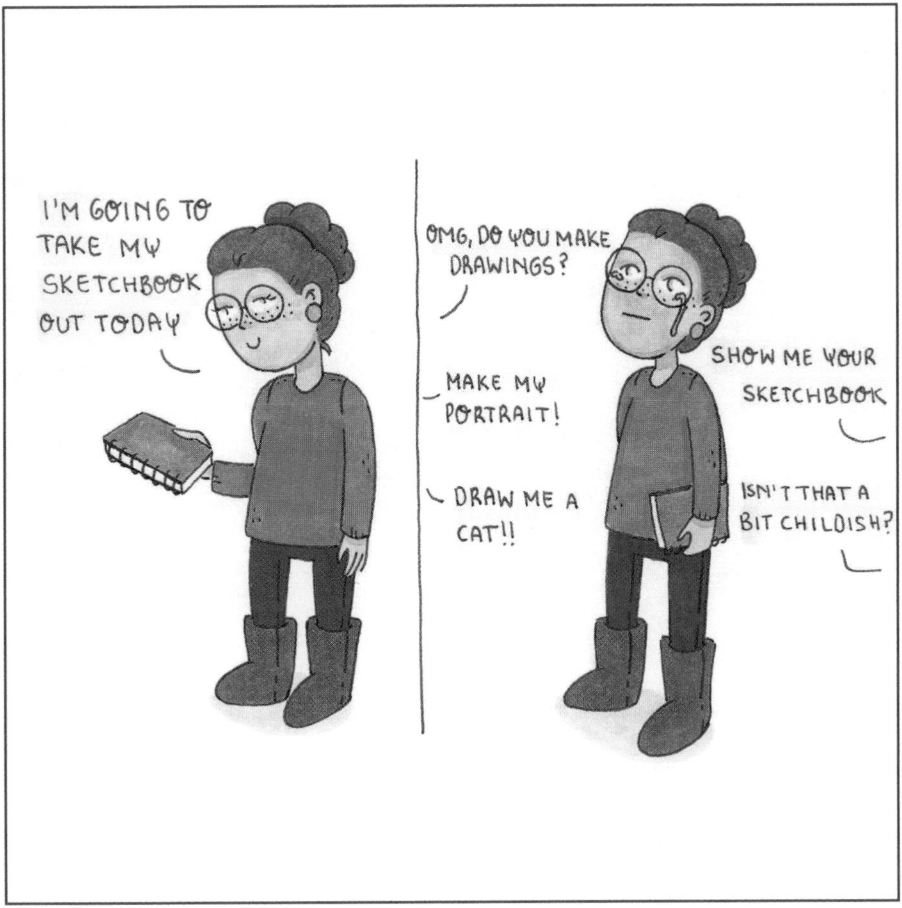
I'M GOING TO TAKE MY SKETCHBOOK OUT TODAY
OMG, DO YOU MAKE DRAWINGS?
MAKE MY PORTRAIT!
DRAW ME A CAT!!
SHOW ME YOUR SKETCHBOOK
ISN'T THAT A BIT CHILDISH?

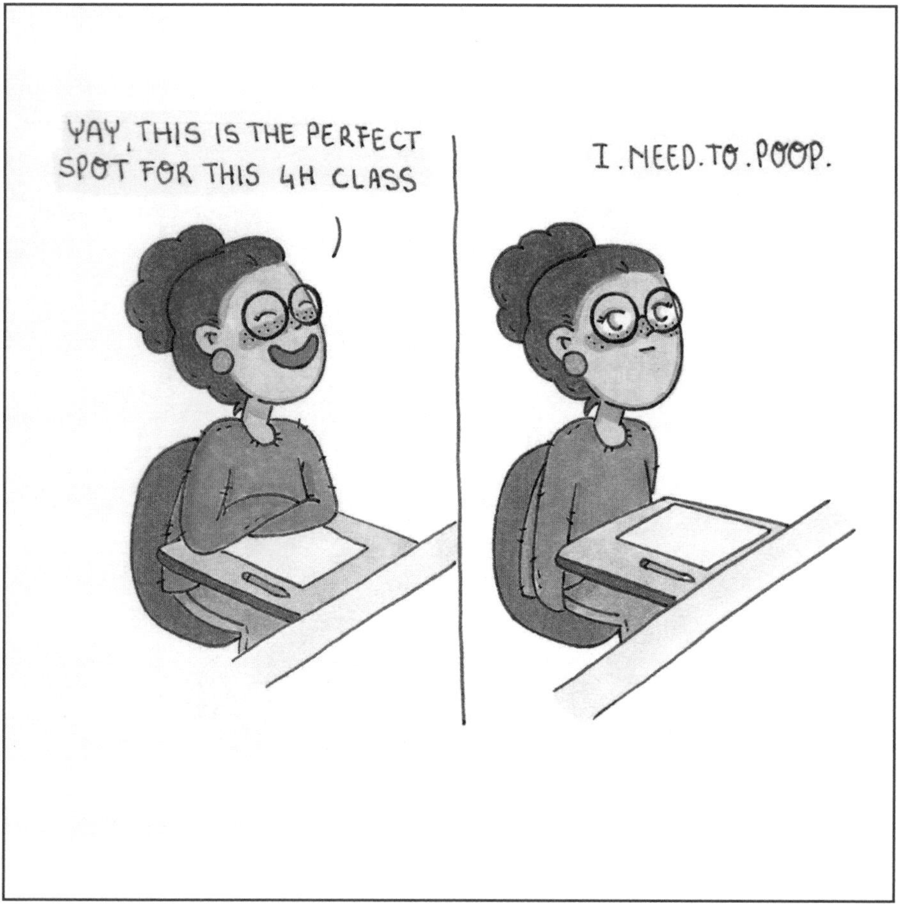
YAY, THIS IS THE PERFECT SPOT FOR THIS 4H CLASS
I.NEED.TO.POOP.

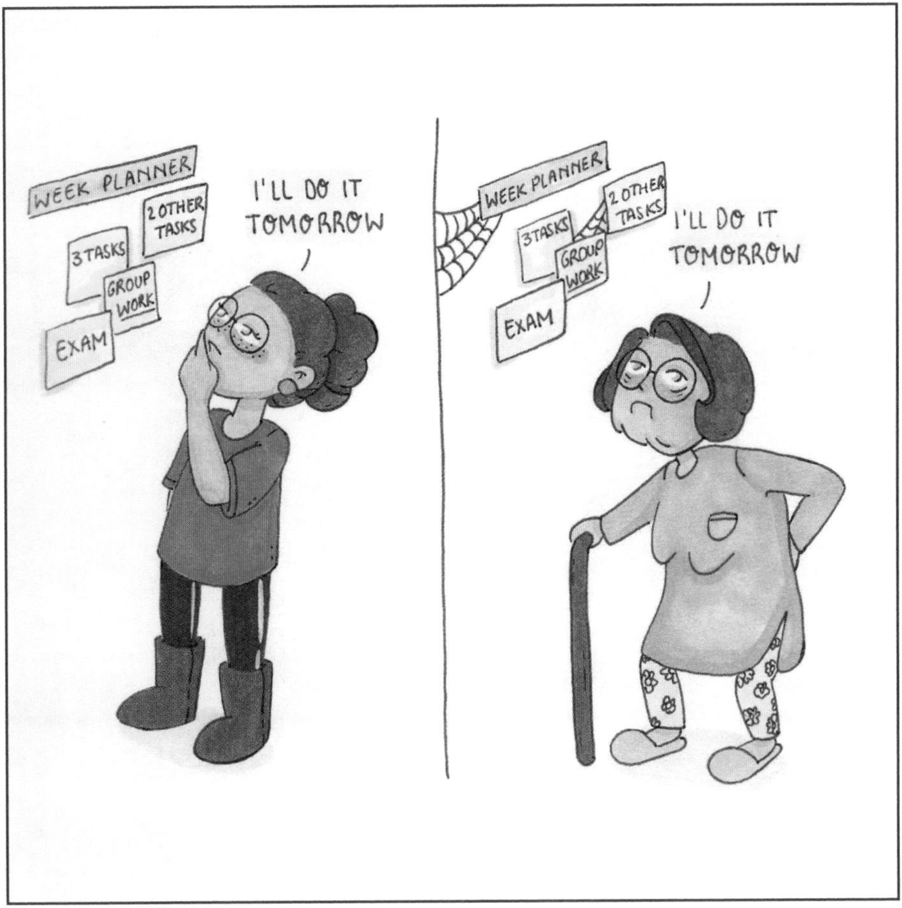
WEEK PLANNER
2 OTHER TASKS
3 TASKS
GROUP WORK
EXAM
I'LL DO IT TOMORROW
WEEK PLANNER
2 OTHER TASKS
3 TASKS
GROUP WORK
EXAM
I'LL DO IT TOMORROW

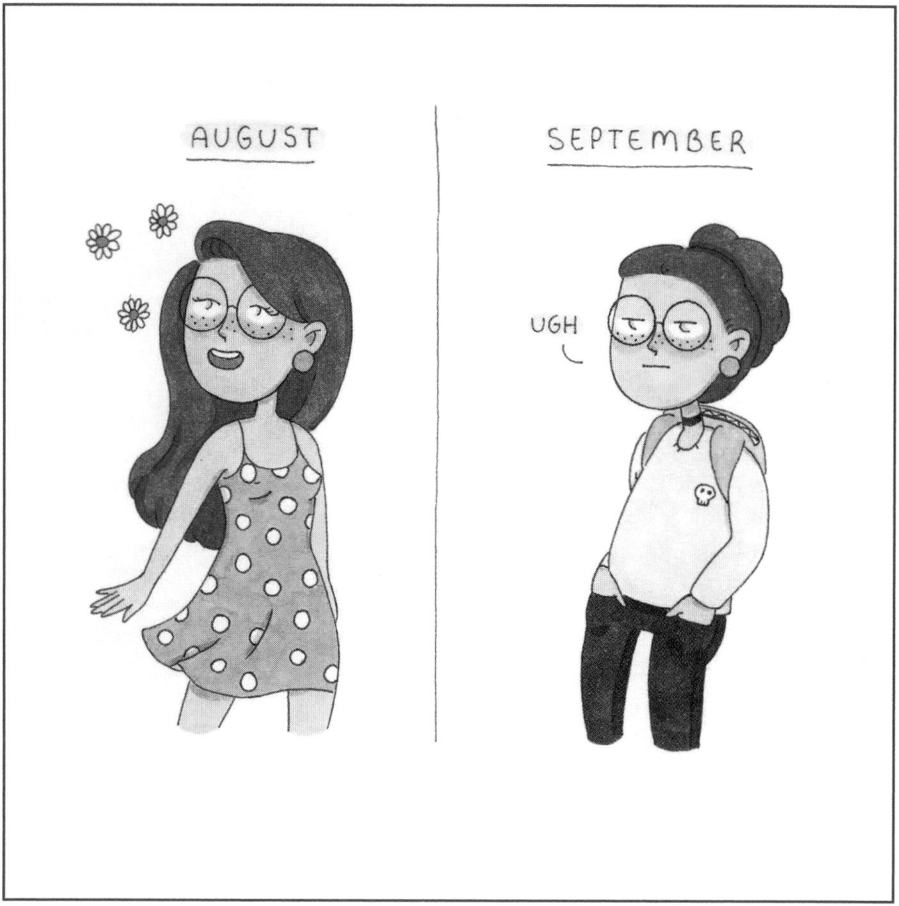
AUGUST
SEPTEMBER
UGH

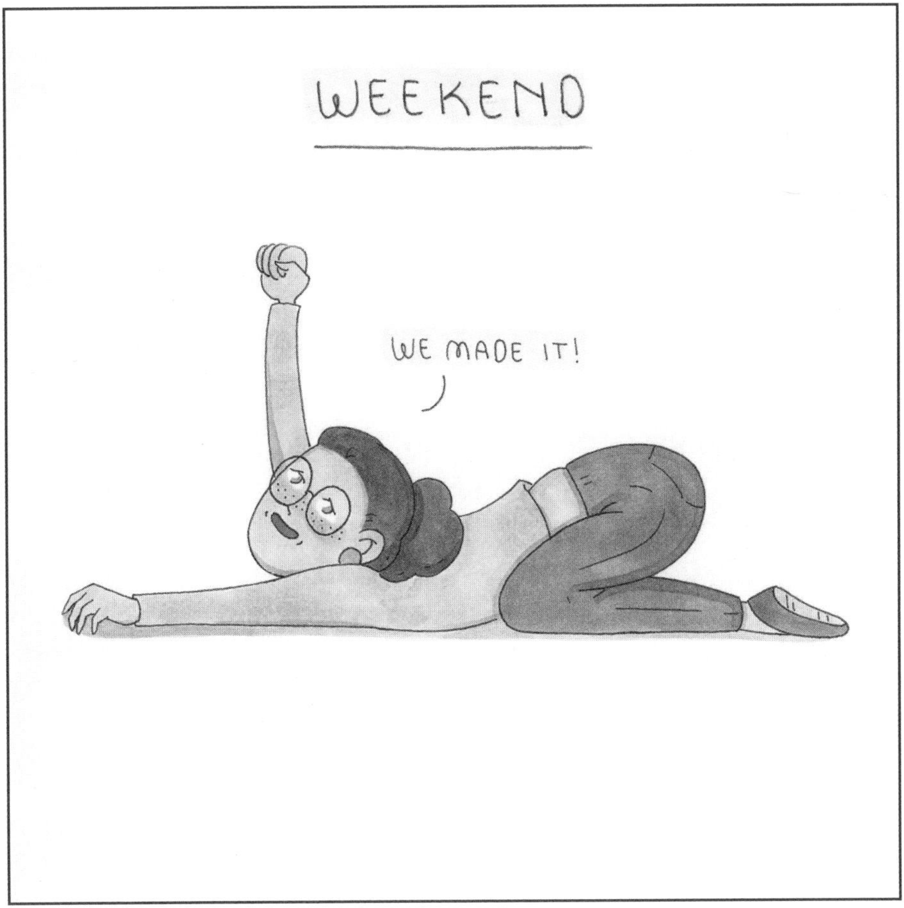
WEEKEND
WE MADE IT!

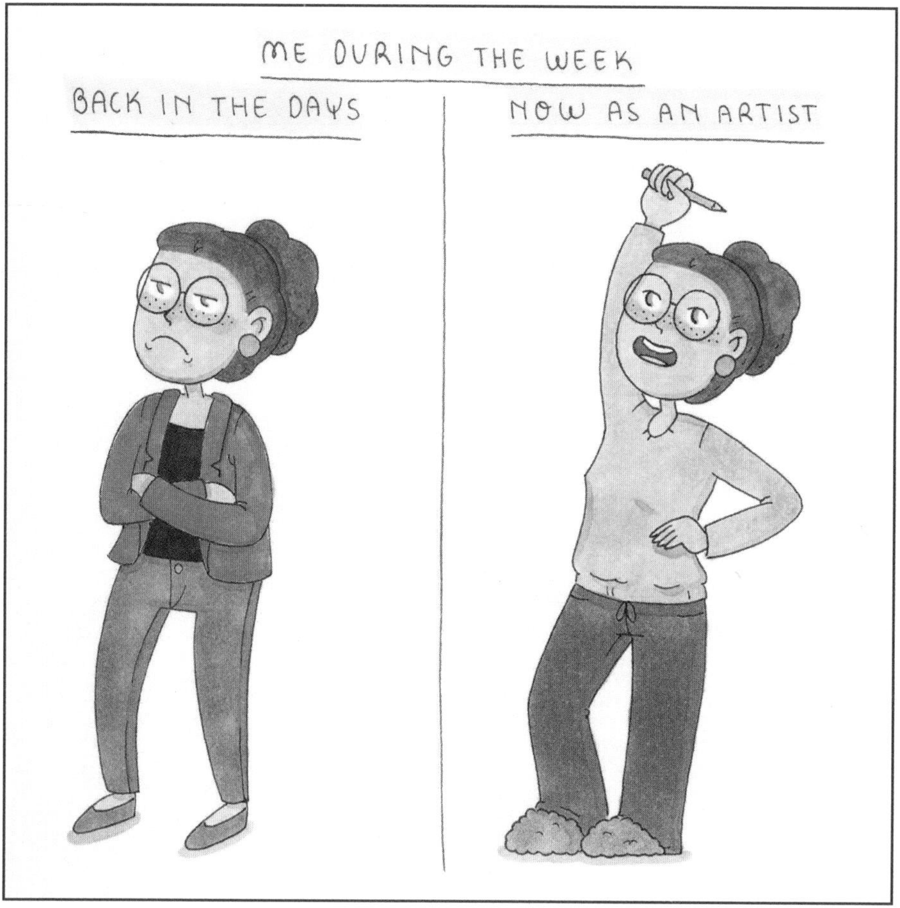
ME DURING THE WEEK
BACK IN THE DAYS
NOW AS AN ARTIST

Answering your Q's...

I wouldn't be writing this book without you, readers, so there's no way I could exclude you from my book! You made my dreams come true, you believed in me, gave me a decent future, made sure I was doing okay, and supported me in every way possible. So this chapter is a tribute to you! Don't worry if your question was not answered, though! I only got to pick out a small bunch. But I do love you very much! And I always will.

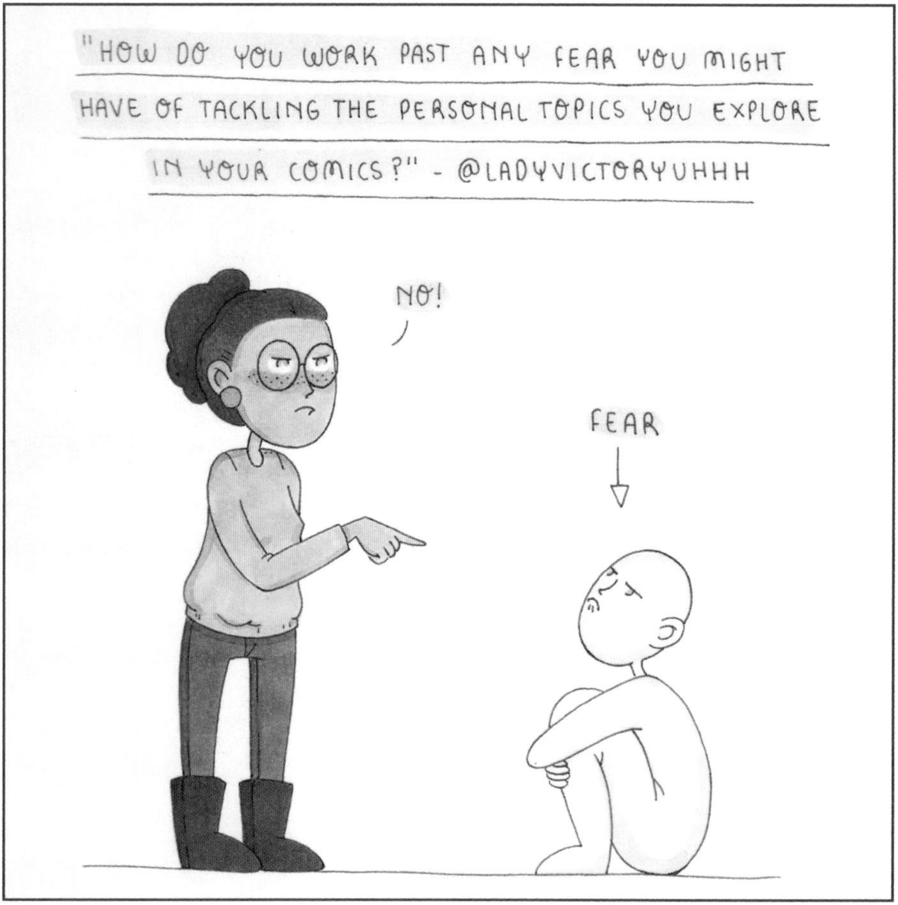
"HOW DO YOU WORK PAST ANY FEAR YOU MIGHT HAVE OF TACKLING THE PERSONAL TOPICS YOU EXPLORE IN YOUR COMICS?" - @LADYVICTORYUHHH
NO!
FEAR

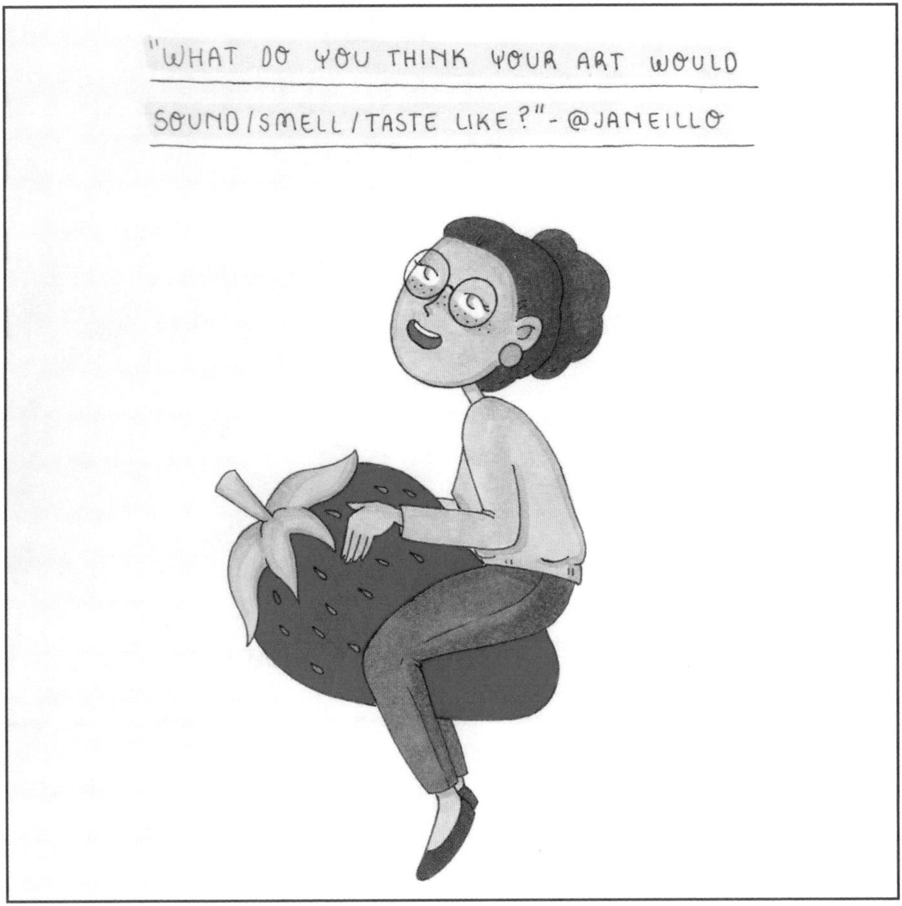
"WHAT DO YOU THINK YOUR ART WOULD
SOUND/SMELL/TASTE LIKE?" - @JANEILLO

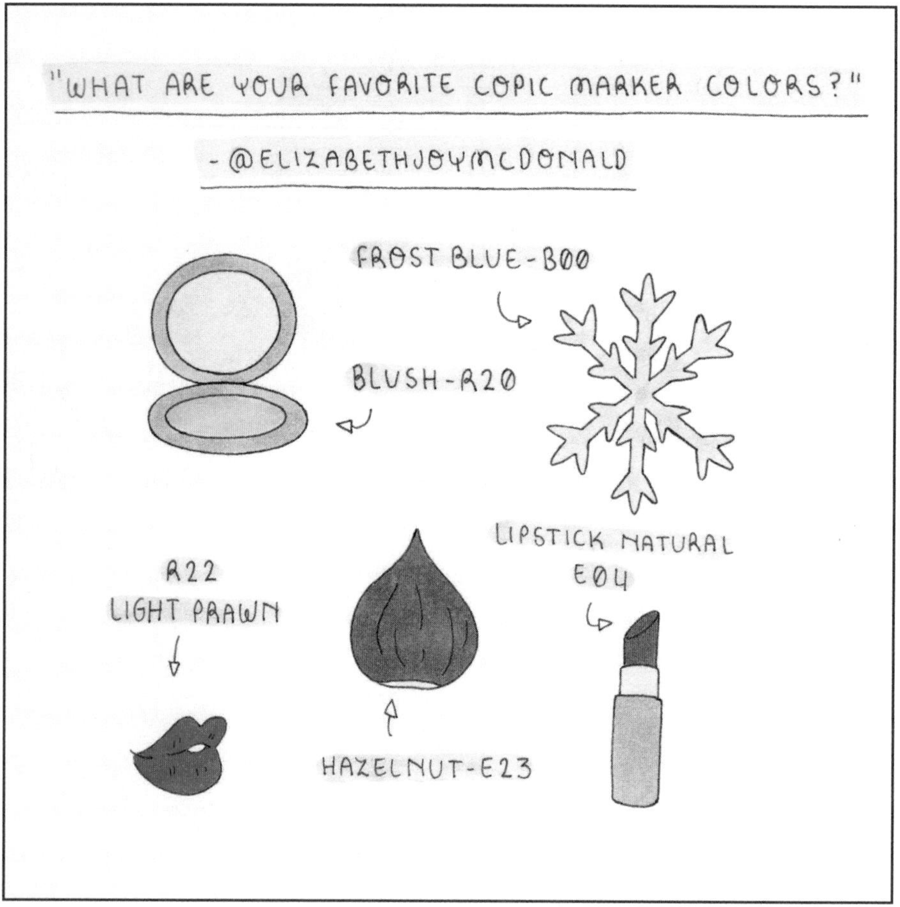
"WHAT ARE YOUR FAVORITE COPIC MARKER COLORS?"
-@ELIZABETHJOYMCDONALD
FROST BLUE-B00
BLUSH-R20
LIPSTICK NATURAL E04
R22 LIGHT PRAWN
HAZELNUT-E23

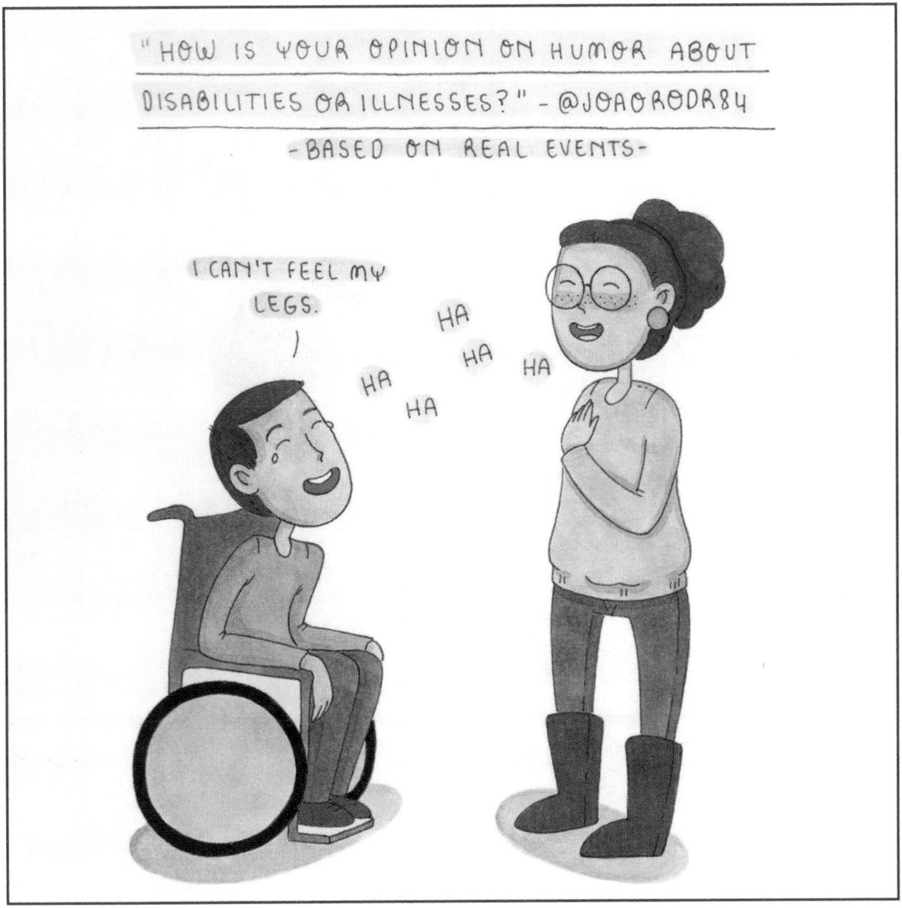
"HOW IS YOUR OPINION ON HUMOR ABOUT
DISABILITIES OR ILLNESSES?" - @JOAORODR84
-BASED ON REAL EVENTS-
I CAN'T FEEL MY LEGS.
HA
HA
HA
HA
HA

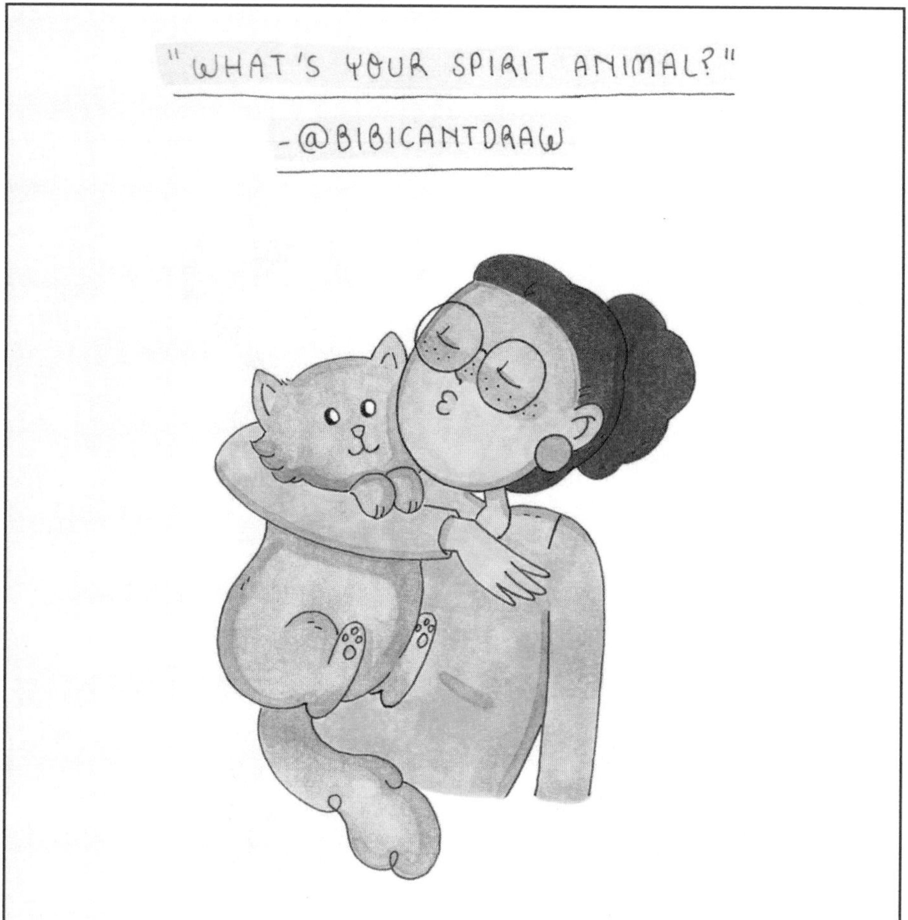
"WHAT'S YOUR SPIRIT ANIMAL?"
-@BIBICANTDRAW

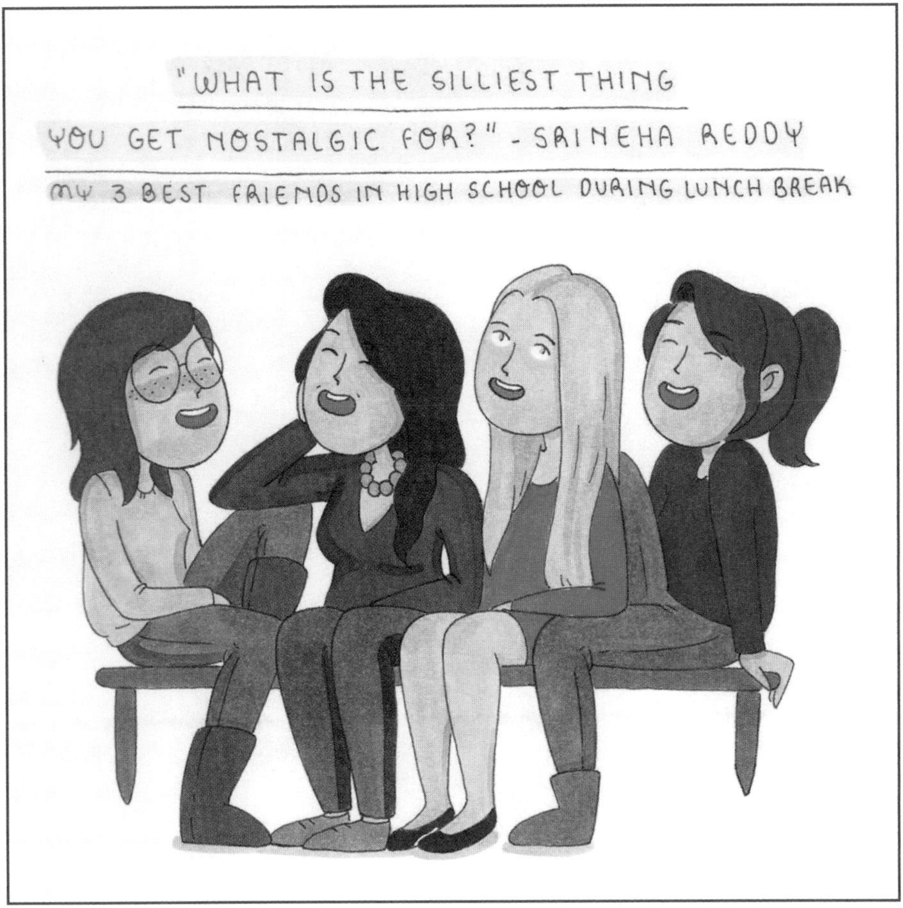
"WHAT IS THE SILLIEST THING
YOU GET NOSTALGIC FOR?" - SRINEHA REDDY
MY 3 BEST FRIENDS IN HIGH SCHOOL DURING LUNCH BREAK

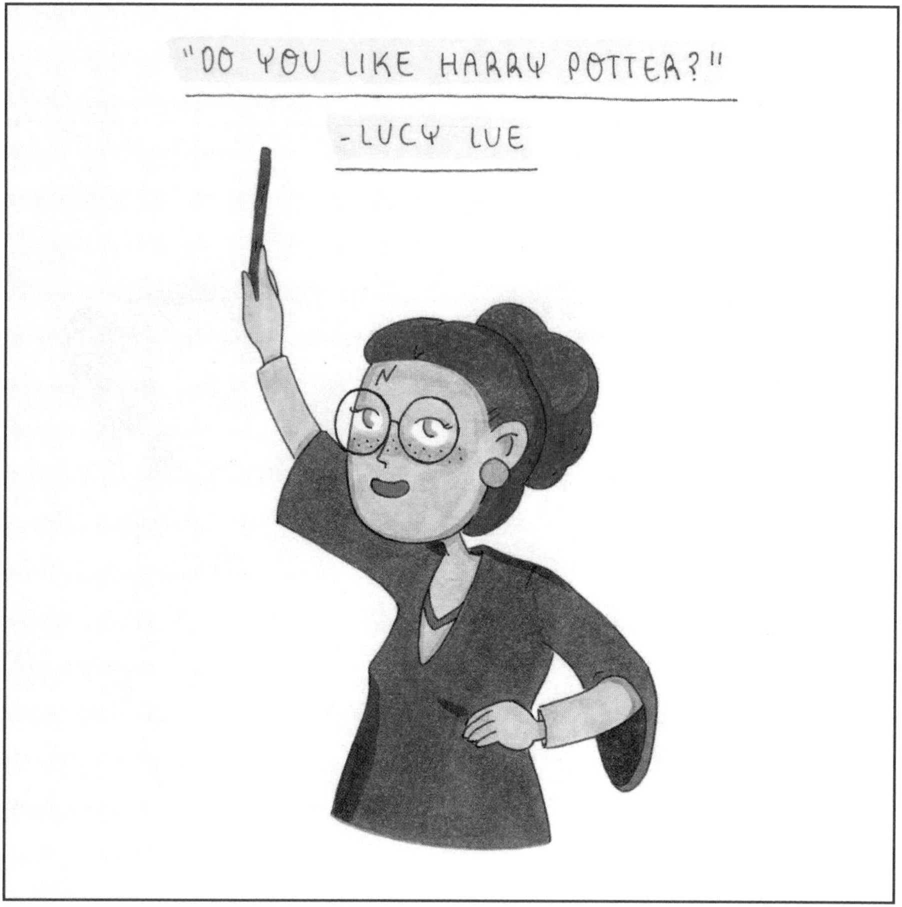
"DO YOU LIKE HARRY POTTER?"
-LUCY LUE

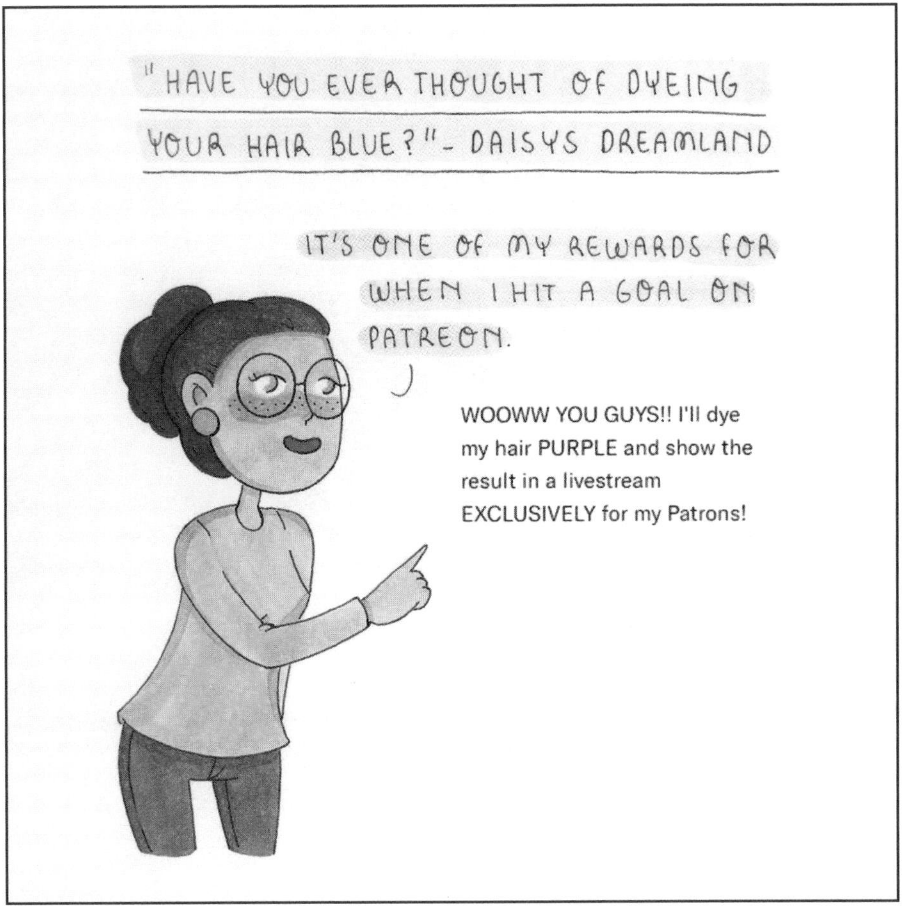
"HAVE YOU EVER THOUGHT OF DYEING YOUR HAIR BLUE?" - DAISYS DREAMLAND
IT'S ONE OF MY REWARDS FOR WHEN I HIT A GOAL ON PATREON.
WOOWW YOU GUYS!! I'll dye my hair PURPLE and show the result in a livestream EXCLUSIVELY for my Patrons!

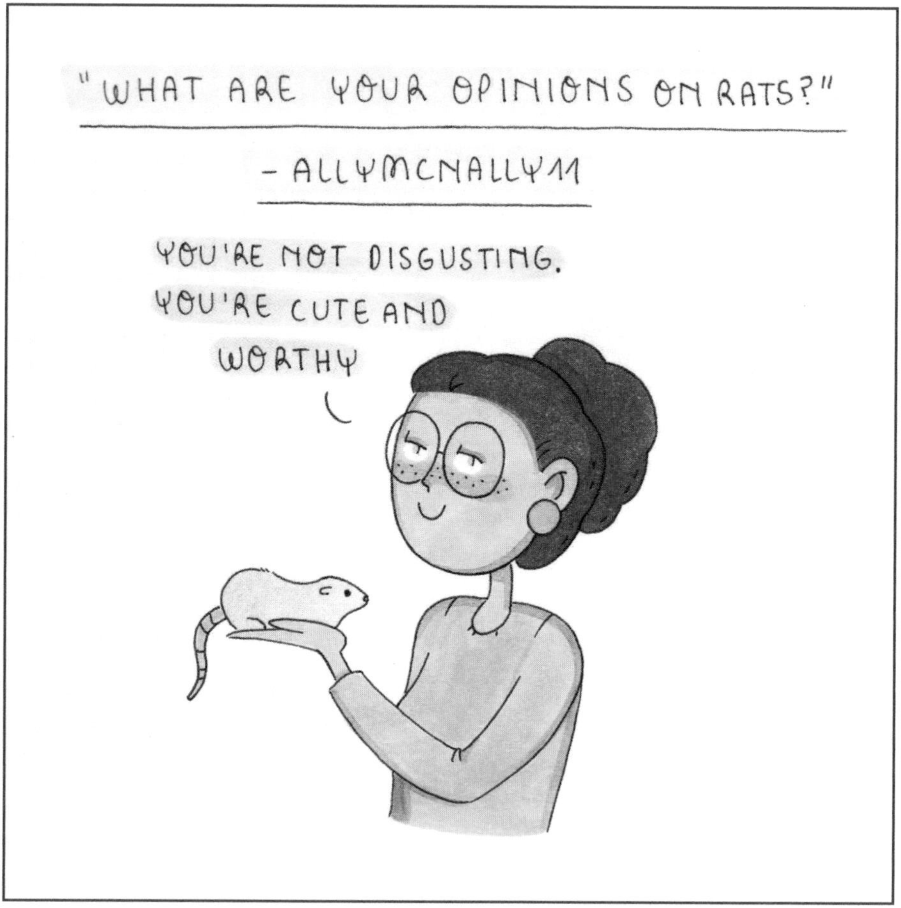
"WHAT ARE YOUR OPINIONS ON RATS?"
- ALLYMCNALLY11
YOU'RE NOT DISGUSTING.
YOU'RE CUTE AND
WORTHY

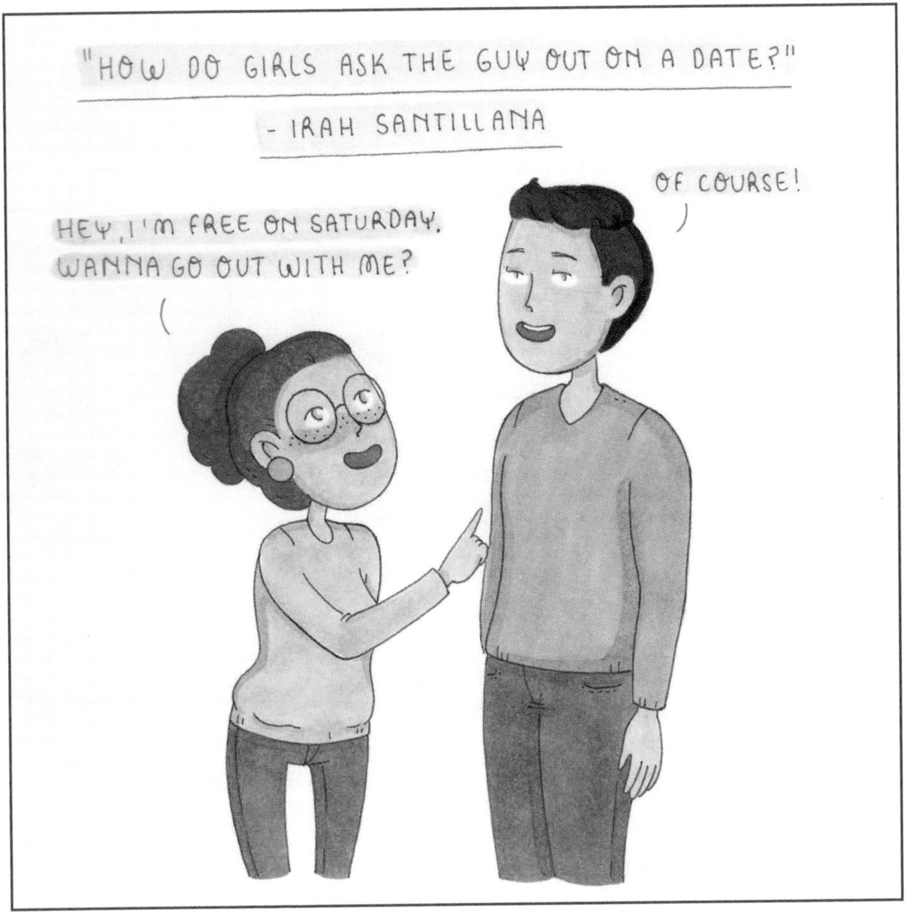
"HOW DO GIRLS ASK THE GUY OUT ON A DATE?"
- IRAH SANTILLANA
OF COURSE!
HEY, I'M FREE ON SATURDAY. WANNA GO OUT WITH ME?

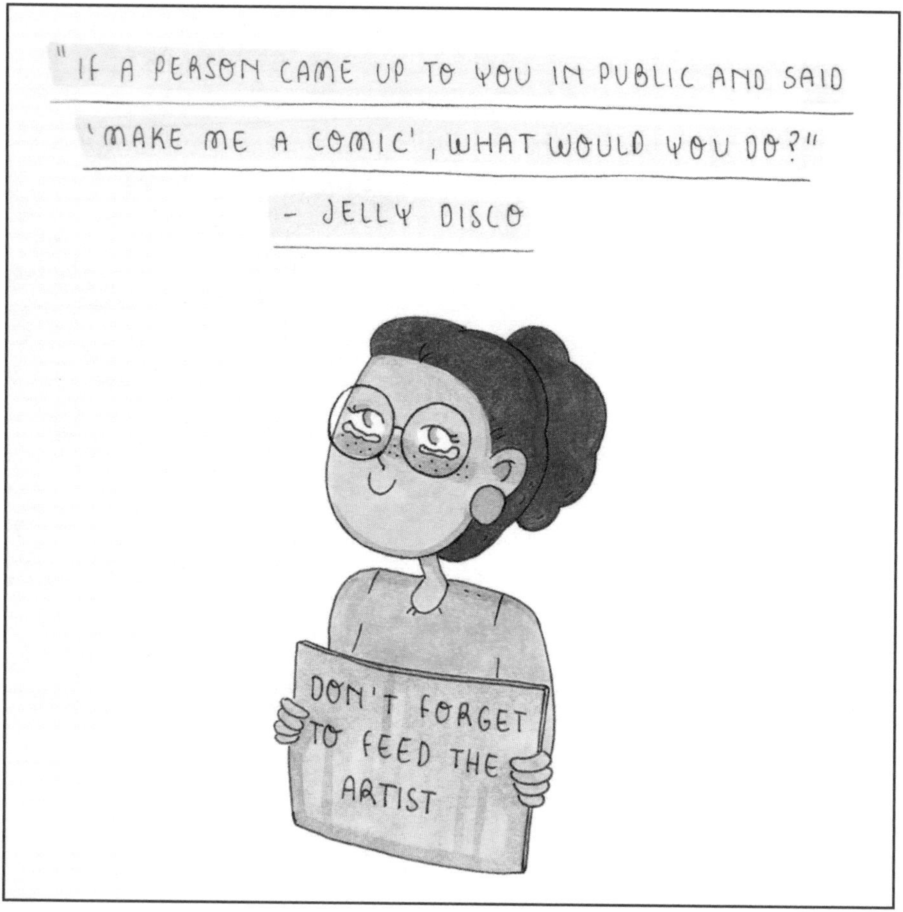
"IF A PERSON CAME UP TO YOU IN PUBLIC AND SAID
'MAKE ME A COMIC', WHAT WOULD YOU DO?"
- JELLY DISCO
DON'T FORGET TO FEED THE ARTIST

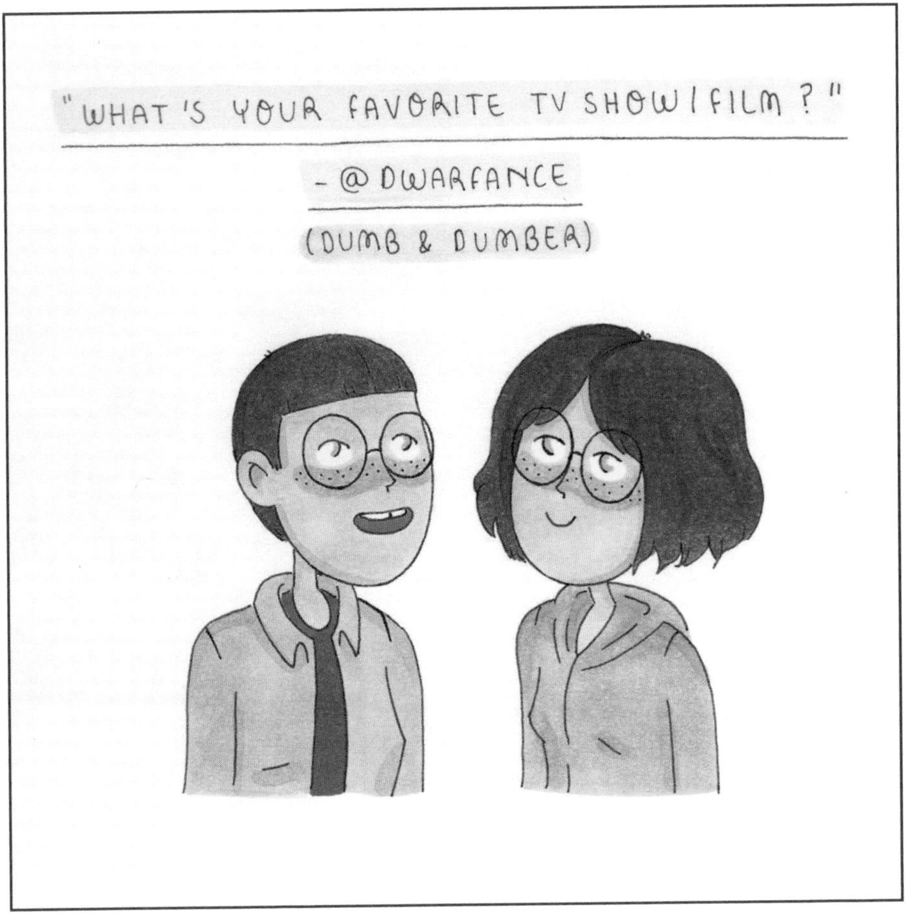
"WHAT'S YOUR FAVORITE TV SHOW/FILM?"
- @DWARFANCE
(DUMB & DUMBER)

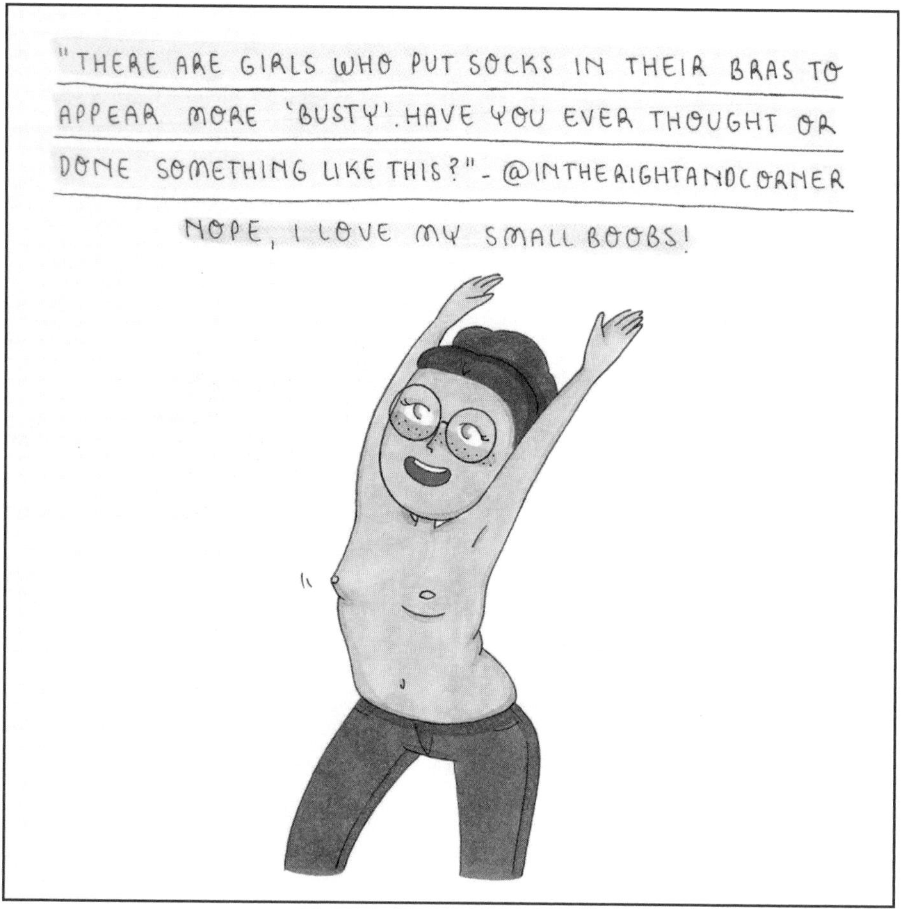
"THERE ARE GIRLS WHO PUT SOCKS IN THEIR BRAS TO APPEAR MORE 'BUSTY'. HAVE YOU EVER THOUGHT OR DONE SOMETHING LIKE THIS?" - @INTHERIGHTANDCORNER
NOPE, I LOVE MY SMALL BOOBS!

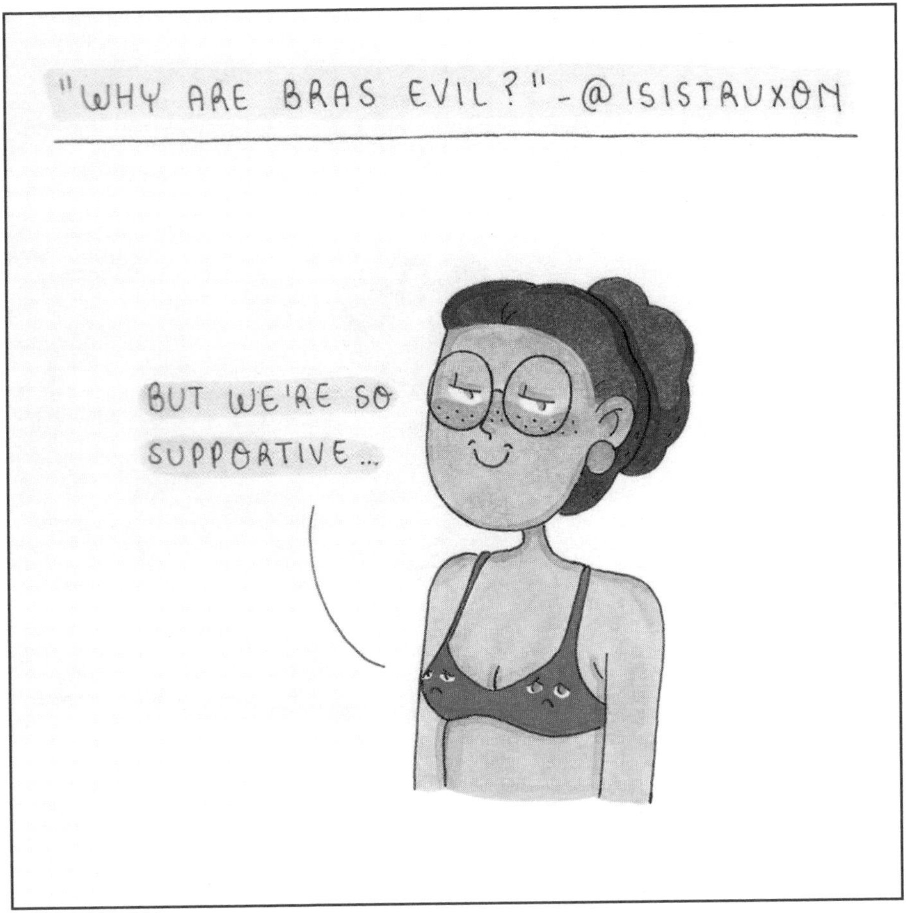
"WHY ARE BRAS EVIL?" - @ISISTRUXON
BUT WE'RE SO SUPPORTIVE...

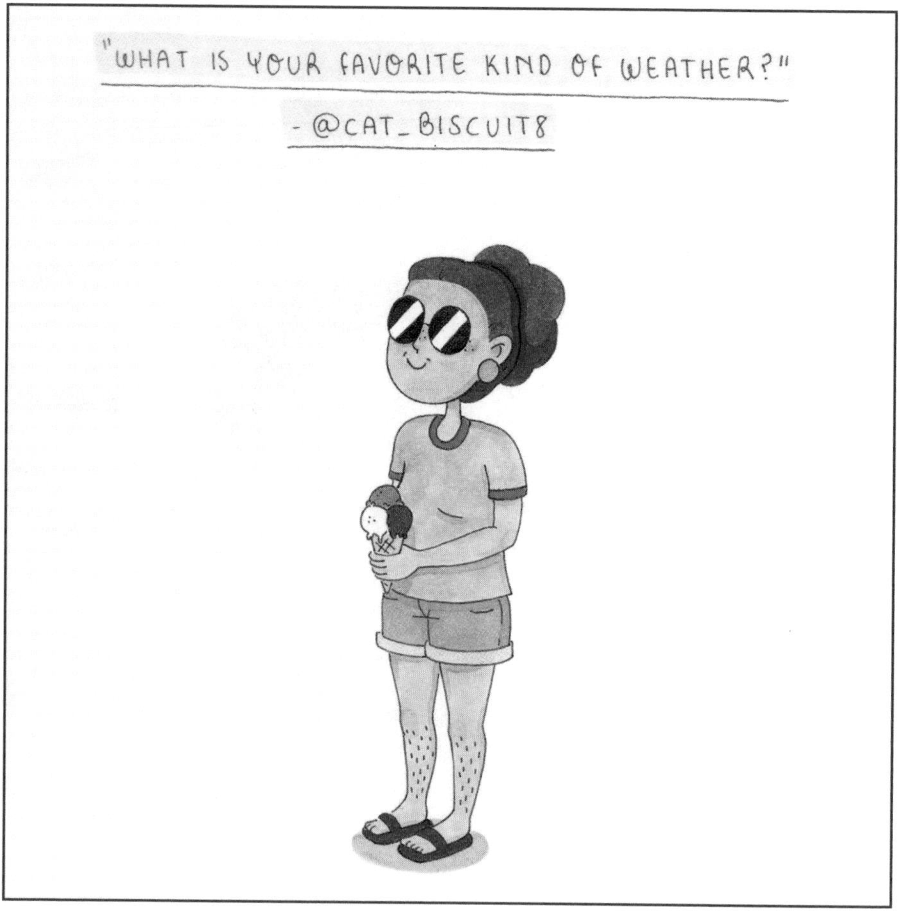
"WHAT IS YOUR FAVORITE KIND OF WEATHER?"
- @CAT_BISCUIT8

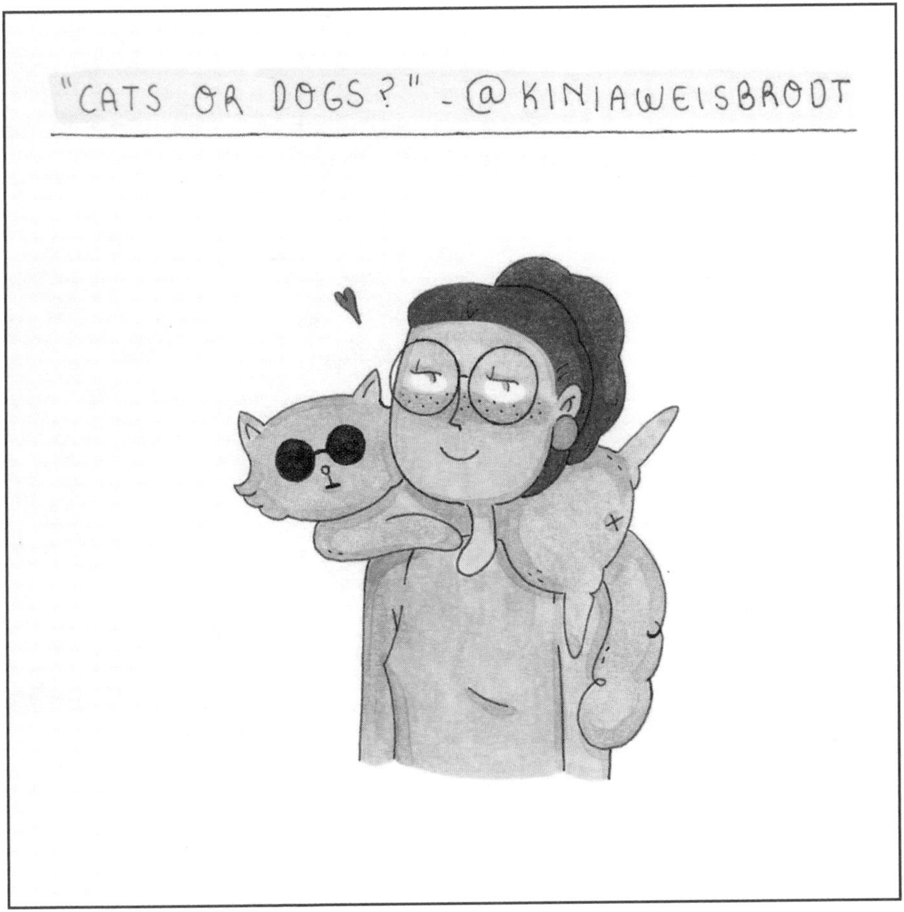
"CATS OR DOGS?" - @KINIAWEISBRODT

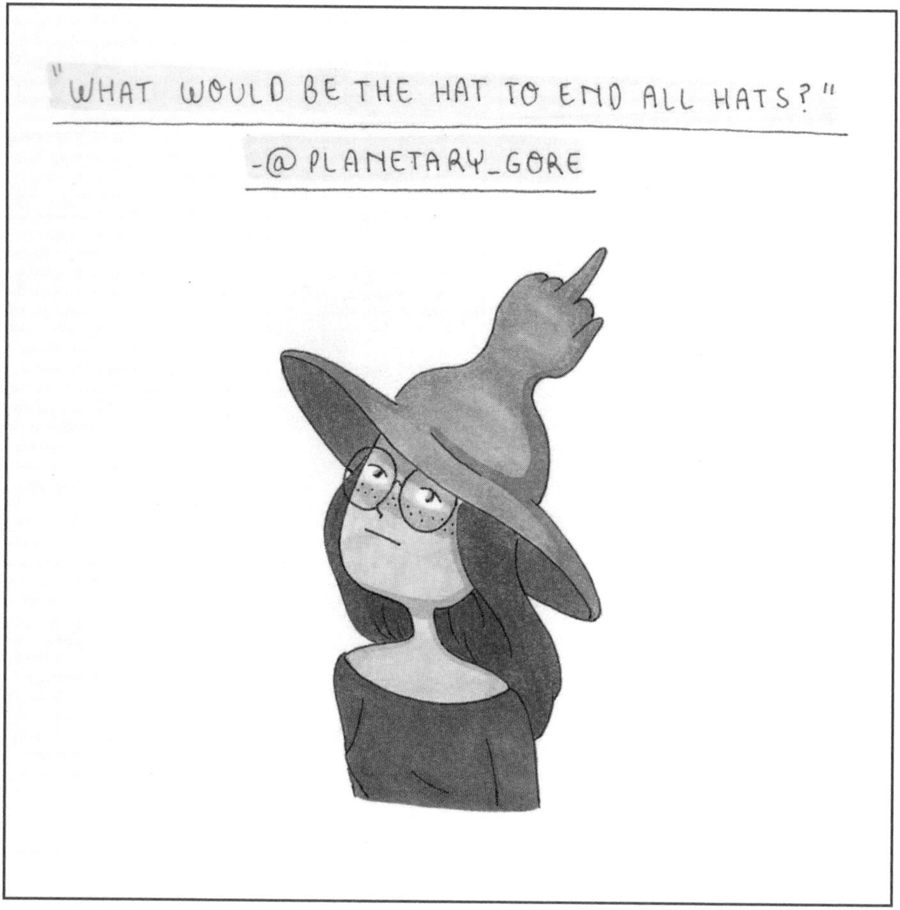
"WHAT WOULD BE THE HAT TO END ALL HATS?"
-@PLANETARY_GORE

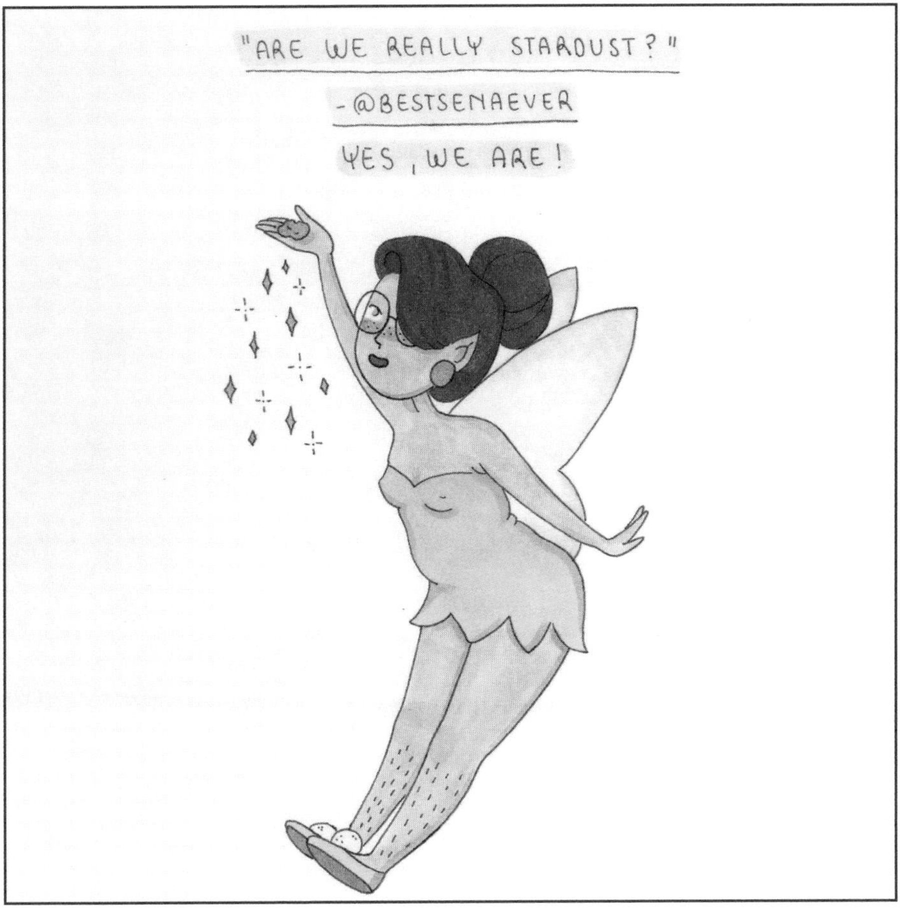
"ARE WE REALLY STARDUST?"
-@BESTSENAEVER
YES, WE ARE!

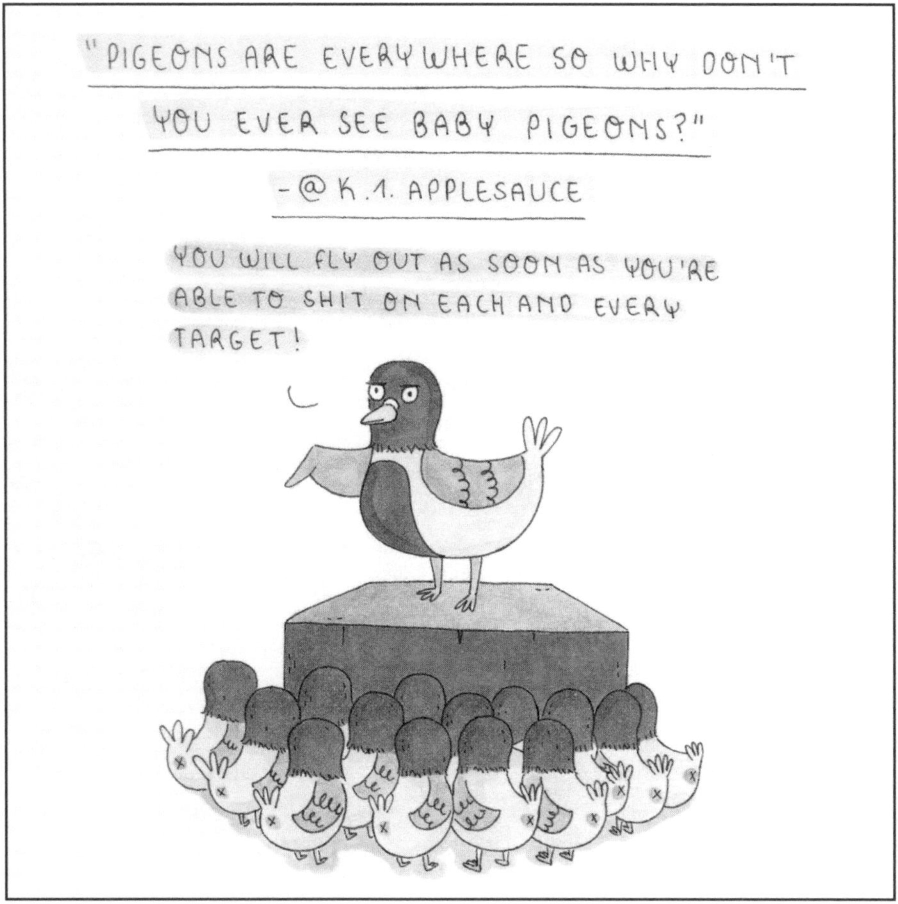
"PIGEONS ARE EVERYWHERE SO WHY DON'T YOU EVER SEE BABY PIGEONS?"
-@K.1. APPLESAUCE
YOU WILL FLY OUT AS SOON AS YOU'RE ABLE TO SHIT ON EACH AND EVERY TARGET!

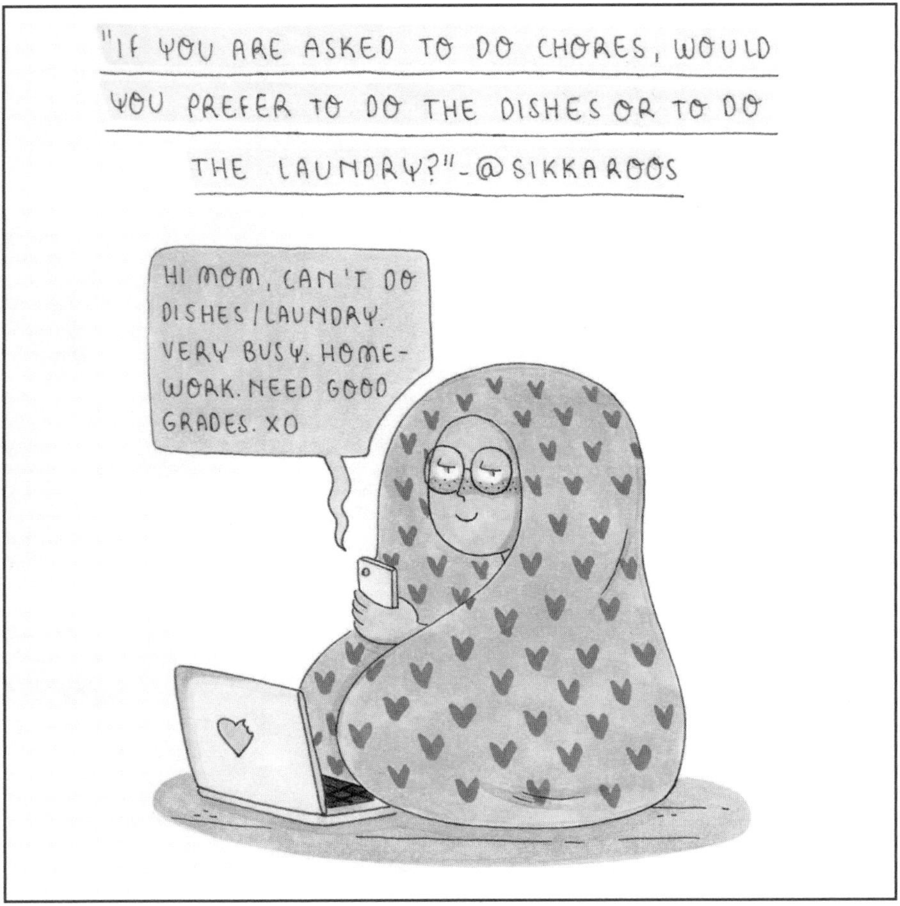
"IF YOU ARE ASKED TO DO CHORES, WOULD YOU PREFER TO DO THE DISHES OR TO DO THE LAUNDRY?" - @SIKKAROOS
HI MOM, CAN'T DO DISHES/LAUNDRY. VERY BUSY. HOMEWORK. NEED GOOD GRADES. XO

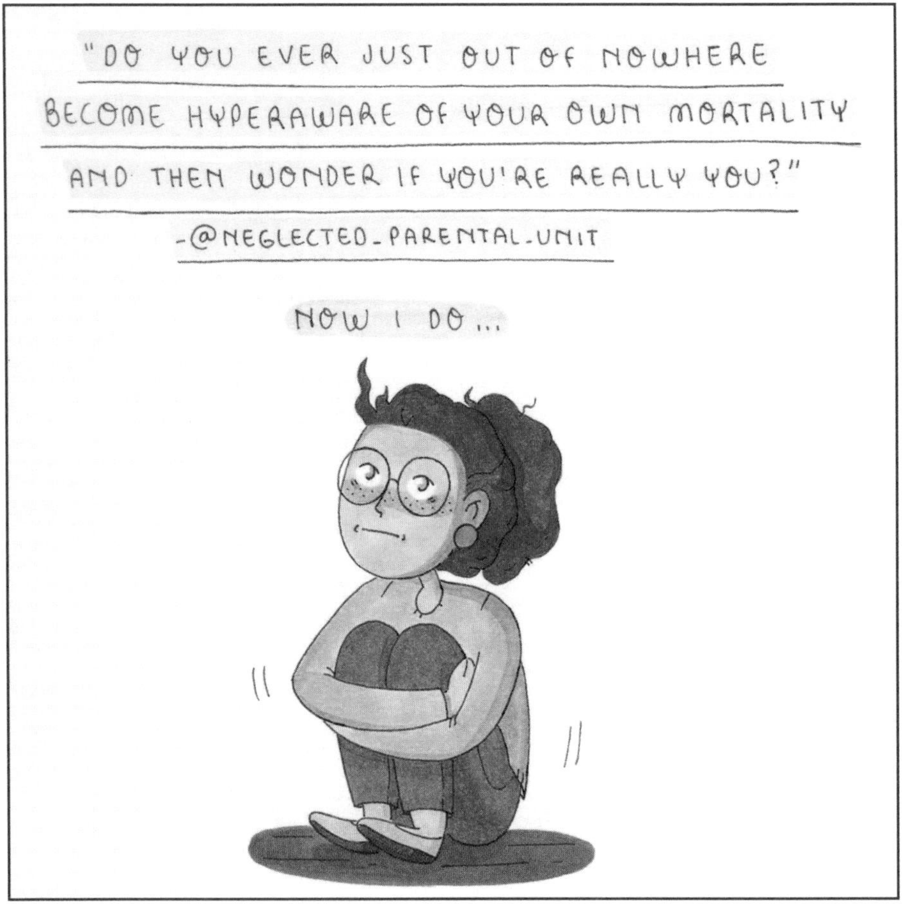
"DO YOU EVER JUST OUT OF NOWHERE
BECOME HYPERAWARE OF YOUR OWN MORTALITY
AND THEN WONDER IF YOU'RE REALLY YOU?"
-@NEGLECTED_PARENTAL_UNIT
NOW I DO...

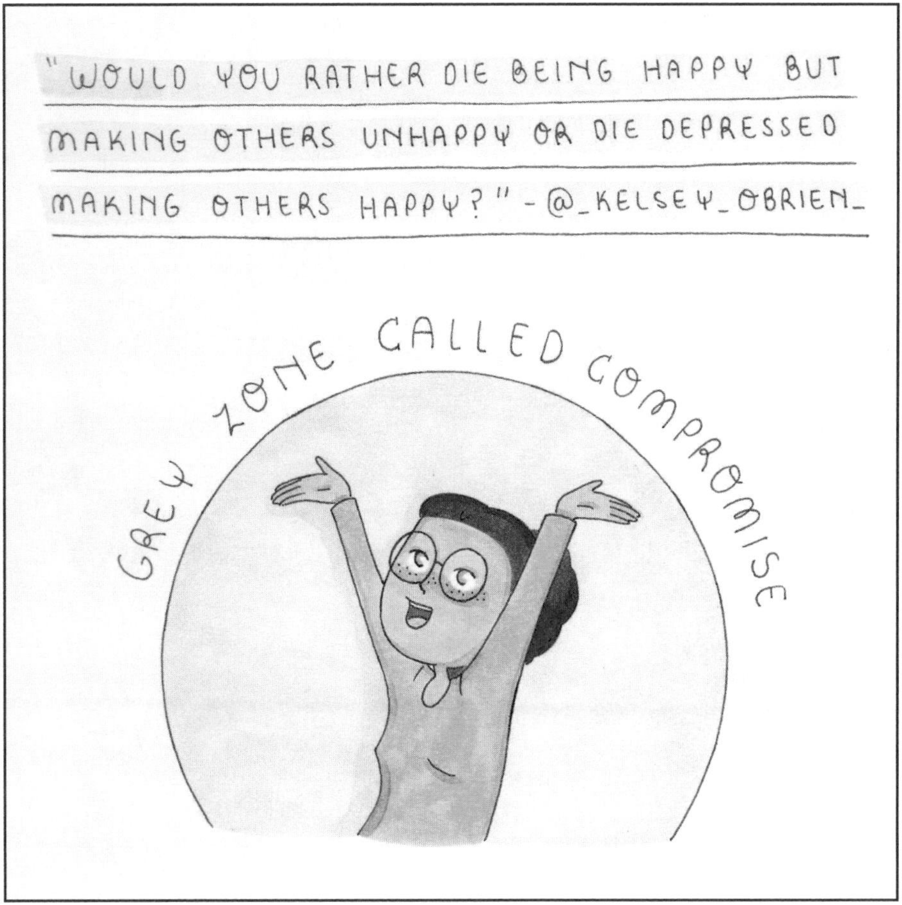
"WOULD YOU RATHER DIE BEING HAPPY BUT MAKING OTHERS UNHAPPY OR DIE DEPRESSED MAKING OTHERS HAPPY?" - @_KELSEY_OBRIEN_
GREY ZONE CALLED COMPROMISE

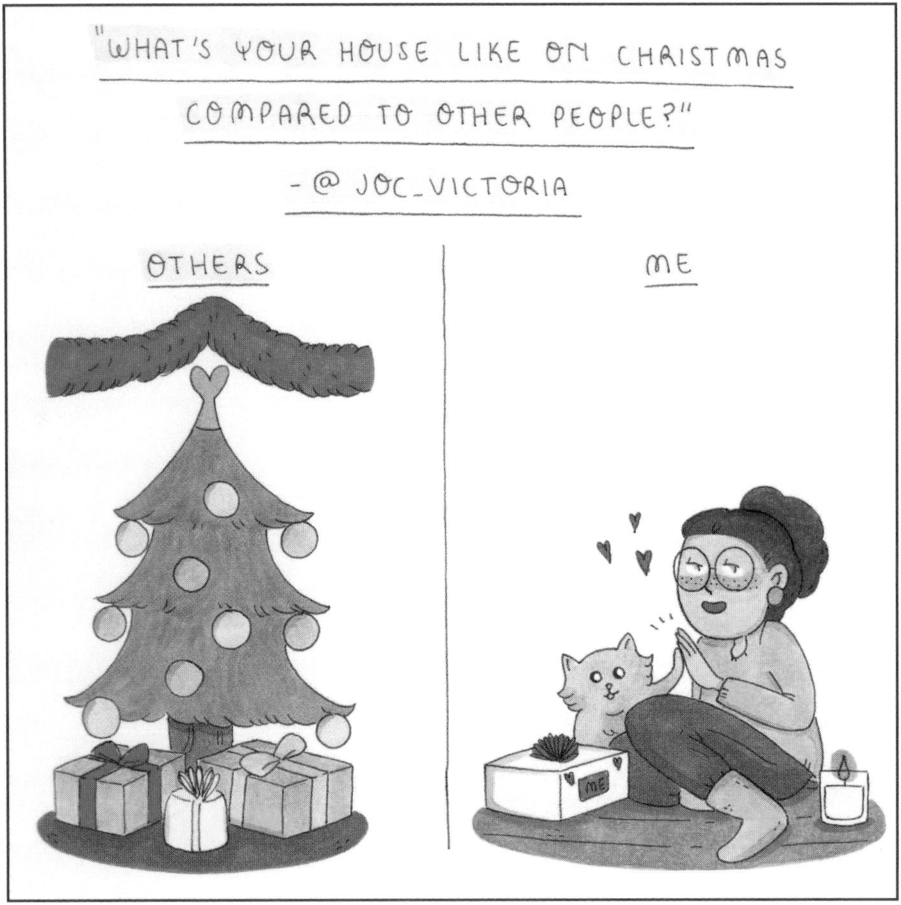
"WHAT'S YOUR HOUSE LIKE ON CHRISTMAS
COMPARED TO OTHER PEOPLE?"
- @ JOC_VICTORIA
OTHERS
ME
ME

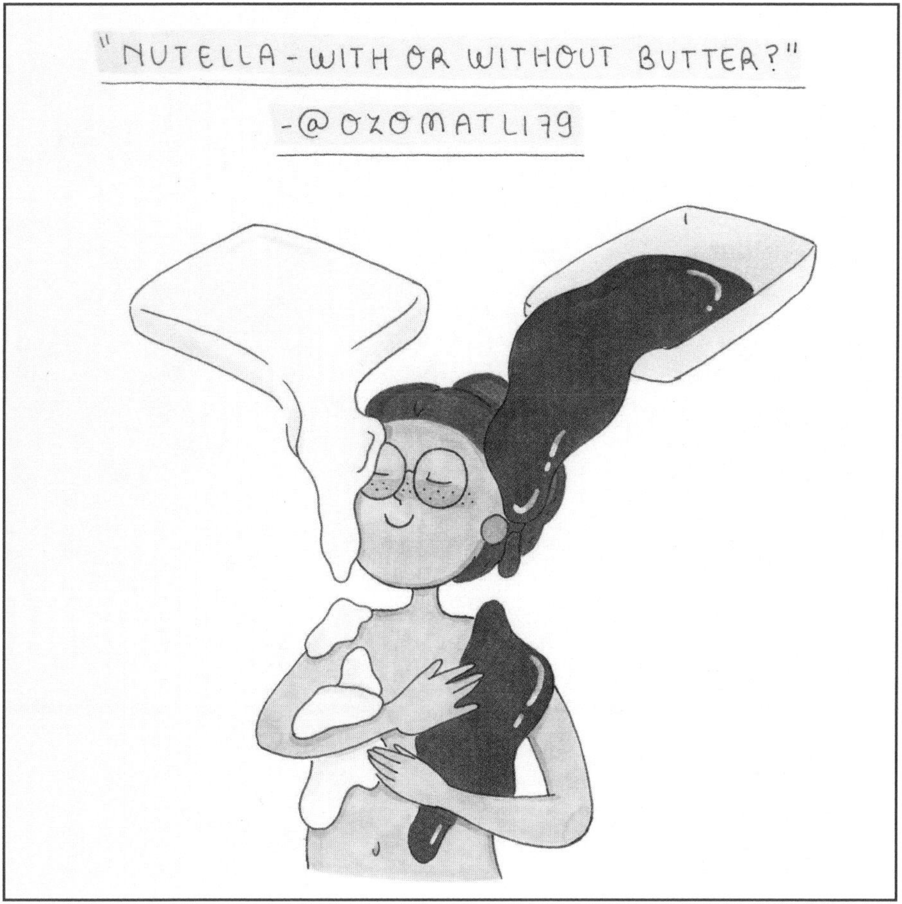
"NUTELLA-WITH OR WITHOUT BUTTER?"
-@OZOMATLI79

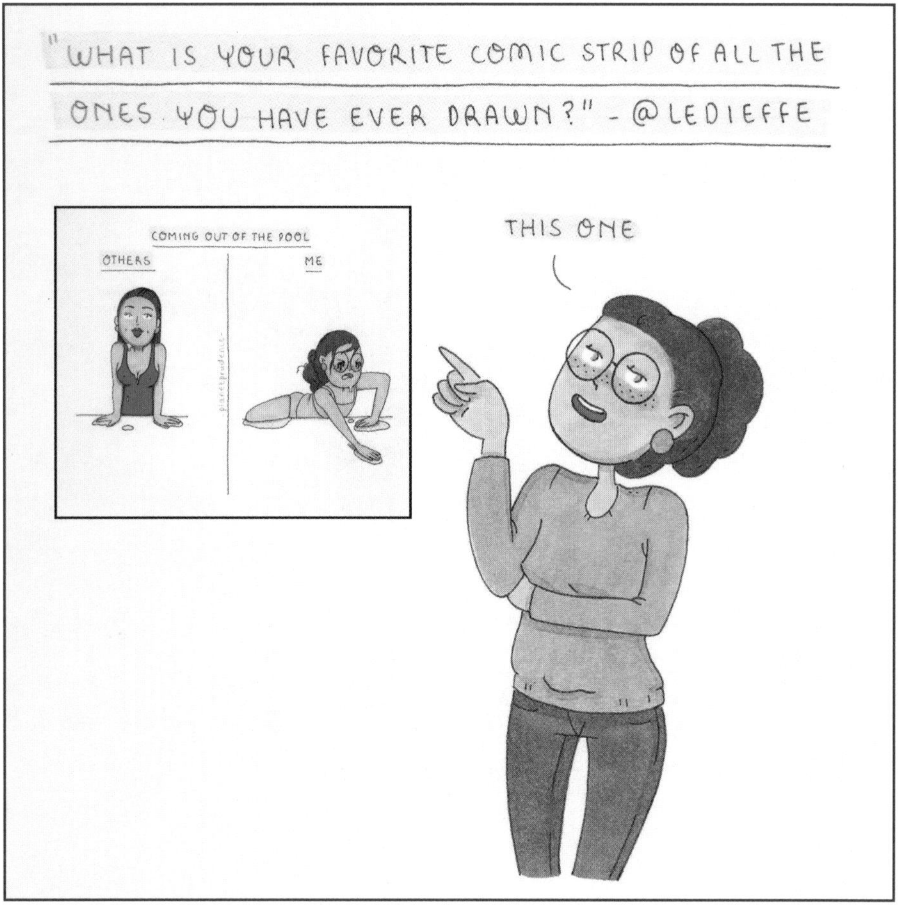
"WHAT IS YOUR FAVORITE COMIC STRIP OF ALL THE ONES YOU HAVE EVER DRAWN?" - @LEDIEFFE
COMING OUT OF THE POOL
OTHERS
ME
THIS ONE

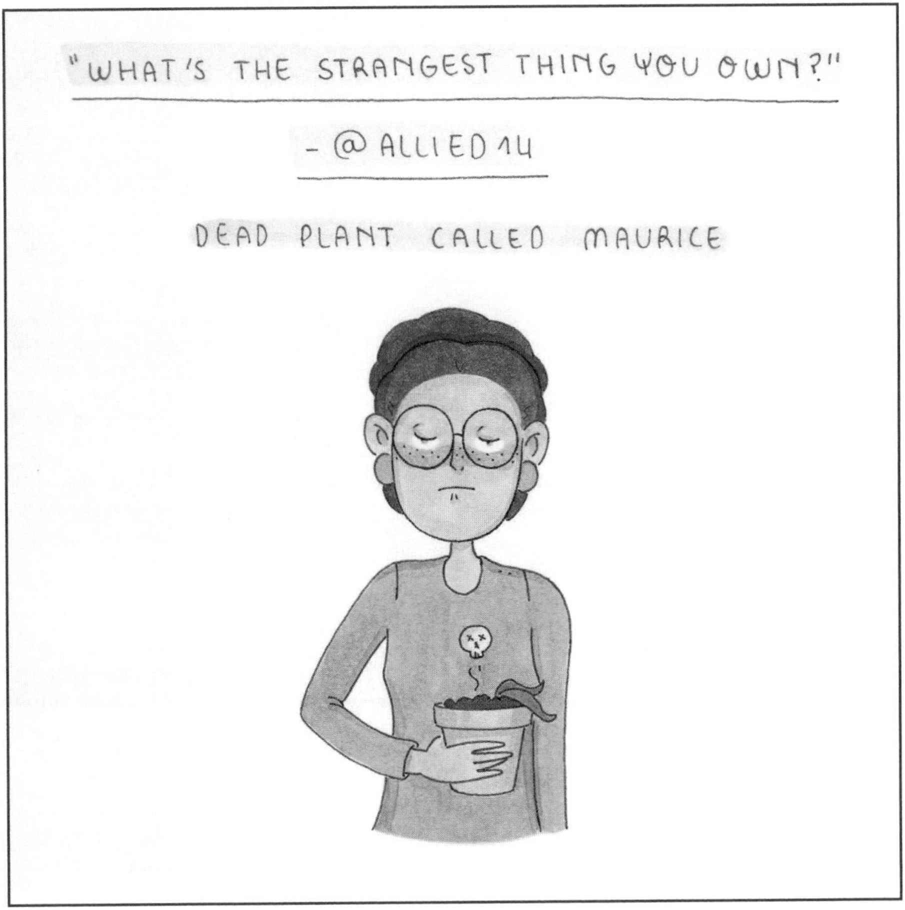
"WHAT'S THE STRANGEST THING YOU OWN?"
- @ALLIED14
DEAD PLANT CALLED MAURICE

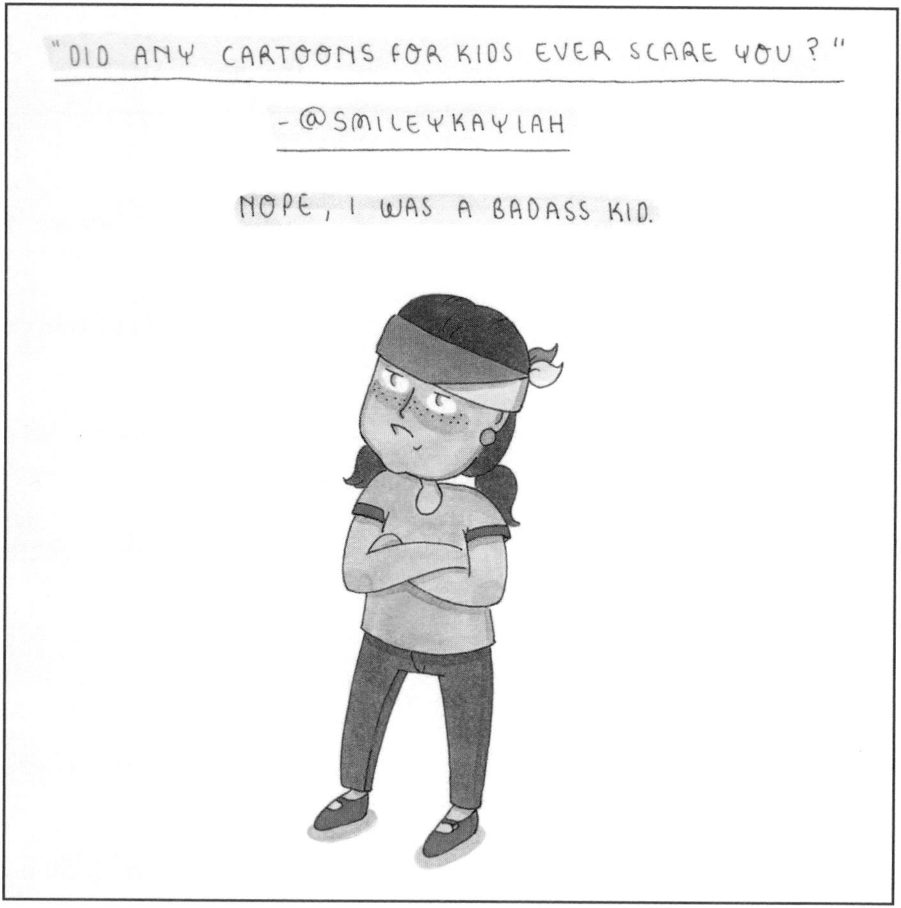
"DID ANY CARTOONS FOR KIDS EVER SCARE YOU?"
- @SMILEYKAYLAH
NOPE, I WAS A BADASS KID.

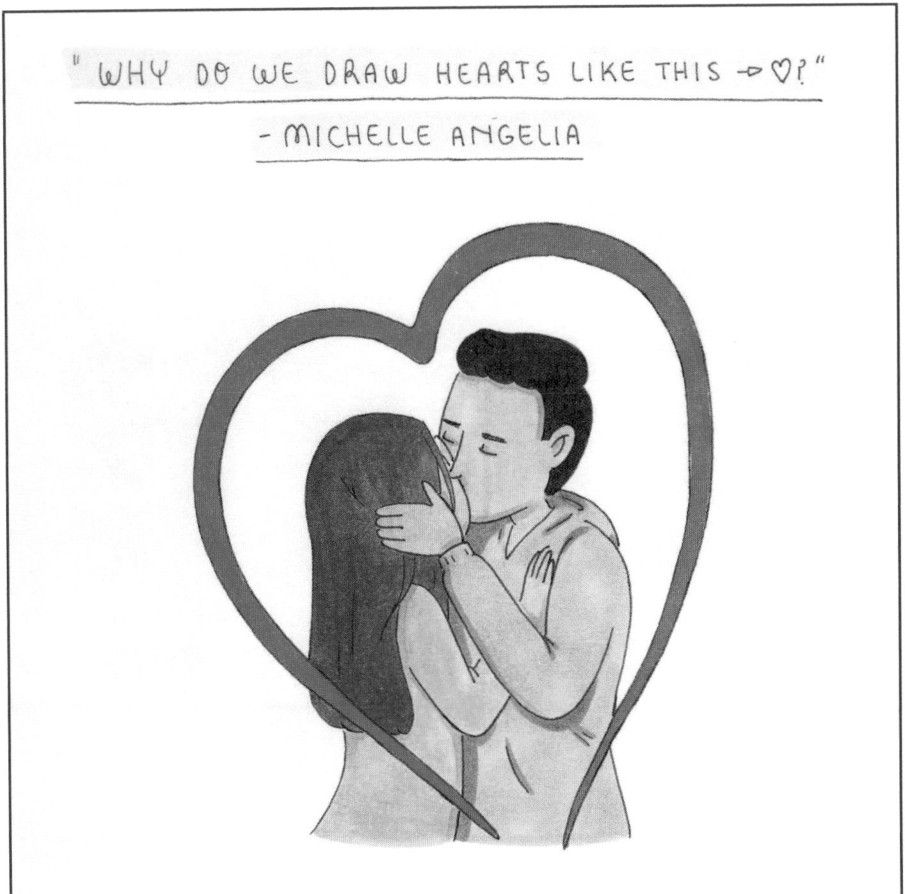
"WHY DO WE DRAW HEARTS LIKE THIS →♡?"
- MICHELLE ANGELIA

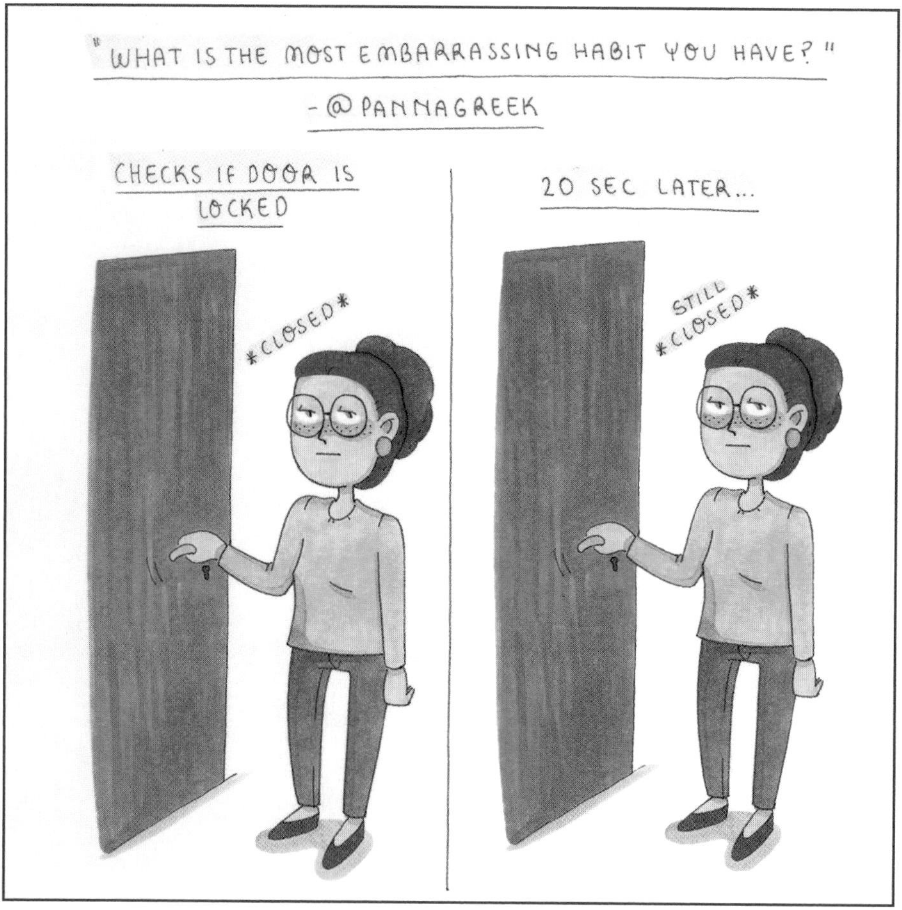
"WHAT IS THE MOST EMBARRASSING HABIT YOU HAVE?"
- @PANNAGREEK
CHECKS IF DOOR IS LOCKED
CLOSED
20 SEC LATER...
STILL *CLOSED*

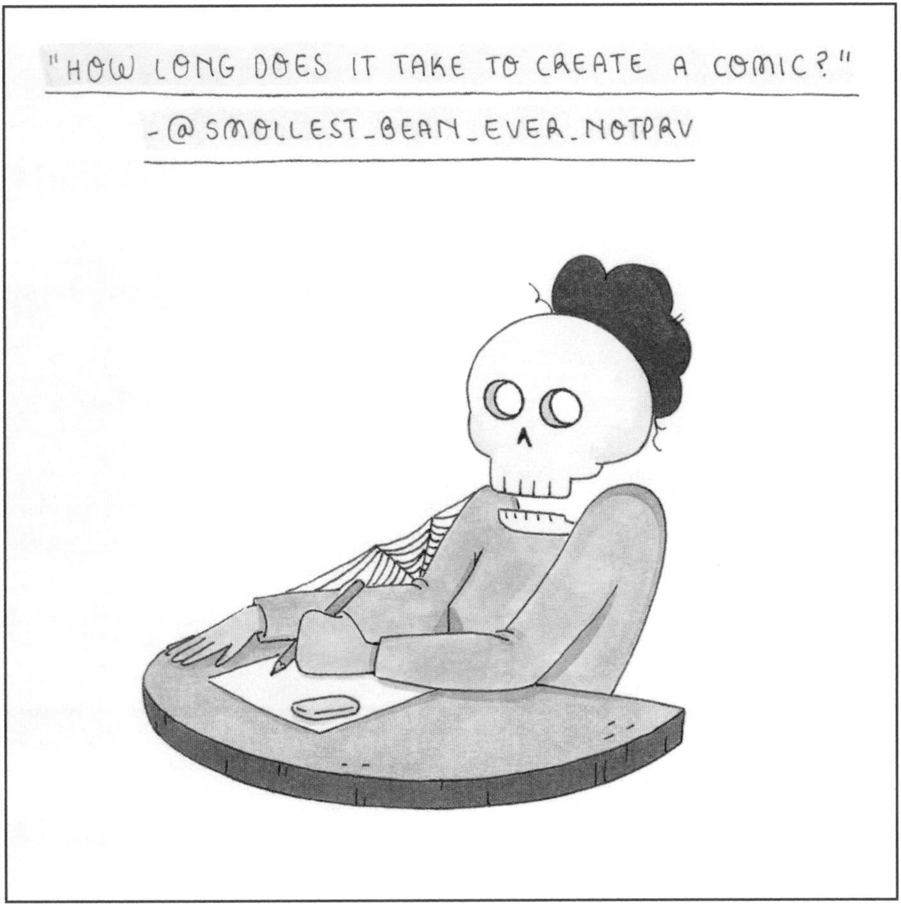
"HOW LONG DOES IT TAKE TO CREATE A COMIC?"
-@SMOLLEST_BEAN_EVER_NOTPRV

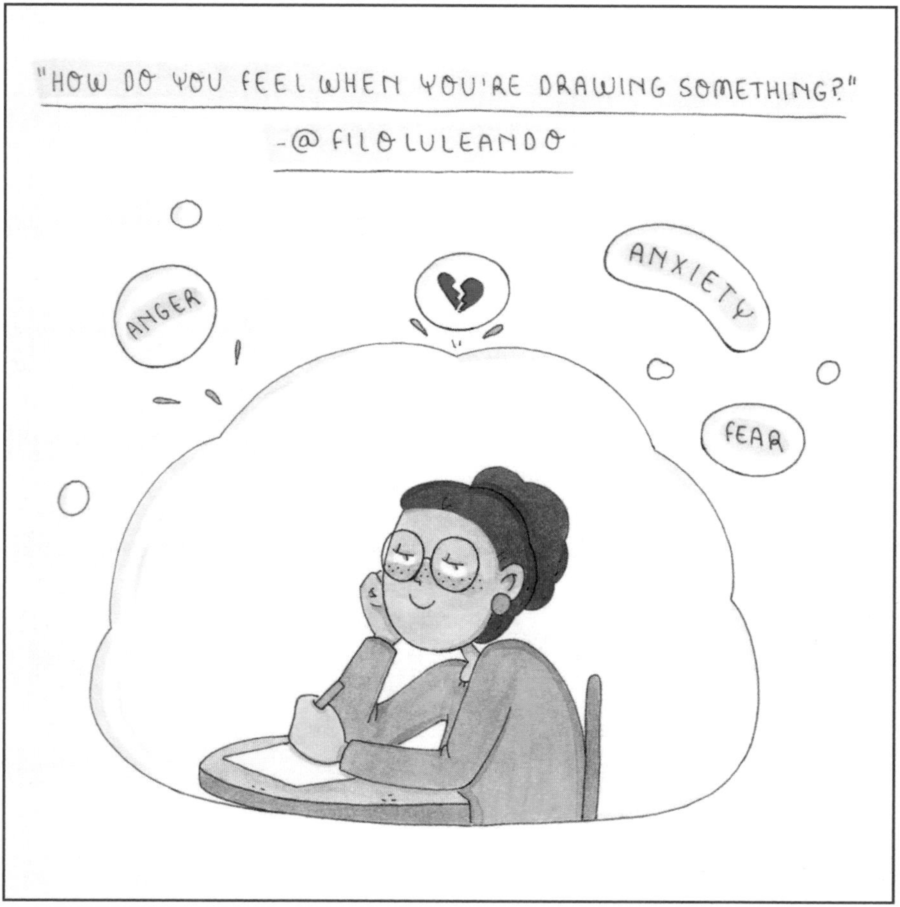
"HOW DO YOU FEEL WHEN YOU'RE DRAWING SOMETHING?"
-@FILOLULEANDO
ANGER
ANXIETY
FEAR

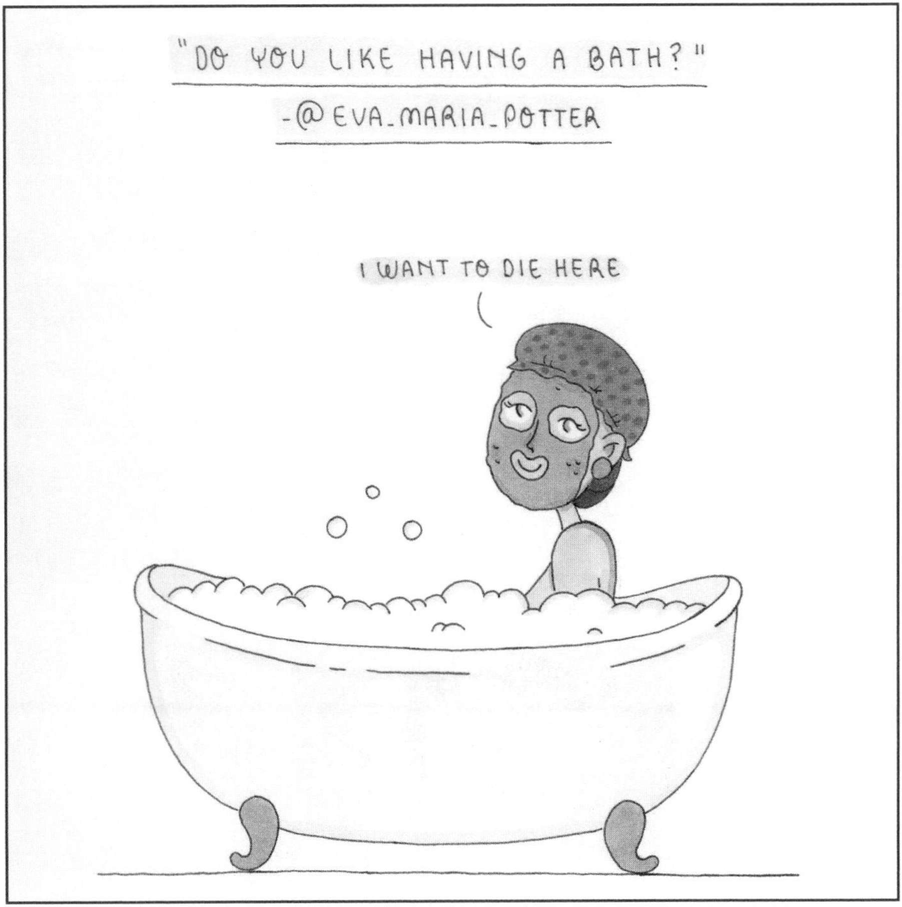
"DO YOU LIKE HAVING A BATH?"
-@EVA_MARIA_POTTER
I WANT TO DIE HERE

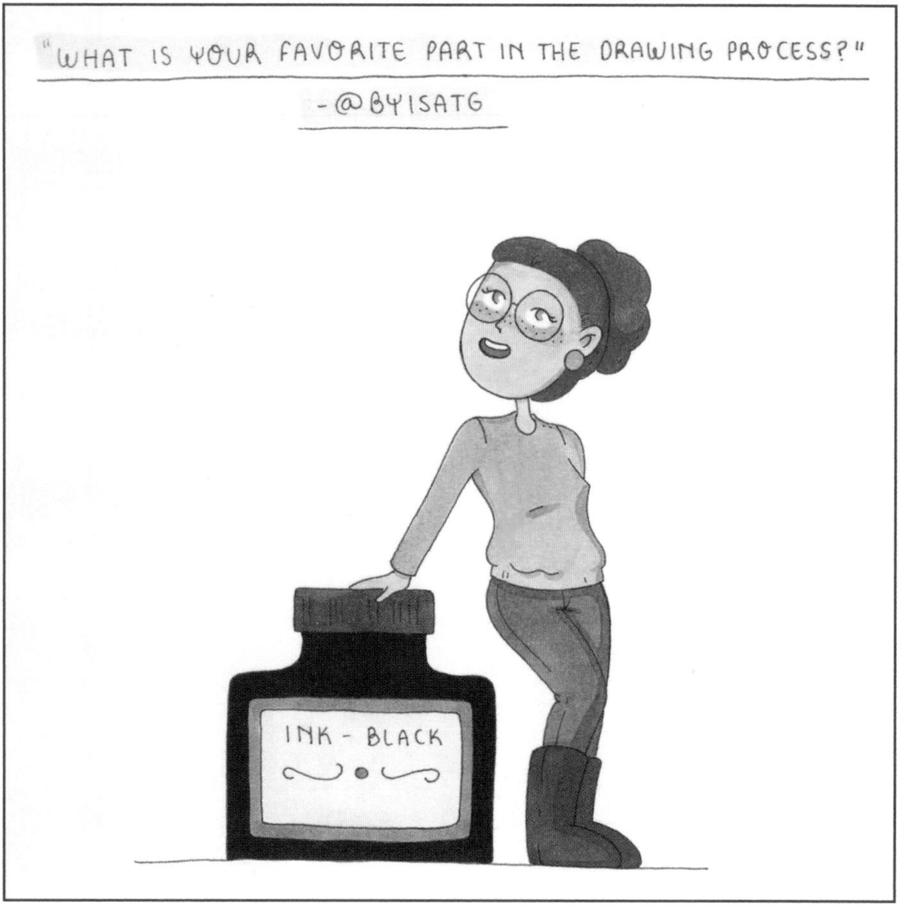
"WHAT IS YOUR FAVORITE PART IN THE DRAWING PROCESS?"
-@BYISATG
INK - BLACK

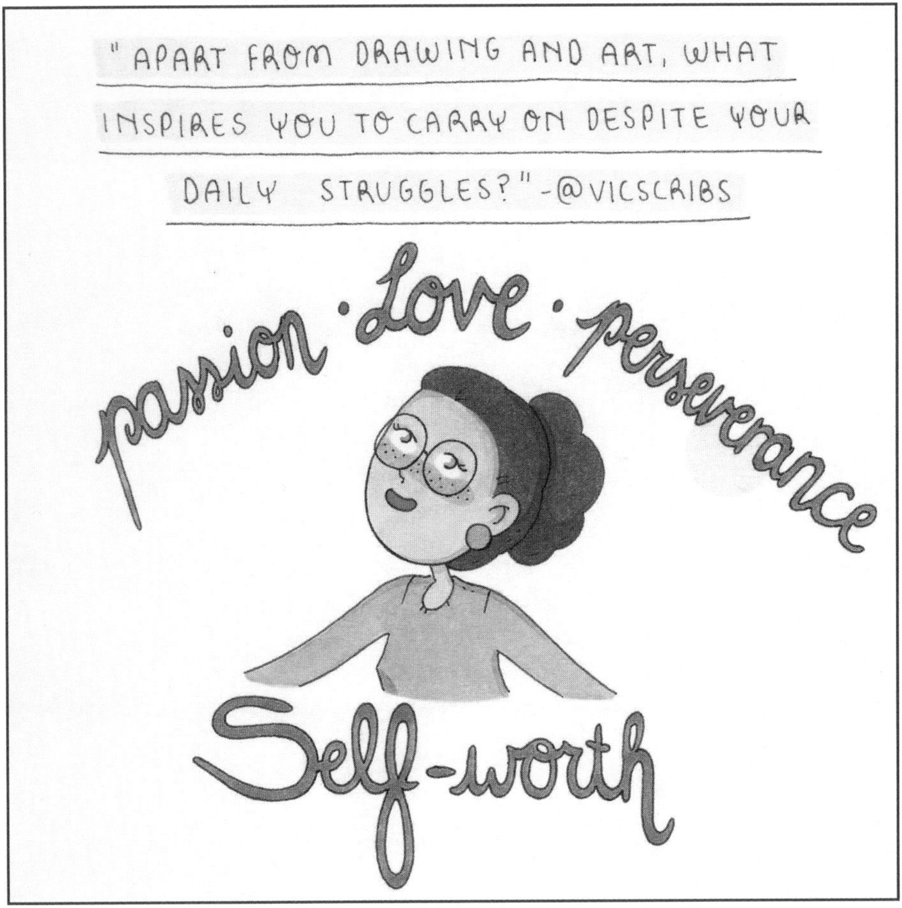
"APART FROM DRAWING AND ART, WHAT
INSPIRES YOU TO CARRY ON DESPITE YOUR
DAILY STRUGGLES?" -@VICSCRIBS
passion · Love · perseverance
Self-worth

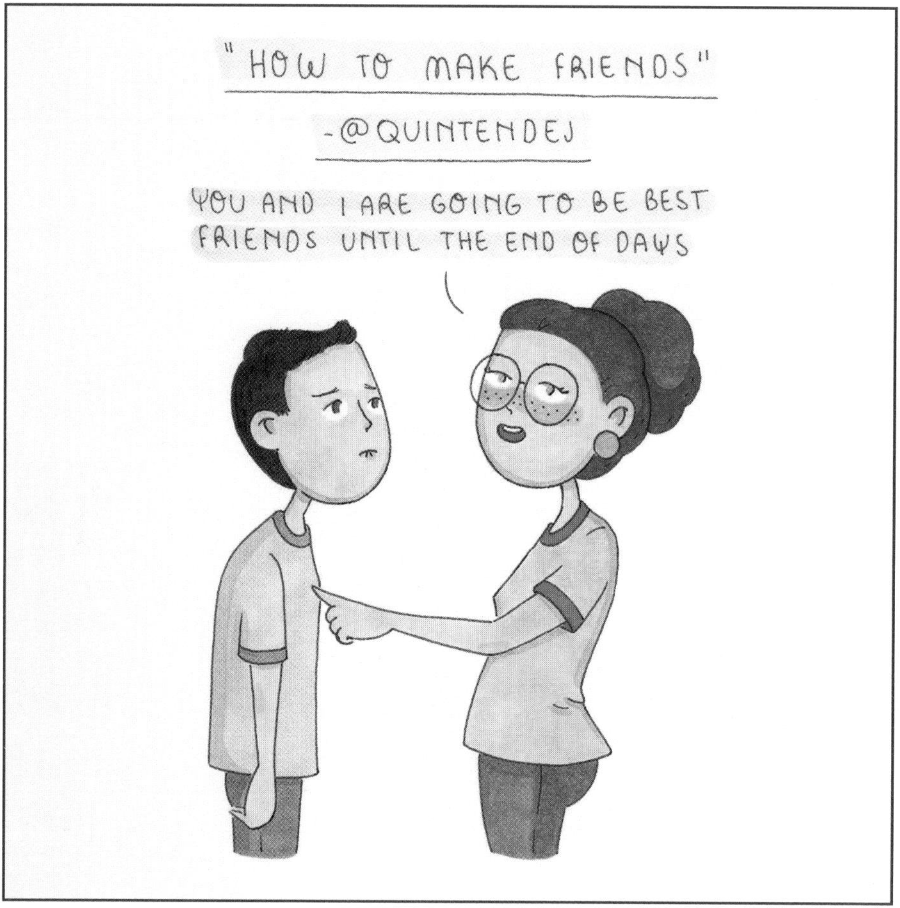
"HOW TO MAKE FRIENDS"
-@QUINTENDEJ
YOU AND I ARE GOING TO BE BEST FRIENDS UNTIL THE END OF DAYS

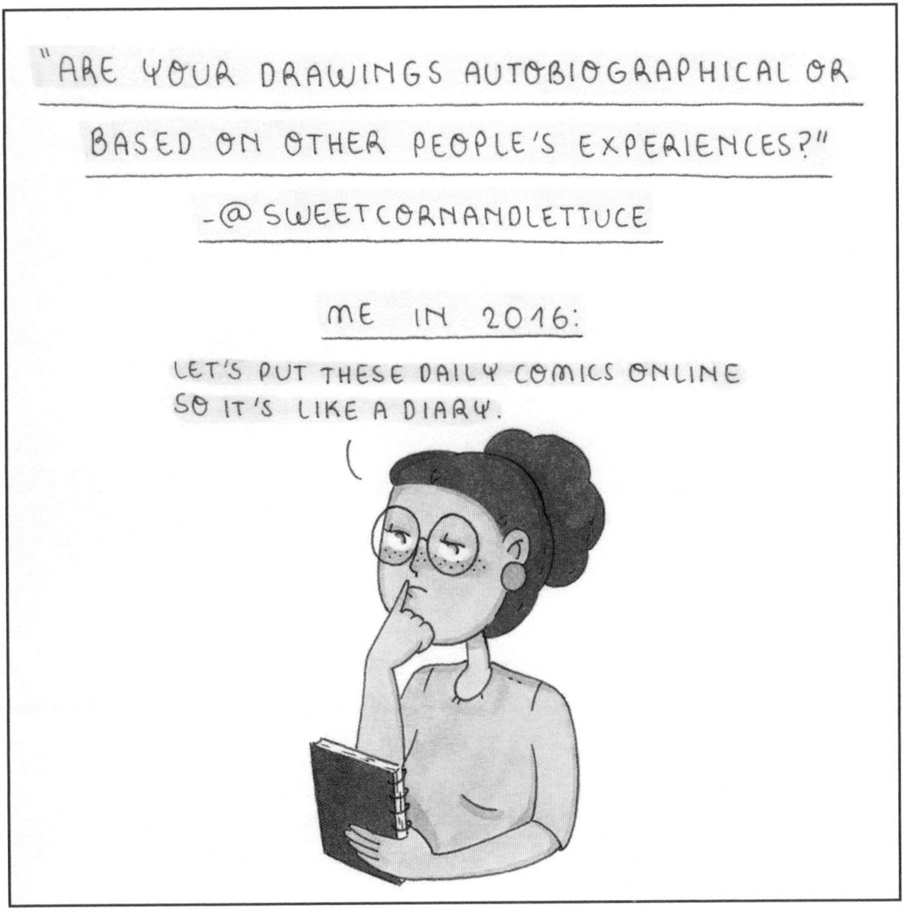
"ARE YOUR DRAWINGS AUTOBIOGRAPHICAL OR
BASED ON OTHER PEOPLE'S EXPERIENCES?"
-@SWEETCORNANDLETTUCE
ME IN 2016:
LET'S PUT THESE DAILY COMICS ONLINE
SO IT'S LIKE A DIARY.

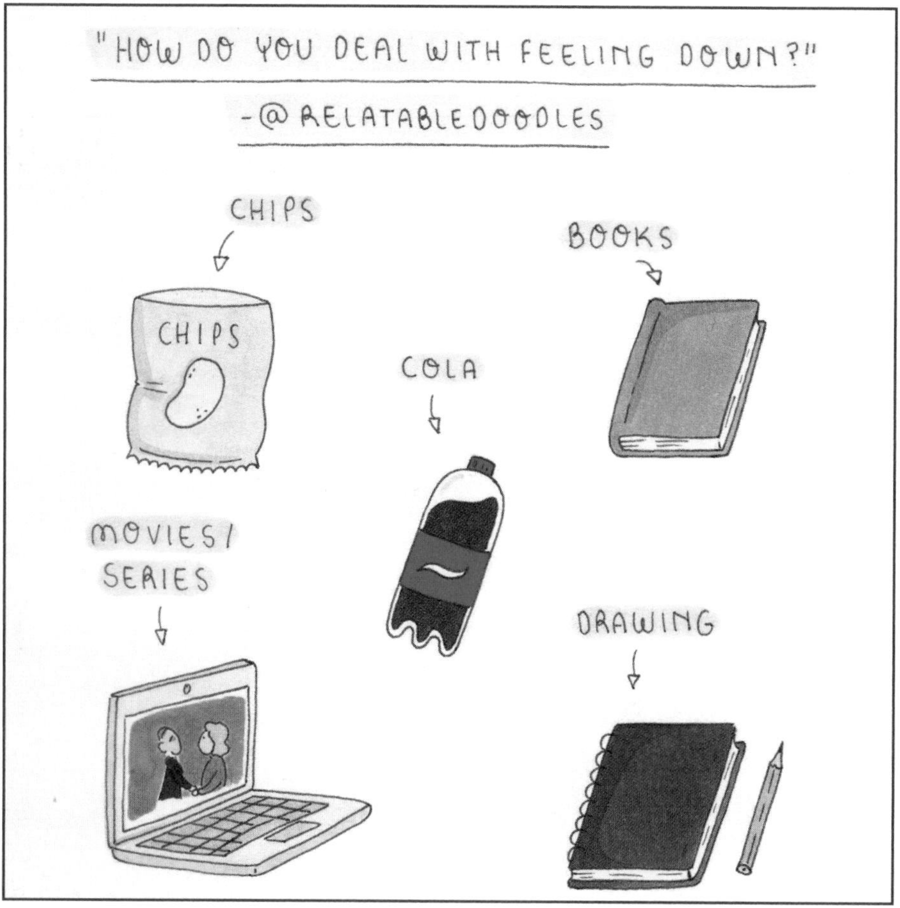
"HOW DO YOU DEAL WITH FEELING DOWN?"
-@RELATABLEDOODLES
CHIPS
CHIPS
BOOKS
COLA
MOVIES/
SERIES
DRAWING

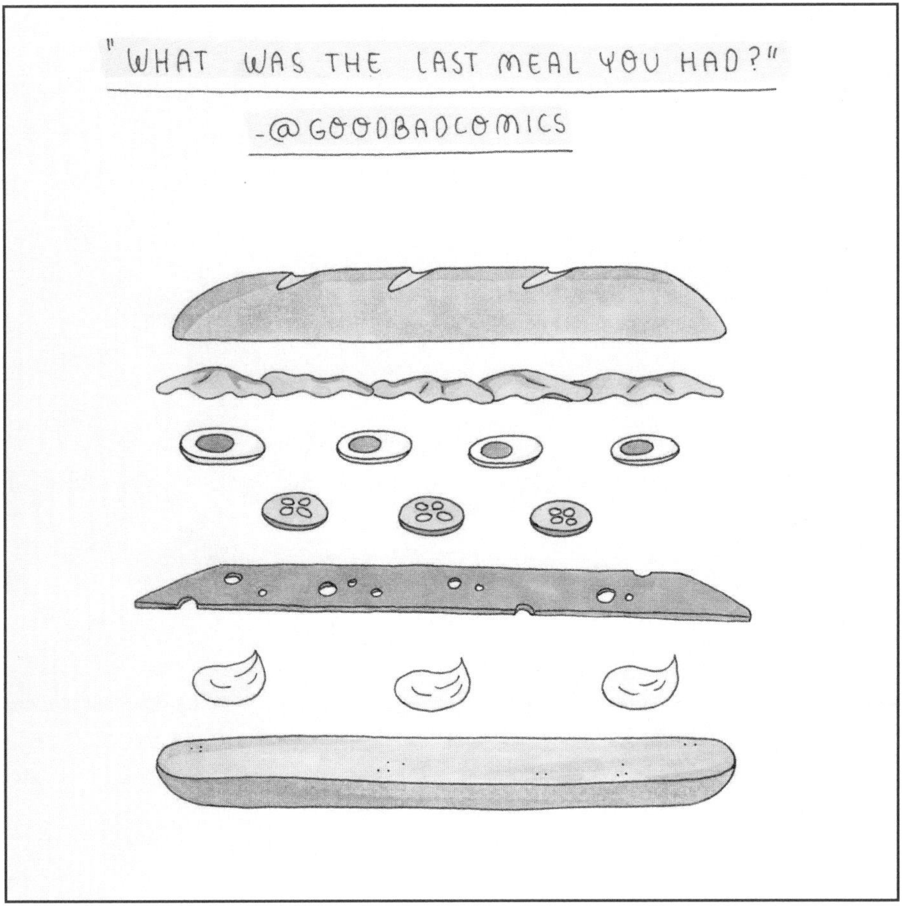
"WHAT WAS THE LAST MEAL YOU HAD?"
-@GOODBADCOMICS

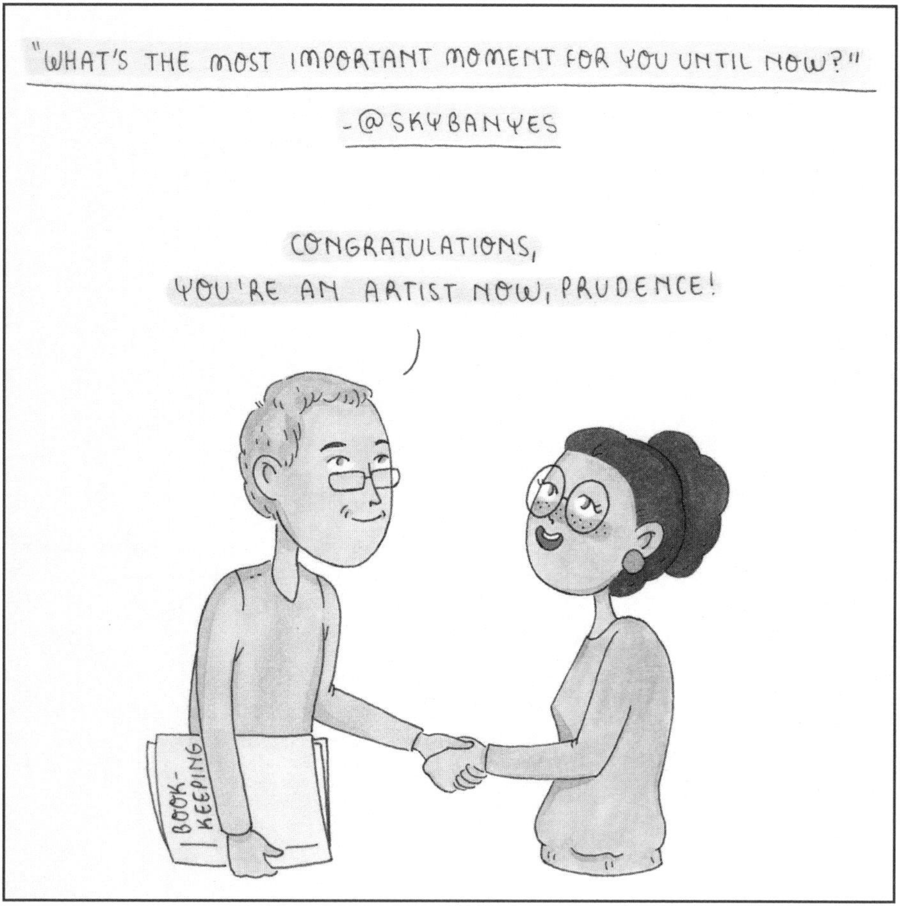
"WHAT'S THE MOST IMPORTANT MOMENT FOR YOU UNTIL NOW?"
-@SKYBANYES
CONGRATULATIONS,
YOU'RE AN ARTIST NOW, PRUDENCE!
BOOK-
KEEPING

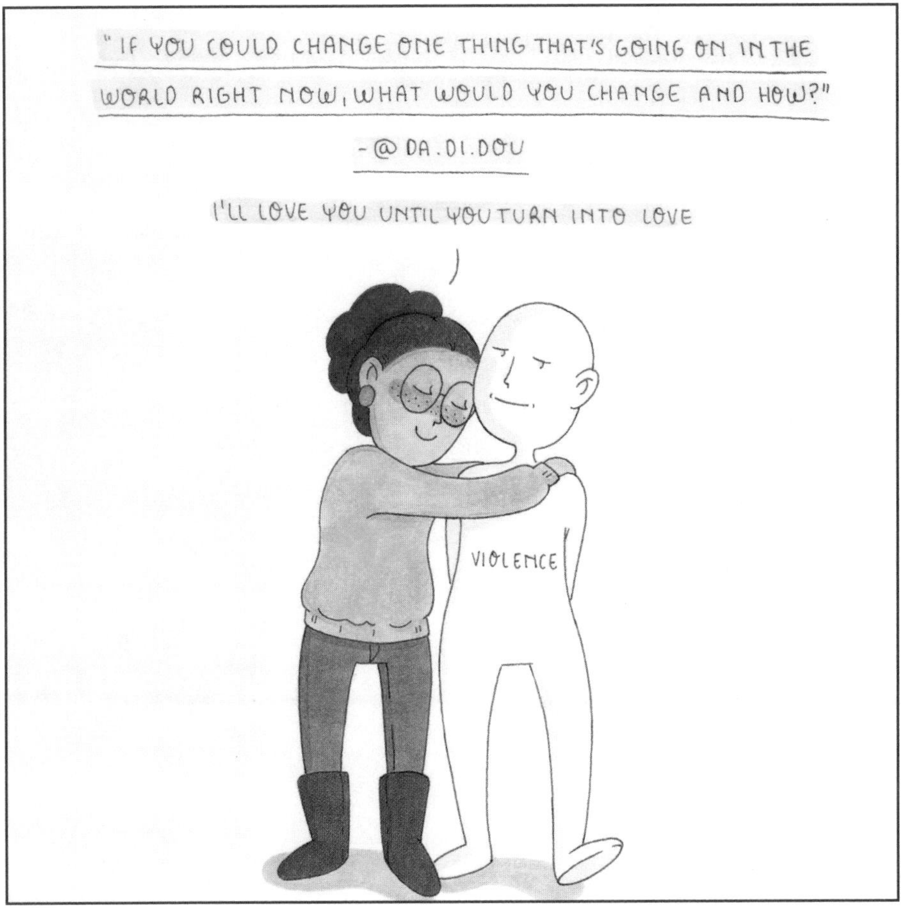
"IF YOU COULD CHANGE ONE THING THAT'S GOING ON IN THE WORLD RIGHT NOW, WHAT WOULD YOU CHANGE AND HOW?"
-@DA.DI.DOU
I'LL LOVE YOU UNTIL YOU TURN INTO LOVE
VIOLENCE

Conclusion

At the time of writing, this book is still under construction. I can't even believe there will actually be a Planet Prudence book in stores soon. I'm so grateful for the opportunity to share it with you. I feel like the luckiest woman in the world right now.

Now that you're at the end of the book, you'll likely have an opinion about it. I can only hope the opinion is positive (you can tell me what you think on social media, I won't bite, I promise!) But whatever your opinion is, this book was created for your enjoyment and laughter. So, thank you for giving it a chance. I hope you enjoyed it.

This book wouldn't be here without the endless support from my readers, their faith in me, and their love for my work. So, thank you all very much! Thank you for making my days brighter. I'm enjoying my life and doing what I love most...all because of you!

website: www.planetprudence.com and
tip jar: www.patreon.com/planetprudence

Thank You!

I won't write a huge thank you letter that includes everyone, because I wouldn't be able to get it to fit in one book. But I do want to write a special thank you to Erwin from Busch & van der Worp for supplying me with Copic Markers. He has made my life as an artist a lot easier and I am incredibly grateful for him!

I also want to thank my closest friends, who have been through every high and low of the past year. You know who you are—and thank you for the laughter, love and the tears. I hope to spend eternity with you!

A special thank you to my aunt, who I've spent the last few days with and who encouraged me to finish the book in time, even though my personal life is a mess at the moment. And last but not least: thank YOU! You, holding this book, because without you, there would be no **Planet Prudence** and there would definitely be no book. I can't thank you enough for your immense support and your love.

I wish I could give each one of you a hug in person!

Author Bio

Prudence Geerts is an illustrator, dreamer,
and cat-hugger based in Bruges, Belgium.